Accounting for Improvement

Form 14 PC28

Other books of interest

ANYANE-NTOW
International Handbook of Accounting Education & Research

BURNS & NEEDLES
Accounting Education for the Twenty-First Century: The Global Challenges

CHAMBERS
Accounting Thesaurus

GUTHRIE
International Developments in Public Sector Management & Accounting

Related Pergamon Journals*

Accounting, Management and Information Technology
Accounting, Organizations and Society
European Management Journal
International Business Review
Journal of Accounting Education
Long Range Planning
Scandinavian Journal of Management

*Sample copy available on request.

Accounting for Improvement

Sten Jönsson

Emerald

United Kingdom – North America – Japan – India – Malaysia – China – Australasia

JAI Press is an imprint of Emerald Group Publishing Limited
Howard House, Wagon Lane, Bingley BD16 1WA, UK

First edition 2007

Reprints and permission service
Contact: booksandseries@emeraldinsight.com

British Library Cataloguing in Publication Data
A catalogue record for this book is available from the British Library

ISBN: 978-0-08-044608-0

INVESTOR IN PEOPLE

Contents

"There's glory for you!"

"I don't know what you mean by 'glory'", Alice said.

Humpty Dumpty smiled contemptuously. "Of course you don't – till I tell you. I meant 'there's a nice knock-down argument for you'".

"But 'glory' doesn't mean 'a nice knock-down argument'", Alice objected.

"When I use a word", Humpty Dumpty said in a rather scornful tone, "it means just what I choose it to mean – neither more nor less".

"The question is", said Alice, "whether you can make words mean so many different things".

"The question is", said Humpty Dumpty, "which is to be master – that's all".

Lewis Carroll: *Alice's Adventures in Wonderland*.

Preface

For most people accounting is like a bad conscience. On the day of reckoning everything will be revealed and sanctions will be allocated without due consideration to the adverse circumstances that prevented exposition of the true self. The problem is that accounts do not allow explanations! They just show figures calculated in a standardized way and accumulated across bad and good days. We want to look good and discount the bad days.

We devote a lot of energy to whitewash. We cover up – and we cover up that we cover up – making some things undiscussable, as Chris Argyris (1982) says. What cannot be discussed cannot be improved, at least not intentionally.

The most frequent argument against accounting figures is that they account for history whereas management is for the future. The primary task of managers is to make the best of the current situation with a view to the future. To brood over spilt milk is not for managers; anyway the accounting figures do not show the true picture, they just show financial aspects, not the bright expectations. People who worry about accounting figures lose their drive, and it almost becomes a duty to ignore them, at least if there is no bonus system coupled to them. Take professionals – doctors or R&D managers – it is below their dignity to take account of accounts. Professionals are supposed to apply their knowledge to unique situations, finding solutions that nobody could have planned in advance. Under such circumstances accounts showing that, for example, a surgeon has passed a budget limit are just beside the point. Accounts are for accounting departments and the less managers are bothered with them the better.

It is easy to recount hundreds of lines of reasoning against paying attention to accounting figures. But after several hundred years we still use the Italian double-entry bookkeeping to keep track of financial situations. In private and public organizations, small as well as large accounting reports are produced regularly at much expense and with disparaging comments about those who produce them. The reason for this is probably that double-entry bookkeeping is an excellent instrument to record and store transactions between people with opposing interests. Financial accounting by 15th-century merchants to keep records of their debts and claims has developed over the years into comprehensive cost accounting systems to describe complex networks of responsibility centres in global corporations.

The drive toward standardization and efficient use of computer capacity seems to have caused the inhibition of experiments with modelling of causality in cost structures in the accounting system itself. The result may well be the loss of relevance that Johnson and Kaplan (1987) so eloquently expose. The accounting figures are no longer useful for strategic decision-making because the allocations of overhead costs do not mirror the true cost-drivers in the business. Managers turn elsewhere for their relevant information and the accounting department goes on cranking out cost centre reports that are used only to harass people instead of encouraging them to improve.

What of accountants? If accounting has to do with bad conscience and a future day of doom, what are they? Priests or hangmen? Are they the ones who execute the sentence or are they there to coax managers into repentance and improvement? In the latter case they had surely better get out there among the people and spread the word. It seems as though they have remained in the halls of power too long. The academic accountants have not been of much help, preaching that systems and analyses are the solutions rather than everyday actions. When systems and analyses are focused, rational choice amongst constructed alternatives – in a world in abundance of interesting choices – is called forth. A more realistic image would be that of people doing what they usually do without realizing that there are problems or choices, and even if they did realize, they would be someone else's problem.

Is this gloomy picture a true one? In case it is gloomy what went wrong and what can be done to improve the situation? These were questions we took with us on our improvement mission. The task was to see how accounting was used and how it could be used more effectively. We found people that were eager to get going and take up challenges, but they were held back by hierarchy and the slow pace. Once they were set free (even within the limits of freedom one can enjoy at work) they achieved improvement: every project we were engaged in was a very profitable one. It is a matter of taking initiatives and, above all, allowing others to try better ways and then to evaluate the outcome. Nothing spectacular happened in the cases reported in this book, but people enjoyed participating in improvement work. Solutions were different, most victories were small and seemingly insignificant in the larger picture of global competition, but they were carried out – not just talked about. Certainly, there were setbacks, but there were always ways to overcome them if team members felt the support of the rest of the team and if management showed trust. People are very resourceful when it comes to inventions – if they are allowed to be. Not all proposed solutions are brilliant but they are all worth discussion. One can learn a lot from finding out what is wrong with an idea.

Our method was that of action research with modest intervention. The term 'modest intervention' was invented by Peter Checkland in a conference comment to one of the chapters. I found 'action research' descriptive and to the point. Somebody said that if you want to find out how something works, try to change it. Action research does just that. The researcher goes into a situation in order to start processes which can be observed. The experimentalist does the same thing, except that in the perfect experiment only the variables under study and the dependent variable are allowed to vary. Everything else is under control – *ceteris paribus* as we usually say. But in real-life organizations everything else is seldom under control. On the contrary, it is changing or even playing against our intentions. Therefore the experiment will not provide much knowledge of value, unless, and this is a crucial point, we assume that there are general laws 'of nature' which guide our behaviour (like preferences or attitudes). If we could determine these behavioural laws we would be able to control people so they would do what we wanted them to do. Fortunately that is only a dream since people are not governed by general laws, but have a free will and the ability to construct solutions in social interaction. Even the experimenter cannot be sure that he or she is in control. We have all heard the story about the mouse in the maze saying: "Oh boy, have I got this guy well trained! Every time I press the bar he gives me cheese!". But this situation could also occur in action research since it assumes that people construct unique solutions in situations which cannot be exactly replicated. Therefore, we cannot aspire to find general laws even if they exist. Action researchers carry out an experiment and observe a great deal of variables over an extended period and then try to make sense of the observations. It is in this context that the term 'modest intervention' should be used. In order to set things in motion there has to be some intervention, some change which will cause participants to act to restore equilibrium or embark on a path of development.

It could, of course, be imagined that the researcher slipped into a situation without being noticed, but such opportunities are rare. What we can do is avoid barging in and dominating the situation so that all we observe are the effects of our own personality or bungled efforts. If we want to observe more natural processes in organizations we should intervene no more than is necessary to set processes in motion. That is why we like to call this approach action research with modest intervention.

The first thing in coping with a situation is to find out what is going on. This is not an easy task for the researcher or the participants. The thing to do then is to talk about it. Do you see what I see? What do you think? Do you mean like this? A little higher? All right, what next? We give accounts of what we see and get accounts back. This is how we orient ourselves. We have discursive minds (Harré and Gillet, 1994). We construct our conceptions of the world we are dealing with in discourse. And the action researcher observes how people go about constructing order. We can only observe what people say and do, not what they think. So we register what they say and do and try to find patterns, agendas and habits in interpretive analysis. Such analysis cannot provide proof of general laws, at most it is an illustration and interpretation that will provide us with a vocabulary to use in the discussion of what we have observed. A good vocabulary allows us to communicate and reach an understanding; which is not a modest achievement.

This book is a report from a series of action research projects (with modest intervention) carried out by researchers in the accounting department of the Gothenburg School of Economics and Commercial Law over a period of almost 10 years. Our programme was to study the use of accounting information in improvement work on the operational level in large organizations. When we started we did not know of the word *kaizen*, but now it could be said that we have studied *kaizen* in Swedish organizations. Most of the fieldwork has been reported in Ph.D. theses, but there has not yet been a summary of the achievements of the programme. This book attempts to provide such a summary.

The fieldwork has been done by Anders Grönlund, Stefan Schiller, Rolf Solli and Olle Westin of the accounting department in the Gothenburg School of Economics and Salvador Carmona, then at the University of Sevilla, now at the University Carlos III in Madrid. Salvador has been a visiting scholar in Gothenburg and we consider him part of our team. My own role in these projects has been as advisor and coach. Doing fieldwork over long periods is often frustrating. Most of the time all researchers in this kind of research feel overwhelmed by the enormous amounts of data that accumulate and sometimes the projects seem to go astray due to the most trivial reasons. That is when the coach steps in to give the fieldworker a pat on the back and send him or her back out there again.

We do need more research on accounting in action and fieldwork is essential for the growth of our knowledge.

But what kind of knowledge can we get from this kind of ethnographic study of one organization or a part of an organization? What are the main conclusions? What are the theses which these studies warrant? Do these studies just provide stories and anecdotal evidence? If I were to pick out a main theme that I would like the reader to keep in mind it is the double-entry meaning of accounting.

Organizations are institutions in the sense that they are sets of habits and practices, cultures, as it were. These practices stem from individuals' experience and from difficult to visualize 'taken for granted' routines. The mechanism by which experience is translated into practice and concepts is storytelling. We account for our experience through stories and get them accepted by our colleagues. These stories are enriched and condensed into principles and practices. In this way accounting is a fundamental, verbal, organizational activity. By doing what is accountable we conform to organizational norms. By conforming to organizational norms we behave responsibly, and responsible people are held accountable. By doing the accounts and providing acceptable justifications for deviations from plans, we confirm our membership and our role in the organization. The accounting which relates to responsibility centres in organizations is a technical activity which communicates according to the code of the conceptual financial models of the firm contained in the accounting system. That is part of the total accounting that goes on in the organization, but just a part of it. To understand the role of accounting in organizational improvement work one must understand accounting in terms of stories which drive the process. If this book succeeds in conveying this insight I will be pleased.

The main contributors to the joint efforts of the programme are the field researchers mentioned above, but there are many others. First, thanks go to the organizations which have allowed researchers in for such extended periods in what must be considered rather risky projects; Volvo, the Road Authority of Sweden, the municipality of Falköping and the city of Gothenburg. There were also many sources of funding for all the projects. The main sponsor has been the Swedish Work Environment Fund, but the Bank of Sweden Tercentenary Foundation and Humanistic–Social Science Research Council (HSFR) have also provided funds together with the

Gothenburg School of Economics and Commercial Law and its donated funds.

Individuals have influenced the text in ways that they never intended or will recognize. Friends like Barbara Czarniawska-Joerges of Lund University, Dick Boland of Case Western Reserve University, Norman Macintosh of Queen's University, Kingston, Jan Mouritsen of Copenhagen Business School, Olov Olson of the School of Public Administration, University of Gothenburg, and Jeremy Dent and Anthony Hopwood of London School of Economics have contributed in discussions. I have stolen their ideas without shame, after all that is what friends are for. Several researchers for the accounting department have been involved with our programme and in seminars. The field researchers of the project which have been used in the text have been mentioned. Others who have participated are Urban Ask, Christian Ax, Lars Erik Bergevärn, Inga Lill Johansson, Staffan Johansson, Anders Källström, Marie Lumsden and Ulla Törnqvist. Thomas Polesie made an extra contribution by substituting for me while I was on leave.

Thanks to them all.

Sten Jönsson

1

A preview: controlling through trust

Illustration

I was surprised that Anders was able to get started so quickly. After all, one must expect that large, serious firms like Volvo would be suspicious of outsiders barging in wanting to experiment with the provision of accounting information to machine group operators in their most quality-sensitive component plants. Possibly the school had generated some goodwill over the years, perhaps the ideology of the research project was well in line with the development of participative forms of organization that has been going on for a long time in Volvo. Anyway, here was Anders, the fieldworker in the project, reporting the first victory in his doctoral thesis project. Anders had found a very able partner in Börje, the foreman of the drive-shaft line of the heavy vehicle section of the Floby plant. Börje had relatively recently finished a one-year training programme for foremen organized by Volvo Components as part of their fabrikör-programme. *(Fabrikör is an old-fashioned name for an independent machine shop owner that one could find in small towns in the old days. Well-rounded waist, cigar-smoking, running the shop in a participative manner, but with undisputed authority – a pillar of society.) Volvo Components wanted foremen to assume greater managerial responsibility and was in the process of decentralizing still further, investing considerable amounts of money in a training programme to support the establishment of these local managers who could make good use of the systems developed under more Tayloristic auspices.*

Börje and Anders had agreed that the project should run by doing things, not just by talking, and that one should start by doing something easy that would ensure victory. Attention was drawn to the cost item 'cutting tools'. There was a negative deviation from standard in the last cost report and something needed be done. Börje had a meeting with the two shifts on the drive-shaft line, after having introduced the project, and Anders attention was focused on the cutting tool 'problem'. The two lathes on the line have rotating heads with the capacity for five cutting tools that have several sharp edges that work on the shafts. These tools can be turned to use another edge when the first is blunted. If a shaft is processed with a blunt cutting tool it will not pass the quality standards. The decision was to do a follow-up on cutting tool consumption: the standard might be wrong. Just counting the number of tools that were used and how many shafts were manufactured would probably help people get ideas about improving the operation.

The project budget allowed for part-time help from outside. Arne, a semi-retired old hand in the Production Technology department was asked to help. The operators would note the number of shafts that had been processed by every cutting tool when it was time to exchange it (it would not do any good to count the number of shafts for every edge of every tool; just how many shafts every tool would yield). Arne would collect these paper-and-pen data for each shift and compare them with the standard according to the technical specification of the operation. The price of cutting tools was also included for two reasons: to improve the awareness of the costs of these small bits of hardened steel that tend to slip through your fingers when you are applying them to the lathe head, and secondly, to get figures that could be compared to the cost item reports.

After three days the first follow-up was ready. Five types of cutting tools were used, 574 shafts had been processed and 52 cutting tools were used. The standard said that 74.3 cutting tools should have been necessary. The first report in the project looked like this:

Table 1.1 *Cutting tool consumption, production department 5026, early September 1984*

Tool type	1	2	3	4	5	Sum
Standard cons.	22.9	17.2	11.4	11.4	11.4	74.3
Real cons.	19	14	9	6	4	52.0
Price/tool	20	28	15	21	18	
'Savings'	78	90	36	113	133	450

They were 450 Swedish kronor (Skr) below standard on cutting tools for these three days and that meant Skr0.60 per shaft. "So what!" said production engineers at a seminar a year later when we presented the project. "Don't waste our time! How many shafts does that line produce a year ... ? Ten to twenty thousand? And you saved Skr0.60 per shaft! Peanuts! Is that what you spend project money on? Look! We restructure whole plants and set up group technology solutions and save millions! Give us a break! You are playing out of league!"

Well, admittedly not very much had been achieved. The 'savings' were insignificant and we did not know why they had occurred. Perhaps the standards were too high (but how could they be when they had been set by those expert engineers who know everything?). What had been achieved was on another level. Attention had been focused on the cost of cutting tools. There was a set of figures to discuss. Operators told Anders that they were not surprised. They had a feeling that the standard was set too high on these tools.

Other things happened.

This book is about how people with operative jobs can take command of their work situation and improve it in quality as well as efficiency. It is meant to persuade, and it is written by someone who is persuaded by faith as well as six years of field research. Improvement means to learn from experience and find better ways of solving the task laid before you. It is not very difficult once you get started and it is fun. The difficult part is to break away from routine and boredom. Then you can try to see things from a different angle, experiment, register what happens and reflect on that outcome. What caused it? How can undesired outcomes be prevented and good ones enhanced?

In most organizations there are very powerful mechanisms to prevent all kinds of experimentation, at least unless it is authorized from the top. It is a nightmare for a middle manager to have irresponsible subordinates fool around with the production process (remember Chernobyl?) – it might go awry. Middle managers are supposed to be in control. One might go as far as stating that their function in the organization is to deliver certainty – to convince the top of the organization that the goods will be delivered as planned, to assure them that things are under control (although they seldom are completely). These mechanisms are based on our needs to reduce uncertainty, organizationally as well as socially, and they must be considered natural and possibly even good. Therefore, acts that initiate change must have impetus or the resistance must be weakened by considerable infusions of trust.

The problem is that learning in itself is a stabilizing factor. It generates patterns of behaviour that tend to petrify into habits that may be so self-evident and 'normal' that they become almost unnoticeable.

To tell it like it was – sorry – is

This book will include a lot of storytelling, an activity which is not well liked in academic circles. "How do I know that you are not making all this up", the critics say, "we do not want to be told fairy tales, we want facts and figures". True measures of the world as it is, one might say.

Well, that is not an easy thing to do since people act on the world as they see it and this book is about people at work. The world as they see it might not be what the researcher sees because people read situations differently. The researcher sees the world through his or her theoretical formulations and people at work see it through their experiential knowledge. The question whether there really is a true world to be seen out there once we get rid of our prejudices and ignorance is a philosophical one that should not concern us now. Of course, it is going to pop up sooner or later when it is time to draw conclusions from the stories about to be told. Then it will be necessary to ask if there are generally valid lessons to be drawn from these stories; that river will have to be crossed when we get there. Hopefully the stories will be convincing enough to make the crossing effortless. (By the way! Have you been to Italy lately? Did you cross the Rubicon – just south of Rimini if I remember correctly? Not much of a river to cross, was it? Almost like a ditch. A great symbolic act by Caesar crossing it, but it could not have been much of a physical adventure. *Alia acta est!*)

To justify the storytelling to academic colleagues and to suspicious down-to-earth readers the ideology behind this choice of reporting must be explicated. This will take some space even if it is kept to a minimum. It is necessary to talk about communication, representation of truth, and what constitutes meaningful statements about the world. It was discussions about these that lay behind the birth of this project.

What can be said and what can be done

Some things simply cannot be said. It is almost impossible to explain to your child how to ride a bike; it is not even enough to show how it is done. Our children will have to try by themselves, with discrete support from the parent initially. By the same token the conductor of a symphony orchestra may have difficulties in getting his or her intentions across to all sections of the orchestra. It is trial and error, reactions, humming and body language. Professional musicians not only have to pay attention to the conductor, they also have to listen to each other and adapt so that the sound and the pauses are right in performance. Machines do what they are programmed to do nowadays, except for some things like fitting threading screws together without damage. I remember visiting a Volvo gearbox plant some years ago. We passed a tired-looking robot with a transparent cover and my host told me:

> "Oh, yes, we are trying to get this robot to assemble the fifth gear. There are eight or nine parts and it can handle them beautifully, but it can't feel like the human hand when the threading of the ring fits the axle. It just screws it on and damages the parts too often."

They were at a loss trying to program this robot to have a delicate enough feeling for fit; I hope they have solved it by now. If they haven't they have learnt a lot from trying.

On the other hand, a good orchestra can do wonders in cooperation with a good conductor, but it couldn't take the intervention of a rationalization expert. Humphrey (1994) picked up the following allegory from a reflecting officer in the probation service of England and Wales, a service that was in the process of being rationalized and provided with a Financial Management Information System in Thatcher's United Kingdom:

> For considerable periods the four oboe players had nothing to do. The numbers in this section should be reduced and the work spread more evenly over the whole piece thus eliminating peaks and valleys of activity. All the twelve violins were playing identical notes; this is duplication. The staff of this department should be drastically cut. If a larger volume of sound is required, it could be obtained by means of amplifying horns or sounding boards. Much effort was absorbed in playing of demi-semi-quavers; this seems to be an unnecessary refinement. It is recommended that all notes be rounded up to the nearest semi-quaver. If this were done it would be possible to use trainees and lower grade operatives more extensively.
>
> There seems to be too much repetition of some musical passages. Scores should be drastically pruned. No useful purpose is served by repeating on the horns something that has already been handled by the strings. It is estimated that if all redundant passages were eliminated the whole performance time could be reduced to 15 minutes and there would then be no need for an intermission.

Indeed, but how could the members of the orchestra persuade this rationalizer about the need for repetition in a symphony? In principle it is impossible since the two parties see different things in a symphony. Communication can only be established if special efforts are devoted to it. Consider the symphony as a message sent by the orchestra to its audience (including one rationalization expert). The meaning of that message is not contained in the message itself – it emerges in the receivers when they enjoy what they hear. It is probably a different experience for everyone. This 'emergent view' of information in linguistics (Moore and Carling, 1982), which simply says that the message contains no information until it is given a meaning by the interpreter, has fundamental consequences if it is accepted. The earlier, and still dominant view, the 'container view', holds that a message is encoded information and what the receiver has to do is to decode it. The information is contained in the message. If the receiver knows the grammar of decoding of meaning, the message will be clear. Communication is really a question of grammar! If we could only find or construct a universal grammar, people could communicate across all languages!

The emergent view, on the other hand, maintains that meaning comes before grammar. A statement is first understood and then it can be subjected to conceptual and structural analysis. This means that the message cannot be said to contain the message, it emerges in the interpretive act performed by the receiver. The interpretive act is not usually any great effort. A person 'sees' the message as a matter of recognition. Only during our first period of reading do we have to struggle to put letters together to make words and to help us in that undertaking we are taught to pronounce every letter. When we understand what pattern the sequence of puffing and stuttering sounds seems to lead us to, we say the word we think this sounds like and look up at our teacher with a smile and expectation for a confirming nod. We have to say it before we believe it. As the organizational theorist Karl Weick has said: "How can I know what I think until I see what I say!"

The important thing about this view in linguistics is that the meaning of the message emerges in the receiver. This means that the sender does not have complete control over the outcome of the communicative initiative. The experiential background knowledge of the receiver may have a significant impact.

A further complication is that the message cannot contain instructions for its own interpretation. Such instructions would have to be sent in a separate message, like "The following message is true and should be acted upon with the utmost urgency". Secret messages remain secret only when the code books are provided through channels other than those used for messages. To break the code one has to try possible interpreting patterns or get hold of the code book. The holy books of the word need a cadre of individuals with specific qualifications to, as it were, lay out the text for us. In a ball game one needs experience to be able to interpret the signs given by the coach or other players. The observer may learn to see a correlation between signs given and the subsequent pattern of behaviour in the game, but it is much easier to have someone explain them as the game goes on. It directs attention and makes it much easier to see the essentials of the game.

Human beings have a remarkable ability to see patterns and thus to learn. It is easier to discover patterns if we have an extra channel of communication against which to check our senses. I happen to be very fond of the connotations of the following little scene from the world of hunting:

First hunter: Hey, do you see the moose over there?
Second hunter: Oh my God, don't shoot! It is our friend Peterson!

We see something, we check our preliminary interpretation with a colleague through a different channel (use audio channel to check the visual impression), and we avoid shooting Peterson. This 'stereo' type of communication is more common in organizational life than we realize and managers should use it consciously. Communication through more than one channel is useful to confirm interpretations and to direct attention. Controllers should pay attention not only to the design of systems and report layouts, but also to the interpretive schemas that these reports encounter. They should talk to the users of economic information about the content and other aspects of the reports in order to include them as natural parts in decision-making contexts.

Forging patterns of interpretation

Most of what we do in organizational life is routine. We repeat similar procedures in familiar situations and we are at a loss when completely new situations emerge. When we do not quite know what to 'make' of a situation we can test our interpretations by acting upon them and registering what happens. The accumulation of observations would be quite burdensome for our memory if we were not able to pack data densely in the form of information generating concepts and associations. Imagine what number of registrations of data on a facial expression would be necessary to allow a reasonably certain interpretation that this is an expression of surprise! Still we are able to detect these expressions, and there are people that are able to control a large number of muscles in their face to project an expression that will be interpreted as (a happy) surprise by other parties, although they are not surprised at all.

The data management capacity that human beings display every moment is amazing. This is proof of a powerful cognitive apparatus at work. Repeated appearance of items in our focus of attention will give rise to associations (Wilson, 1980) that tend to link concepts together into patterns related to our experience. I, personally, tend to think of concepts in terms of atoms that have a number of potential links that may be activated in a formation of 'molecules' and larger complexes of associations like the following: fish – fishing rod – hook – boat – water – bite … , which indicate that my fishing experiences do not consist of trawling at sea, or angling for trout in mosquito-infested mountain creeks.

The formation of concepts and stable links between them (associations) is assumed to be achieved through repetition. Repeated confrontation with similar situations makes us first able to recognize the similarities and to form associations. The physical counterparts to these associations are neurons in our brain (this is doing violence to the complexities of cognitive psychology and neurophysiology and I apologize for that) which upon repeated 'firings' are 'primed' in the sense that repeated firing increases the likelihood of another firing. Hereby associative 'paths' are *established and maintained by use.*

Learning will be seen as the priming of associative links in this book. There will be many reasons to come back to this conception during the course of the storytelling.

Establishing rules of behaviour

The fact that senders and receivers of messages may see different information in the same message obviously is an organizational problem. The efficiency of organizational action might be served if senders and receivers of messages tended to agree on the proper interpretation of what is said inside the organization. To focus the mechanism through which this is achieved we may turn to social philosophers like Wittgenstein and Winch. When Winch discusses what separates meaningful behaviour from events and *ad hoc* movements in time and space he refers to Wittgenstein (1953) and concludes that meaningful behaviour consists of an act that is governed by the application of a rule. Two criteria are involved here: first the actor must be able to give a reason (an account) for an action, and second the actor must be bound by his or her action now to do something (behave consistently) in the future. Winch maintains that only if these criteria are met can the actor's behaviour be said to have a sense.

This is probably not at all clear and has to be elaborated. Regarding the first criterion one could ask why the actor has to make an account for the action. An actor could perform an action without paying attention to it as an action or without having formulated an account in advance. That is true, but Winch requires that the actor must have the capacity to offer an account for it and that account must be reasonable and compatible with other evidence. The account may not necessarily be an accurate one but it should be recognizable as a reason. "I was just playing without paying attention to what I was doing" is an account of a mishap that may be accepted as a reason. The second criterion in this case might be a promise to be more attentive in the future. That is, the reason for the action contains a commitment to a rule that will be followed in the future. The public announcement of respect for the rule by using it in the account for the action serves to make the actor more predictable in the future. The account for the act confirms the actor's intention to apply the rule in the future. Action is self-display and an announcement of intentions for the future. Interaction between individuals automatically generates patterns of behaviour that are fairly stable and predictable. This allows specialization within the group and teamwork.

The trouble with action is that you might lose face

The only way to learn who we are is to do something and see what people say about it. It is a slightly frightening proposition that we have to live with. The reactions of others constitute our mirror. We are torn between two urges, to establish our identity, and to avoid disappointment. The trouble is that in seeking the one we risk the other.

Knowing oneself and liking what one knows form the basis for self-confidence and citizenship. From childhood we test behaviours and develop those that meet with approval. Our parents, 'the boys', teachers, and colleagues at work are significant senders of value judgements. To extract an evaluation we have to carry out an act, that is do something that appears meaningful to our audience. (An act which can be accounted for and which signals commitment to a type of behaviour.) Disapproval is usually a setback and it forces us to make decisions about whether to abandon the type of behaviour that was exposed or to explain our intentions more clearly. Intentions relate to responsibility as well as identity. To 'come of age' means to be recognized by society as a person to be held responsible for his or her actions, a person who is suited to enter into contract with. Someone to be trusted.

All this requires interaction. We have to act in order to elicit reactions. And there is this awful risk of disappointment. The others might signal that we are the scum of the earth or simply that we are not worthy to participate on an equal footing in the game going on or about to be played. So we have a strategic problem. How can a favourable judgement be promoted? The two extreme strategies are: (1) to try to dominate the environment and thereby control reactions; and (2) to avoid disapproval by avoiding doing anything. Hannah Arendt (1978; see also van Gunsteren, 1976) tells us that both strategies are bound to be self-defeating. If we manage to dominate our environment we will not get honest reactions from it and we will end up with a distorted view of ourselves. The excesses of dictators, in larger or smaller format, may be amplified by the absence of controlling negative feedback. The other strategy, to avoid action in order to avoid disappointment, is also self-defeating because it means giving up the project of forging an identity. By giving up the self and joining the crowd a person assumes anonymity and irresponsibility, which sooner or later lead to distorted behaviour and lack of self-control.

So, what are we to do? Well, there is only one solution and that is courage! The need to have an identity as a responsible, trustworthy person is so important that we have to take the risk. Social life is taking the risk of losing face in order to get feedback from others on who we are. Perhaps people in organizations could consciously help each other to take these risks by giving positive feedback to good performances. Such feedback obviously cannot only come from pecuniary incentive schemes; not even in the most genuinely profit-seeking organization. It has to be given in interaction in problem-solving situations, spontaneously and immediately related to the act. Frequent and mutual interaction of this kind inside a group can generate an atmosphere of willingness to face problems and seek their solutions, a sense of active experimentation in order to learn whether things can be improved.

Learning to learn

Once a person is recognized, and has accepted the role as a responsible person who can be trusted with sensitive tasks, that person is ready to learn from experience. Experiential learning (Kolb, 1984) includes cycles of concrete experience, reflective observation, abstract conceptualization and active experimentation.

Kolb starts his book on experiential learning by stating that:

> Human beings are unique among all living organisms in that their primary adaptive specialization lies not in some particular physical form or skill or fit in an ecological niche, but rather in identification with the process of adaption itself – in the process of learning. (Kolb, 1984, p. 1.)

This project has embraced that attitude all along. Human beings have this extraordinary talent of learning only if given a chance, and, if they are used to being held responsible for actions that they initiate. Kolb works in the tradition of Piaget (development), Dewey (pragmatism) and Lewin (democratic values) and seems to fit Scandinavian organizational life nicely. The structural model of experiential learning he uses is quite simple and is illustrated in Fig. 1.1.

This view of the learning process is built on two pairs of modes of learning. First the apprehension–comprehension pair, which represents two different processes of understanding the world. Comprehension is conceptual interpretation and symbolic representation of experiences. One might picture this as 'seeing the world through the glasses of a model', the concepts of that model determines more or less what is seen. Apprehension is reliance on tangible, immediate experience with its felt qualities. Perception and imitation are examples of learning through apprehension, while mental imagery or modelling is learning through comprehension.

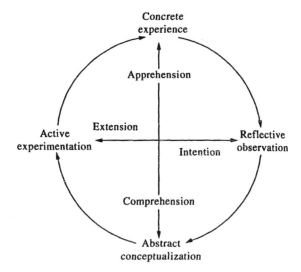

Figure 1.1 The structure of experiential learning according to Kolb (1984, p. 42).

Touching and seeing the table is apprehension, trying to define what essential features constitutes the concept 'table' is comprehension.

The other pair, extension–intention, represent two ways of transforming concrete apprehensions or symbolic comprehensions. We apprehend something moving behind the bushes on our hunting trip. It is big and bulky and makes a certain kind of noise. We reflect upon this observation transforming it intentionally to fit with the concept 'moose'. Not being completely sure about our conclusion that we are seeing a moose we venture to extend our knowledge by whispering to our colleague "Do you see the moose over there?". The answer ("Oh my God, don't shoot! It is our friend Peterson") meant an extension of our knowledge of the facts which was tested through another pair of eyes (we could also have sneaked closer to get a better look) and we avoided shooting our friend Peterson.

The learning process includes going through cycles of concrete experience (registering with our senses), reflective observation (making sense of what we experience), abstract conceptualization (classify and define) and active experiment (design and carry out plans). It is a basic assumption throughout this book that effective learning requires whole cycles. An organization that separates concrete experience (operations) from abstract conceptualization (planning) is likely to be a poor learner. The same goes for individual members of the organization. Operational excellence and quality improvement presupposes that the responsible individual is allowed to extend current knowledge through participation in the whole cycle. To some extent difficulties to be physically present at all times can be compensated by dialogue.

Trust

The extent to which a person relies on information received through dialogue depends upon trust. The choice between trusting what I see with
my own eyes ("The big bulky thing behind the bushes looks like a moose")
or what my colleague exclaims ("Oh my God, don't shoot! It is our friend
Peterson!") might not be a difficult one, but it could be thought to be
dependent upon how much experience I have of seeing mooses on hunting
trips. If my experience is plentiful I am likely to trust my judgement more
than if this is my first hunting trip.

Trust relates to a person's sense of being familiar with the situation.
Knowing 'the rules of the game' means that the person feels able to:
(1) recognize the situation; and (2) forecast future possible states. Under
such conditions a person will feel 'in control' and may be willing to react
to the situation, for example by carrying out an experiment to learn more.
If, on the other hand, the situation is unfamiliar the propensity to act is
normally smaller.

Garfinkel (1963) illustrates the content of the 'trust' concept by designing
experimental situations of distrust. He starts with a game situation. There
are, for instance a number of basic rules in tic-tac-toe. They give rise to
a set of constituent expectancies that make sense of game situations. If a
player then breaks the rules by placing his mark, not in a square but on
the border between squares there will be confusion. The opponent will
look up and say something like "What do you mean by that!". If the rules
of the game are breached there will be vigorous efforts by other participants to normalize the situation by bringing the game inside constituent
expectancies. Garfinkel found that the players who were most frustrated
were those who tried to restore the game while retaining the original rules,
while those players who were able to see a redefinition of the game and
adapt to that were less frustrated.

The frustration in the face of 'cheating' in games can, as we all know,
be quite strong. The game situation is defined precisely by the mutual
expectations of players to abide by the rules and there usually is a clear
definition of what constitutes a winning situation which gives the game its
goal direction. Cheating ruins 'everything', that is the sense of the game.

In organizational life situations are more fluid and difficult to apprehend
in all their complexities. Still we exert vigorous efforts to 'normalize' when
we perceive the game to be out of bounds, and we are anxious to establish
rules of the game when they seem to be lacking. This is done chiefly by
behaving in a way that is meaningful to the others in the group, that is to
do things that can be justified (accounted for) in a reasonable way, given
the organizational situation, and by committing ourselves to consistent

behaviour through our actions. In this way we become people that can be counted on to fulfil a role and to be useful partners in interaction.

Against this background it seems reasonable to assume that trust comes before rationality in organizational settings. This is an assumption that will colour much of what is said in this book. Only then can organizational members devote their full attention to the pursuit of cost or quality improvement when they have achieved a stable role setting, that is a team situation.

There is another aspect of trust beside the feeling of being in control or knowing what the rules of the game are and that is personal trust in terms of goodwill. This aspect of trust relates to the sharing of ownership or confidential information. We can trust somebody in the sense that we rely on his or her advice, or we can trust somebody to take care of our most precious assets. In both cases it is a matter of granting someone partnership in our personal sphere. We put, as it were, part of our life in somebody else's hands. An important way to maintain trust is, obviously, not to take advantage of such a situation. Like other relational concepts, for example friendship and love, trust is an implicit contract that vanishes once it becomes explicit. If one starts to make a list of everything one has done for a friend and tells him or her that there is a balance that should be corrected it is likely that the relationship will suffer. These relations are unconditional and once conditions are introduced the relationship suffers. On the other hand, if there is an imbalance in terms of one partner exploiting the relationship, the unconditional nature of the relationship is not likely to remain.

It seems possible to regard trust as something that can be accumulated over time and which yields benefits. If not maintained properly it will deteriorate. If mismanaged it can vanish over night. The mutuality of trust makes it an interesting concept. Obviously it is not a zero-sum game for those involved. It can grow for all partners at the same time. It also can be expected to decrease transaction costs within an organization.

Rationality

Trust is a normative concept in the sense of Habermas (McCarthy, 1984; Habermas, 1984). That means that it is established in dialogue between participants that are serious and intent on reaching an understanding. Normative knowledge arrived at in such a manner implies an obligation to those standards. Participation entails commitment to follow the rules even at a cost.

Rationality, on the other hand, is a more complicated concept to classify. It is normative in the sense that rationality is assumed to be the norm of all organizational members, but it is also instrumental in the sense that it entails goal direction. Rationality has come to represent explanations of behaviour where stable preference orderings dictate optimizing choices. But rationality is also implicated in science itself. A large part of the truth-value of a scientific text lies in its ability to exhibit a rational–logical path from problem to solution. We do not write research reports to describe the actual progress of the research project, but to give an account for the reasons why the proposed solution is the rational one for the stated problem. Reports are made to look more rational and logical than the research process actually was.

In organizational sciences the members of organizations are assumed to behave rationally, which is necessary if decision-making is to be depicted in mathematical form and optimal choices found through derivation. "Only behaviour that can be expressed in equations can be subjected to scientific study" an economist explained to me in a discussion of methodology in a social science research council meeting. Since he was so sure about the definitions of his world there was not much to add and, one might think, not much to learn for him either. One might ask whether learning is at all possible in a rational world. If people are assumed to know all the available alternatives beforehand, and are sure about what they want, then it appears that there is not much need to spend time trying to find out how things function.

But in this imperfect world, which we all know from experience through reflection on concrete observations, we often do not know what we want or what is expected of us. We do not know what alternatives are available and what outcomes they might entail. But still we do not act blindly. Instead we act routinely. We do what we usually do and if the situation is new to us we ask for instructions (or wait and see). If we are surprised by outcomes or by obstacles in our projects we try to 'normalize' the situation by matching goals to outcomes. We redefine situations, we cover up and we manipulate to be able to appear rational. Normally this is not such a great problem because the world of expectations is a fairly robust one where games are defined with wide safety margins and shrouded in routine. There is almost always a reasonable explanation for most outcomes and we are able to save our rational face. But there are of course situations where rationality makes demands on us which we have difficulties coping with, either because they are too important to ignore or too blatantly at odds with our own statements. Argyris (1982; Argyris *et al.*, 1985) tells us that people cover up and that people cover up that they cover up. That is not a very good starting point for learning since the denial of the cover up makes things that are crucial for a problem solution 'undiscussable'. In organizational life there are many subjects that are undiscussable because of our need to appear rational.

Brunsson (1985, 1989) has uncovered many of the mechanisms of organizational behaviour that relate to the need to appear rational. One way of avoiding losing face is separation. An organization may separate talk about problems from decisions which, in turn are separated from action. In this way people that talk about problems can go on talking about problems in an utterly unrealistic way in one part of the organization, while carefully worded and perfectly justifiable decisions are taken in other parts, and, finally, something is done about it in still other parts of the organization.

We find the most obvious illustrations of this mode of organizing for rational appearance in the public sector. There are specially designed halls in the public sector for talking about problems, with special arrangements for the public to sit in and listen. Such halls are called parliaments or city halls. Then there are ministries, for example of education, where important decisions, concerning certain areas of activity, are taken, and, finally, there are agencies, for example state universities, where activities are carried out to make the best of the current situation. Sometimes we all ask ourselves whether it is the same world that is talked about, decided on and acted upon. The same phenomena can be found in all large organizations. They are only more directly visible in the public sector organizations because there it is necessary to make a 'public' display of the process of management of our common interests, just because they are common. Many of the positions held in the public sector are positions of trust and the business of the public sector is to serve the public. The public sector must exhibit democracy at the top of the organization so that citizens may see that their representatives work relentlessly to promote their goals and put their problems on the agenda. The majority of the parliament must show that it is implementing the programme it was elected to carry out. Therefore decisions have to be taken in a visible way. Talk is cut off and decisions are taken by thumping the table with wooden clubs. Activities on the operational level, for example courses on organizational behaviour at universities, are carried out in the same way this year as last year, hopefully in an efficient manner. One might wonder if it is at all possible to keep this together in one logical and meaningful sequence. The odds that there will not be a perfect correspondence between talk at the top and action at the bottom of the organization are overwhelming. Still, this may be a very intelligent organizational design. By keeping the activities – talk, decision and action – separate, the organization allows for learning along the line and adaption to real situations. Sometimes there are administrative reforms to signal that the organization is worried about the difference between talk and action.

As mentioned above these are phenomena that can be found in all large organizations. It is not enough to be rational and efficient, the organization must also appear to be rational and efficient. That is why some problems may become undiscussable. To see organizations as conglomerates of hypocrisy, cover up, separated talk, decision-making and action, etc., may invite cynicism, but it may also help us to reach a realistic understanding of large organizations. Large and small organizations do have an image of rationality to uphold, not because they want to deceive the environment but because they want to maintain an identity, to be a possible partner in business, to be able to act as a responsible entity in the future.

Making action meaningful

We did pay some attention to the notion of meaningful behaviour above and there it was concluded that meaningful behaviour includes being able to account for actions and it also includes a kind of commitment to following the same rules in the future, that is to be predictable. If organizations are aware of the fact that this kind of interpreting of their actions is going on all the time it is only reasonable to expect that these organizations devote considerable attention to helping the environment to get the interpretations 'right'. This might be called 'identity management'. An important factor in that management obviously is the presentation of praiseworthy goals, before and after action. An assumption that we took with us in the projects in the Accounting for Improvement programme was that a good way of presenting goals is to show results that point in the right direction. Results themselves are convincing goal statements that compel the group to continue the trend. However, planning and development of explicit goal statements may get in the way of progress in early stages of improvement work.

Crisis

Sometimes the discrepancy between the managed identity and actual performance becomes so obvious that it is not possible to cover up. Then there is crisis. The identity or image as well as performance have to be repaired, often at great loss of prestige and trust.

Abandonment of old myths and basic beliefs in how things work are not easy, especially in situations of uncertainty and lack of knowledge. In a crisis situation, where these conditions dominate, the only thing that is certain is that the old ways of doing things do not work. There is ample evidence of that! There is a push away from the old patterns, but there is little knowledge about what should be done instead. This is very frustrating, but something all organizations encounter now and then (Jönsson and Lundin, 1977; Hedberg and Jönsson, 1977a, b). The need to maintain the usual patterns of behaviour and the rules of the game makes organizations rather slow in abandoning obsolete strategies, not because they are stupid but because of the way they learn by encoding experiences (Levitt and March, 1988; Van de Ven and Polley, 1990) into routines. This standardization through encoding makes organizations predictable and trustworthy, but stable. Stability is needed because organizations have an identity to manage.

The stability, which the organization stands for in the eyes of its environment, also provides the organization with inertia. It is not desirable for organizations to surprise their environment all the time and the cost for being dependable is inertia. Even if the organization wanted to change with the turbulent environment there are at least two kinds of inertia that relate to manoeuvrability: delayed insight, and delayed action. The first kind is a consequence of the fact that organizational members, like other human beings, tend to organize their experience in patterns and treat deviations, if they are at all discovered, as errors that will be corrected in due time. Vigorous efforts to maintain patterns and to discount discordant signals can be expected in any organization, but especially in successful ones.

The second kind of organizational inertia comes as an effect of difficulties of communication in large organizations. If everybody in the organization cannot see the reason why change is necessary with their own eyes, the experience and the reasons why change is necessary have to be explained to them. It simply takes time to achieve concerted new action across levels and functions in large organizations.

Of these two kinds of inertia, the most troublesome to deal with is probably the delay in insight. Our way of learning from experience is by standardizing successful behaviour in a way that makes it more self-evident and even subconscious. It simply becomes 'how it is'. We do not bother to explain to ourselves every time we go through the routine why we do it and how it came about. Like the routines at home it is comfortable, reassuring and relaxing to have routines, and, nota bene, most of the time it is quite efficient.

But then something changes in the environment. Tastes change, demand is saturated, a substitute or invention occurs that gradually changes the basis for the routines of the organization. Abrupt and clearly visible changes are rare. No, change comes creeping up on the organization, and time and time again one is astonished by how far it can go before an organization realizes the need for change. First there are deviations from plans that can be explained as temporary errors, then there are persistent deviations that will be explained by the business cycle, government policy, low-priced imports, etc., that will eventually go away when things are back to normal. Then there is uncertainty – what is going on? – which is temporarily relieved (Ericsson, 1978) by cost-cutting efforts (work harder). Then uncertainty reaches a maximum when there is a realization that something is fundamentally wrong and that the organization has been doing the wrong thing for some time. What should one do when the only thing known for sure is that what has been done until now does not work any more? One idea is to listen to advice or explanations. An organization in crisis will be open to advice. Crisis, characterized by maximal uncertainty about the validity of basic beliefs about the nature of the business and environmental conditions, is an opening mechanism to closed patterns of behaviour.

The way organizations break out of a crisis situation (Hedberg and Jönsson, 1977a, b, 1989) is by basing action on the conception of strategy that follows from the explanation to the crisis. The causal links in the reasoning explaining why things went wrong constitute the starting point for a new strategy. They provide a map covering causes and effects that may help in reducing uncertainty to such an extent that action can be resumed. The enthusiasm related to the new-found orientation, and the reduction in uncertainty, provide impetus to action that improves the likelihood of success in post-crisis action. Early success serves to stabilize confidence and confirm the viability of the new strategy. Learning from experience can be resumed.

Crisis, thus, introduces a breach in experiential learning patterns and as such poses a threat to continuous improvement work. On the other hand, it also provides a way out of unproductive situations where the bank of activity ideas seems to be exhausted. To start anew and forget about the stalemated situation, where action seemed to repeat itself without any progress being noticed, can be a relief. It obviously is not to be recommended for organizations or groups to seek crisis consciously, but it should be remembered that crisis contains elements of opportunity as well as threat. The trick is to get out of crises quickly and resume learning from experience.

Summary

This chapter dealt with some of the cornerstones of the view of improvement work that this book seeks to convey to the reader. The concepts will be more fully developed through the stories of the cases and the analysis of them that will follow, but the blueprint given here may help the reader to discover the intentions behind the material and to give structure to it.

First the matter of what can be said and done was dealt with. To achieve 'concerted' action a group, for example an orchestra, has to communicate not only through their words or through the gestures of the conductor, but they must also listen to each other playing and adapt continuously. Acting is also signalling and the meaning of the act emerges in an interpretation by the receiver of the signal. The emergent view of information is central to this book, since it implies that influencing behaviour and learning makes use of multiple channels of communication. It is wise to ask our colleague if he sees the moose we see before we shoot our friend Peterson (who might look a bit like a moose). A controller in a company should realize that it is not enough to design report layouts. It is also necessary to use other channels of communication to influence what information emerges when reports are read. Messages cannot contain instructions for their own interpretation. Meaning emerges in the receiver.

Interpretation means establishing links of association in our minds. We see things, in more than one sense, and associations are strengthened when our actions confirm the links. Associations are 'primed' by repeated use and become structures (cf. Giddens, 1984) in our models or maps of parts of the world. We also establish organizational structures in interaction with others. Meaningful behaviour could be defined as behaviour that can be accounted for as following a rule, and a coincident commitment to future rule-following. By social action we build identities and reputations as responsible persons to be relied upon. But there is always the risk of losing face. We need the reactions of others to find out who we are, but their reactions may not be as favourable as we would like them to be. There is an urge to dominate the environment to ensure favourable reactions in our identity formation process. Individuals may also give up the identity project and prefer to merge with the crowd, at least at work, while emerging as champions of the bowling club instead.

It is furthermore assumed that learning in an organizational context is largely experiential learning according to Kolb's (1984) model. A full cycle of concrete experience, reflective observation, abstract conceptualization and active experimentation may be needed for adequate learning. Perhaps groups and organizations have to learn how to learn from experience.

A basic precondition for learning and improvement is trust. This concept in a sense is an antithesis to rationality as we know it from our textbooks in economics. The rational person is opportunistic, well informed and goal directed, while a trust is established in dialogue and in the consideration of the well-being of others. Trust also has a more technical interpretation in the sense of knowing the rules of the game, being confident that one understands the situation, that one is in control. Being able to form expectancies about the future development of the situation is based on trust.

Then there is crisis. When we register that things do not work, uncertainty is at its maximum because we are not able to state anything with assurance except that what we have been doing until now no longer works. Our strategy does not work and we are at a loss. Such a situation is of course threatening, but at the same time a crisis provides an opportunity to break away from unproductive patterns and start new processes of experiential learning. Perhaps a way of avoiding major crises is to see to it that the organization has frequent reasons to question the wisdom of what it is doing (Hedberg and Jönsson, 1977a, b)!

2

Control through practice and understanding

A theme that has grown in importance through these years of field research on information support for improvement is the insight that communication through several channels is crucial for success. It was with us from the beginning as we adopted the 'emergent view' of information, but it became more obvious over time that it is a necessary precondition for managing differing logics to have multiple channels of communication. Since this has become a major finding, seemingly of theoretical importance, it is necessary to go into some depth on this issue. We have to come to some sort of understanding of how operators (active doers) can combine their operational skills with organizational learning – how they do things with words, as it were. This is not an easy thing to do. I find that the words get in the way of what I want to say, which in itself is an illustration of the problems we are facing here.

We started with the notion of information being an emergent phenomenon in receivers of information. The meaning of a message *emerges* in the interpretative act by the receiver. This does not seem to be a very radical thing to say. It is reasonable to claim that it is the receiver of a message that understands it! But when the 'emergent view' is counterpoised to the 'container view' as Moore and Carling (1982) did, we see the implications.

If we assume that the information of a message is contained in the message, the only problem with communication would be encoding and decoding of data. It may be possible to design a general grammar, the code of all codes, and thus all misunderstandings would be due to decoding errors only. The problem for management information systems designers would be to design reports and train people to read them properly.

If we, on the other hand, assume that messages contain data and that these data become *meaningful information* only when receivers of the message relate the data to their experience in an interpretive act, we gain insight. The same message – data – can have different meanings for different receivers depending on what experience they relate it to. Thus the sender of the message could instruct the receiver on what is the proper interpretation and the relevant experience to apply in this case. But such a message could not be part of the original message, because the instructions would change the character of the message implying a need for further instructions on how to interpret the instructions and so on. We can conclude that a message cannot contain instructions for its own interpretation. These would have to be dealt with through other channels. But the sender, for example a top manager, obviously wants to achieve a specific information change in the receiver and thus has an interest in influencing the receiver's choice of interpretive schema.

In everyday life we use, for example, body language to signal that a statement is meant to be ironic or funny. This can be said to be a use of a second communication channel and a different mode of communication. In organizations different modes of communication may also be necessary to influence interpretations of formalized reports. Then the controller would have to worry not only about the layout and timing of reports but also about how to establish and use other communication channels to responsibility centres. There would also be some difficulties in deciding how to deal with the differences between the financial logics of the accounting system in relation to the operational logics of the diverse activity centres of the organization.

These were our fairly vague assumptions about our study objects at the start. Could existing systems be complemented to enhance improvement in work with communications going through channels other than the reports themselves?

In the fieldwork at the Volvo plant we registered interaction in the production teams and cherished and kept, as archaeological items, notes operators had jotted down during problem-solving sessions. We analysed and discussed what kind of causal maps might have generated the sequences of explanations to problems and suggestions of solutions. Of course it was necessary to document the improvement work that we studied in this way, but we would have missed the interpretive texture of the cases had we not come to realize the importance of the discourse on problems and solutions that goes on beside formal or semi-formal meetings. It is as if work practices are silent until one 'discovers' them.

A particular occasion was important in this respect for this author; during a pause in a final session on the Volvo project we came to talk about what characterizes a good foreman. Per, a qualified operator who acts as team coach and deputy foreman, presented a theory. There was no notepad available and no tape recorder, so the words are not the exact ones; he said that a good foreman is able to see patterns in the noise. When a foreman passes through a machine group the operators will send lots of signals to him about lots of things, including early indications of problems and possible solutions or improvements. During a day there must be hundreds of signals and operators think they have done their 'duty' with these low-key signals. Now it is up to the foreman to do something about it. Responsibility is loaded onto him. A good foreman registers all these signals, but he cannot deal with them as they appear, he must move along. When some signals form a pattern he is able to detect it, and if a pattern is significant he will put it on the agenda. A good foreman does this by announcing to the workforce that "we have a problem". Then he will allow some time for the workforce to think about it and then arrange for a meeting (probably *ad hoc* in the machine group concerned) where the operators will contribute their parts of the solution. "It is quite simple really," Per said, "if you make a public statement that we have a problem with X, the operators will provide their part of the puzzle if they are allowed to participate in the solution. The tricky bit is hearing the signals and seeing the pattern". In this way improvement work is silent or semi-silent.

Articulations come in group processes of problem solving, preferably the ones with success. We could see with our own eyes that activities increased in Börje's team. It was not that they were especially noisy or busy. They would have an occasional meeting between shifts around the time of the cost reports and one could see them talking in groups of two or three on the shop floor. They took initiatives. It was what they did that put us on the track. Following up these activities we would get a story about what had gone before them. The story about the activities and their results would give us an episode in our case documentation. Increasingly we could see initiatives directed towards other organizational units (responsibility centres) establishing customer relations that would influence the other units to more intense internal community building, etc.

In more technical areas like the Road Authority and maintenance the internal processes accompanying identity-building were more oriented towards recovering local planning processes and their relations to every-day production. In the social services department focus was almost entirely on the communication with outsiders and, since the controller and the researcher were perceived as outsiders, the process of identity-building was cast more or less explicitly in terms of commitments and contracts. There is relatively little evidence in the social services case on the internal problem-solving processes involved. We gained the impression that the work groups in the social services exhibited more hierarchy in matters of improvement initiatives than the other units we studied. In the management team of the city district it was possible to register the problem-solving dialogue of the team on videotape, but then the analysis can only cover 2.40 minutes of a specific meeting!

Theorizing on the basis of such anecdotal data may be considered unjustified, but we need theory to deal with the joint processes of system and social integration and the role of communication in these processes. The strategy here will be to start with literature and see to what extent observations or rather impressions get support from some major theoretical works, namely Habermas' (1984, 1989) theory of communicative action and Bourdieu's (1977) outline of a theory of practice.

The problem we have in theorizing about the interaction between a central financially-oriented logic, embodied in information systems like the accounting system, and local activity-based logics often embodied in silent, that is taken for granted, local practices and the work done, is to find an overarching logic that can accommodate both aspects without distorting either of them. It may be quite mistaken to ask for a logic or a theory of rationality (Habermas, 1984, p. 2) that makes it possible to analyse both levels of this two-level concept of organization on its own terms. Still it is necessary if the basic assumption and the prospect of the project is that an adequate analysis of organizational improvement is not possible as long as a monological, top-down approach is used. The context in which the phenomena under discussion are situated determines the interpretations of participants to an extent that we have so far largely ignored in management research. If we are to carry this idea of the frame of reference with us throughout the cases it is necessary to have a frame of reference for the social construction of the environment of organizational learning.

As mentioned, Bourdieu and Habermas seem to offer solutions that will now be explored. It should be noted that the interpretations about to be presented here do not claim to be professional ones as far as the theoretical orientations of these two authors go. They should, rather, be seen as the result of a pragmatic problem looking for a frame of reference.

Bourdieu: 'tradition is silent'

Bourdieu's book *Outline of a Theory of Practice* is based on empirical material in the form of ethnographic studies in Kabylia which was generated under the extreme influences of the Algerian war. Consider, furthermore the fact that an ethnographer's task is to understand the practices of an alien culture and to describe them to members of other cultures in such a way (language and references) that they appear meaningful to them (Agar, 1986). Finally, this book was written to be an argument against the structuralism and the 'theoreticism' that characterizes French social science. These are all reasons to be careful in generalizing in other fields of experience and to other groups of readers.

Bourdieu starts out by commenting upon how the role of the anthropologist as an observer is, "excluded from the real play of social activities by the fact that he has no place (except by choice or by way of a game) in the system observed and has no need to make a place for himself there" (Bourdieu, 1977, p. 1). This dooms the observer to reduce social relations to communicative relations or still worse, decoding exercises. Practices will tend to be looked upon as a spectacle, which is described (mapped) as a portfolio of rules or as a role in a model. The difficulty, then, for the anthropologist is not only to break with the native experience and the native representation of that experience, but also to make a second break, this time with his interpreting practices, and realize that:

> in taking up a point of view on the action, withdrawing from it in order to observe it from above or from a distance, he constitutes practical activity as an *object of observation and analysis*, a *representation*. (Bourdieu, 1977, p. 2.)

This is the first argument in Bourdieu's questioning of the possibility of being objective in studies of organizations or practices. The second step is the discussion of the three modes of theoretical knowledge that the social world can be object to. First there is *phenomenological* (or ethnomethodological) knowledge that sets out "to make explicit the truth of primary experience of the social world, that is all that is inscribed in the relationship of familiarity with the familiar environment, the unquestioning apprehension of the social world which, by definition, does not reflect on itself and excludes the question of conditions of its own possibility" (Bourdieu, 1977, p. 3).

The second type of knowledge Bourdieu calls *objectivist* (of which structuralist hermeneutics is a special case) and it aims to construct "the objective relations (for example, economic or linguistic) which structure practice and representations of practice, that is in particular, primary knowledge, practical and tacit, of the familiar world" (Bourdieu, 1977, p. 3). This can only be done if observers distance themselves from the primary experience and ask the question what (particular) conditions make this experience possible, and assume that the observed actors are unaware of these structures.

The third type of knowledge, which Bourdieu obviously wants to develop, is about "the *dialectical* relations between the objective structures to which the objectivist mode of knowledge gives access and the *structured dispositions* [my emphasis] within which those structures are actualized and which tend to reproduce them" (Bourdieu, 1977, p. 3). One cannot avoid seeing similarities with the reasoning of Giddens (1984) here.

Now Bourdieu criticizes the either/or choice between objectivist and subjectivist approaches that social sciences have allowed themselves to be trapped in. His intention is to focus our attention to the dialectic relations and the structured dispositions mentioned above. He proposes that we can avoid the trap by inquiring into the mode of production and functioning of practical mastery, which makes both description and ('enchanted') experience of a practice possible. Bourdieu illustrates this point by analysing the practice of gift-exchange and the related concept of honour, where he takes us from the 'rules' of honour to the sense of honour. Instead of locking the observed phenomenon into a 'mechanical' model one should consider the difficulties of procuring a theoretical mastery of social practices one has practical mastery of. The more 'alien' a practice the easier to describe it by rules and models, the more practical mastery the observer has of the practice the more cumbersome the description of tact and savoir-faire necessary in everyday life. May we conclude that Bourdieu means that it is more difficult to *articulate* adequately the nuances and possible patterns of the practice – especially to outsiders?

In developing the dialectic between external conditions and internal dispositions Bourdieu introduces the concept *habitus* as systems of durable transposable dispositions. He is anxious to point out that habitus does not stand for practices as mechanical reaction, neither are the practices generated by them completely determined by anticipated outcomes. In fact they tend to reproduce the objective structures of which they are the product. They may generate a series of moves that may objectively be described as strategies without being products of strategic intentions.

Now, if habitus is a socially constituted system of cognitive and motivating structures that tends to reproduce the structures that produced them while generating strategies, it must be considered as granting only a conditional amount of freedom. The external conditions have inculcated dispositions which will engender aspirations that are compatible with those external conditions. The holder of the dispositions exclude some possibilities without examination, as unthinkable, and others because they would not be accepted by external conditions anyway, making a virtue of necessity, or *learning to love the inevitable*. The expectations that habitus give rise to will tend to ignore the restrictions on validity that the implicit assumption of *ceteris paribus* pose. Early experiences colour expectations disproportionately while history is forgotten. "... what is essential goes without saying because it comes without saying: the tradition is silent, not least about itself as a tradition; ... " (Bourdieu, 1977, p. 167).

Bourdieu uses fairly detailed descriptions of Kabylian social life and farming to show how and why submission to collective rhythms is required. The most arbitrary orders become natural. The experience of the natural and social world as self-evident is called 'doxa' (to distinguish it from an orthodox or heterodox belief which presuppose awareness of alternative beliefs). The more stable the structures and the more fully reproduced in the dispositions of a person, the greater the extent of the field of doxa, of that which is taken for granted. Tradition is silent. Principles remain implicit and unformulated because they are unquestioned in a world which has no place for opinion, which is unaware of the very question of legitimacy.

The opening of discourse on the tacit theses of practice is not a purely intellectual operation which phenomenology calls *epoche*, the methodical suspension of naive adherence to the world. To bring the undiscussed into discussion and the unformulated into formulation, a crisis is necessary but not sufficient. Crisis situations, where the everyday order is challenged and with it the language of order, call for an extra-ordinary discourse where extra-ordinary experiences can find expression. The misfit between subjective and objective structures 'destroys self-evidence practically', and the social world loses its character of being a natural phenomenon. The character of social facts can be raised. Private experiences take on different dimensions when they are recognized in an already publicly constituted discourse. This gives them recognition and the right to be spoken of in public. Here the relationship between language and experience is quite clear. When a name is found for what was until then experienced privately, that experience not only finds expression but it is also authorized and legitimated by the group using the language. (This might be illustrated by the way consultancy buzz-words, like 're-engineering', gain acceptance and are commonly used, often with widely different meanings.)

When those dominated by the earlier regime have the opportunity to reject the definition of reality imposed on them through reproduced social structures, power issues become visible. Those threatened by deviations from the status quo will invoke the imperfect substitute for doxa, orthodoxy, that is straight opinion. By instituting an opposition between right and wrong opinion, they mask the more fundamental opposition between the universe of what can be said (and thought) and the universe of that which is taken for granted. If the society in question is structured by class, the struggle for the power to impose the legitimate order of expression is waged in the field of production of symbolic goods, which will contribute to a limitation of the discourse.

The structure of society or an organization and the legitimate order of interaction may be said to be instituted through rules of behaviour. But

> it is not sufficient to say that the rule determines practice when there is more to be gained by obeying it than by disobeying it. The rule's last trick is to cause it to be forgotten that agents have an interest in obeying the rule, or more precisely, in *being in a regular situation*. (Bourdieu, 1977, p. 22.)

Agents do not normally have a pure, disinterested respect for the rule. There is not only the first-order effect of harvesting the profit from practices (for example, the prestige accruing from marrying a child into a high-status family), but also the second-order effects of putting the agent in the right. To earn the respect of other members for impeccable conformity with social and ethical rules is an investment for the future in organized life. The accumulation of symbolic capital is an activity we are all engaged in and it is not easily made compatible with the economic rationality of our rhetoric. Bourdieu illustrates with gift-exchange practices, where the matching of the value of gifts and the timing has to be watched carefully in order to uphold the "sincere fiction of disinterested exchange". In the good-faith economy of the Kabylian lifeworld a man of good faith would not think of selling certain fresh food products, like milk or vegetables, to his neighbour. He gives it away, making relations personal. In this way he establishes client relationships and the client establishes him as a respected member of society. Such relations have to be kept implicit to survive. On a larger scale, strategies of accumulation of honour and prestige, symbolic capital, also produce clients. Symbolic capital has an ambiguous relation to economic capital in the sense that investments in symbolic capital require effort and time, which will have to be exerted at the expense of economic capital accumulation. In other words symbolic capital incurs costs in terms of economic capital. Bourdieu develops this theme to the point of stating that "the theory of strictly economic practice is simply a particular case of a general theory of the economics of practice" (Bourdieu, 1977, p. 177).

This is not the place to argue such a statement, but it is a central issue in this project to inquire about the exchange rate between the symbolic capital of a work group in the form of social network, complementarity of skills, cohesion and trust, and, on the other side, its capability to produce output of economic value to others, for example central management. It seems safe to assume that symbolic capital may function as a buffer in times of crisis, allowing members time to articulate and solve problems of work and production. It may also be assumed that there is a progressive depletion of symbolic capital while unsuccessful problem solving goes on and that successful problem solving will add to symbolic capital and extend the tolerances for ambiguity (caused by crisis). There is a risk in talking about symbolic capital and thereby making it visible, in organizational contexts, since exposure may make it seem insincere and thus without value. On the other hand, we have all experienced what appeals to morale and what common values can achieve in terms of extra efforts in a group.

We borrow from Bourdieu the insight that there are specific difficulties in dealing with and presenting *knowledge as interaction* between context and personal experience, or between the local lifeworld of production and the central and abstract world of finances. We also borrow his concept of *habitus* to denote organizational and personal dispositions that become so natural that they are invisible and thus difficult to articulate. Finally, there is the notion of *symbolic capital* referring to the accumulation of honour, prestige and trust that occurs as a by-product, as it were, of rule-following in social interaction.

Identities are established and maintained in interaction with others in addition to the production of primary services and goods. Investment in symbolic capital takes time and effort and may thus be said to be complementary and to a certain extent a substitute to economic capital. The substitute effect becomes visible in situations where symbolic capital may grant a person or group access to time and resources necessary to solve problems in crisis situations.

Habermas: understanding

Habermas' project is most impressive. He wants to:

1. Develop a concept of communicative rationality that is not limited to the subjectivist, monological views of rationality that have dominated so far.
2. Construct a two-level concept of society that integrates the lifeworld and system paradigms.
3. Sketch, against the background of a wider concept of rationality and the differences in inner logic between lifeworld and system, a critical theory of modernity that redirects rather than abandons the project of reason and rationality in society.

His attempt is metatheoretical in the sense that he uses the theoretical work of others, critically or approvingly, to underpin his solutions. In this sense his observations are as far distanced as they could be from the everyday improvement work that is the subject here. But he has something to say to us that can enlighten our understanding of the observations made during the fieldwork presented here.

Habermas starts out by providing us with a first sketch of rationality. What does it mean to behave 'rationally' in a certain situation or that a person's expressions can count as 'rational'? Must it be based on reliable knowledge? Not necessarily, since knowledge is fallible! But it must be open to objective judgement. Judgement is objective if it is based on a validity claim "that has the same meaning for observers and non-participants as it has to the acting subject himself" (Habermas, 1984, p. 9). Truth and efficiency are validity claims of this kind and the better they can be defended (accounted for) against criticism the more rational they are.

Such an approach to rationality is not unproblematic. It is too abstract in the sense that it does not allow much differentiation, and it is too narrow in the sense that it should deal with other expressions than those of truth and efficiency. There is more to it than this. Who is, for example, to judge what is 'better' in the defence against criticism?

Take the simplest form of rationality. A person, **A**, makes a claim, **p**, which states that if x is done than y will occur – that is descriptively valid. Then **A** states "I want y therefore I do x", which is instrumentally and cognitively rational. If **A** does not fumble, that is instrumentally masters the doing of x, y will occur. Now, if **A** and **B** share the knowledge of what y is and **A** states "we should have some y", and **B** then chooses to do the appropriate instrumental activities (x) to produce y the situation is somewhat more complicated. It involves communicative understanding as well as instrumental mastery. What if there is disagreement as to whether x causes y, or if **B** did not understand that it was y that was wanted? Well, only responsible people can behave rationally. This means that instrumental rationality requires that the person is able to chose among alternatives and control the necessary environmental conditions to achieve stated goals. As to communicative rationality those people are considered responsible who are able, within their communication community, to direct their actions towards generally recognized validity claims. People who are so private in their attitudes and evaluations that they cannot explain them or render them plausible by appeal to generally recognized standards are not behaving rationally. This applies to actions regulated by norms as well as expressive self-presentations and evaluative expressions. The basis is the ability to, under suitable conditions, give reasons for validity claims – to account for them.

Habermas develops a typology of argumentation and arrives at the set as shown in Fig. 2.1.

Forms of argumentation	Reference dimensions	
	Expressions	Validity claims
Theoretical discourse	Cognitive–instrumental	Truth of propositions Efficiency of actions
Practical discourse	Moral–practical	Rightness of norms of action
Aesthetic criticism	Evaluative	Adequacy of standards of value
Therapeutic critique	Expressive	Sincerity of expression
Explicative discourse	—	Comprehensibility of symbolic constructs

Figure 2.1 Types of argumentation (adapted from Habermas, 1984, Fig. 2, p. 23).

A validity claim is an assertion that the conditions of validity of an expression are fulfilled. The meaning of grounding of validity claims is different for different types.

> 'Grounding' of descriptive statements means establishing the existence of states of affairs; 'grounding' normative statements establishes the acceptability of actions or norms of action; 'grounding' evaluative statements, establishing the preferability of values; 'grounding' expressive statements, establishing the transparency of self-presentation; and 'grounding' explicative statements, establishing that symbolic expressions have been produced correctly. (Habermas, 1984, p. 39.)

Obviously this is not an easy task without a prior communality of understanding and of language. To accomplish this a certain order or logic of argumentation is necessary. Habermas presupposes an attitude of cooperative search for the truth and excludes all force except that of the better argument. If considered as a *process*, argumentation "can be conceived as a reflective continuation, with different means, of action oriented to reaching understanding" (Habermas, 1984, p. 25). When seen as a *procedure*, argumentation is seen as interaction, subject to special rules, where participants: (1) focus attention on a problematic validity claim; (2) rid themselves of the pressure of action and assume a hypothetical attitude; and (3) test with reasons, and only with reasons whether the validity claim stands or not. Finally, argumentation can be viewed in terms of its *products*, that is arguments. Here focus is on the properties of arguments, rules of inference, rules about when claims have to be modified, and so on. Habermas maintains that the idea of the ideal speech situation cannot be adequately developed in either single one of these analytical levels. All are involved. In a process view the intuitive intention is to convince a universal audience, in a procedural view it is to end a dispute with a rationally motivated agreement, and from a product view the intention is the grounding of validity claims with arguments. We should take note of the requirement posited by Habermas that it is necessary to relieve oneself of the emergencies of action and assume a hypothetical attitude. This is probably a crucial point in our analysis of the cases – the need to provide for an escape from the pressures of operations when a group is about to start problem solving. This shift from the physical world of operations to the hypothetical world of arguments and back is, as we have noted earlier, constitutive of experiential learning even if Kolb's model may be said to be oriented towards the individual learner.

Of specific importance in the development of the proper attitude for ideal speech situations is the 'decentralization' of world views. Here Habermas refers to cognitive development, as described by Piaget, as the construction of a reference system for the simultaneous demarcation of the objective and the social world from the subjective world, to the extent that if a person is able to manage all three worlds (objective, subjective and social) in a differentiated way, can that person be said to be cognitively mature? It is then possible to form reflective world concepts and open up access to the world through common interpretive efforts. This makes it possible to adopt a *third-person perspective* on a problem. Distance from the subjective, self-evident experience is achieved through an articulation of validity claims that are criticizable and thereby amenable to change in the face of good arguments. Individuals cannot 'step out' of their lifeworld, but they can "free themselves from the fetters of habitual concrete forms of life". How this can be achieved may be said to be the problem we focus on in this book.

The task is finding rational solutions to common problems in organizations. Consider a two-level conception of organization. Such a model of organization will contain: (1) 'system', which represents the financial and profit-oriented measurements and information requirements that follow from the view of the organization as a monological, hierarchically coordinated production unit; and (2) 'lifeworld' which represents daily implementation of abstract plans into operative processes in physical time and space situations with their technical, social and practical urgencies. 'System' and 'lifeworld' views of common problems will differ. 'System' statements will gain meaning from the conceptual structure in which it is cast. An accounting report gains meaning from the structure of the accounting system. The cost centre report shows that there is a deviation from budgeted costs, to the extent that any reason for the deviation implies that the person in charge of this responsibility centre is not living up to his or her responsibility. The 'lifeworld' meaning of the same report may be that there was a breakdown in the robot that transfers semi-finished goods from operation x to operation y, which in turn was due to overheating resulting from inadequate preventive maintenance, etc.

To arrive at a common understanding of how this problem should be dealt with one could, of course, agree that the best thing would be for one of the logics to dictate the terms of argumentation. This would be best if the dictating party knows what is the truth, what is right, and does not see any need for self-expression by other parties. As soon as any one of these conditions is not met, a dialogue, that is communicative action, is necessary, because the meaning of a sentence, for speakers and hearers, is understood when they know under what conditions it is true or valid. To reach agreement – understanding – the parties involved have to behave reciprocally in adapting their thoughts and arguments to each others background knowledge, current situation, concepts and language. In this way they can bridge the gap between the inner logics of 'system' and 'lifeworld' or between 'lifeworlds'. But only if they are sincerely oriented towards reaching an understanding. If one party sets as its goal to win, that is to persuade the other party and avoid being impressed by the arguments of the other party, he or she behaves strategically, that is, is oriented towards success in terms of its own goals. Then communication is distorted and trust will be dismantled.

This view of Habermas is quite a challenge to traditional management control thinking since it allows for different standards of inner logic in different parts of the organization. Surely the overall goal is rational conduct of human affairs, and Habermas has sometimes been called "the last great rationalist" (Habermas, 1984, p. vi), but his concept of rationality is far more complex and thus useful in understanding empirical observations rather than ordinary, monological and instrumental rationalities. If there are differences in inner logic between different parts of the organization then dialogue through communicative action is necessary. Communication inside and between organizational units involves much more than finding the best solution to a given problem. There is also the matter of establishing and maintaining norms of good practice, of giving opportunities for self-expression and of building trust. Of course it matters if the messages that are exchanged are well formed, but the essence of the problem is not to design the best possible report layout to present the output from the most advanced information technology. You can always ask the other guy: "What do you mean by that?" if communication is distorted. It takes time and effort to communicate, but if communication generates learning, trust and improved performance, the time spent on it may prove precious in a positive sense, return on time and effort invested may surpass expectations.

3

The context: Swedish management style, institutions and knowledge of participation and budget control

To understand communication and the implications of the stories that will be told shortly, the reader needs a conception of the context in which these events occurred and the stories developed. We have already claimed that the meaning of a message emerges when interpreted in context. To give an adequate description of what it is like to work in Swedish industry, or in the public sector, which we shall also deal with, is obviously an impossible undertaking. It would be necessary to give a historic account of the development of industry, institutional structures, mentalities and competitive ups and downs of a nation. A sensible person should not even try.

A sketch of Swedish management

The following description is largely based on a current study of Swedish management based on interviews with the most respected industrial leaders. By asking great leaders to tell the story of their careers, and especially about critical incidents that have coloured their view of what good management is, one might gain insights into the core characteristics of the management culture. A by-product of such a study is a multifaceted history of the last 30–40 years of Swedish industry. Here we are interested in this industry as a setting for shop-floor improvement work.

Industrial leaders in any country can safely be assumed to be products of their own environment. The differences between managerial styles in different countries become visible when management is globalized. Swedish management has been characterized by its most prominent leaders as "ambiguous and obscure" (Jönsson, 1995). To illustrate the point of such a summary statement imagine a top management meeting in a Swedish corporation. (Most managers in all nations spend a large part of their time in meetings.) If a foreign manager participated in the typical Swedish meeting he (it would be a male manager) would come out of the meeting with an empty note book and more questions than answers. "Have there been any decisions?", "What am I supposed to do?", "It was an interesting discussion but where is the structure?", "There was an overview of our problems but what are the solutions we are supposed to pursue?". This is the impression we got from descriptions in our business-leader interviews (and it is our experience of faculty meetings).

Somebody said in an interview about this 'Swedishness' in management: "The strictest command you will get is 'See what you can do!'".

This is, of course, a caricature of the core characteristic of the Swedish management style, but there are some truths to point out in it. The style is an expression of the ambition to lead by ideas (vision) and through consensus. The ideal leader is portrayed as a team coach rather than a strong-willed captain. The most celebrated events in the careers of Swedish industry leaders seem to be when a (top management) team is persuaded by the ideas presented by the leader and a new strategy is established and later proven to be functional. The team is present and approving in the images leaders want to present to illustrate how their careers have developed to prepare for the climax of becoming president of one of the major corporations!

Also present in illustrations of the Swedish management style is a tendency towards rough and ready analysis, little planning, and a willingness to take the risk of getting going even if all details are not properly analysed. There seems to be a strong reliance on managers' ability to keep projects together through teamwork on an *ad hoc* basis.

Such a Swedish management style seems to fit with the results of Hofstede (1980) after having measured work-related values in many countries. Four dimensions were indicated as structures of national work values: power distance; uncertainty avoidance; individualism; and masculinity.

Power distance (PD) has to do with to what extent subordinates are of the opinion that employees are afraid to state a different opinion to their bosses and whether they see their own boss as autocratic or paternalistic. It is an expression of the 'distance' between high and low in the organization.

Uncertainty avoidance (UA) is a measure of fear of failure. Its central variables are a tendency to agree with the statement that employees should follow the rules even if they are of the opinion that it would be better for the company if they did not. It also relates to preference for long-term employment. It has to do with the willingness to take risks and the fear of losing face.

Individualism (I) is a dimension in Hofstede's study that is generated by stressing the difference between 'company time' and 'personal time'. The job should give enough free time for the employee to pursue private interests and family life. There is also a strong appreciation of freedom to organize one's own work and appreciation of a demanding job.

Masculinity (MA), finally, is a dimension that relates to career, good pay, and reward for hard work. This dimension is negatively loaded with good relations with your boss, cooperation and job security.

Hofstede's study generated indices along these four dimensions for a large number of countries. Some of them are listed in Table 3.1.

Sweden registers the lowest value on masculinity of all countries reported by Hofstede, and is comparatively low on power distance and uncertainty avoidance, while it is moderately high on individualism. Teamwork seems to go well with Swedish work values. Even risky projects can be undertaken provided that the boss does not get too 'bossy', and the individual gets a decent opportunity to distinguish himself or herself as a valuable team player. Good relations and cooperation are distinguishing values for Swedes if we follow Hofstede.

Table 3.1 Hofstede's (1980) indices on the four dimensions of national work cultures

Country	PD	UA	I	MA
U.S.A.	40	46	91	62
Germany	35	65	67	66
Great Britain	35	35	89	66
France	68	86	71	43
Japan	54	92	46	95
Italy	50	75	76	70
Sweden	31	29	71	5

Institutional factors

When it comes to an institutional setting Sweden as an industrialized nation is characterized by early internationalization, high concentration of industry and a strong welfare state.

Swedish industry internationalized early. In a small country the home market cannot support growth to any extent. The growing company has to find markets and, in a protectionist world, production capacity abroad. The major companies have 75% or more of their investment and employment abroad. The concentration of industry was to a considerable extent caused by the internationalization. The successful exporting company accumulated resources to acquire domestic competitors or to forge cartel agreements. The state did not mind. An atmosphere of deliberation in committees with representatives of the parties concerned developed.

Another aspect of the cooperative bias was a deep-rooted idea of self-sufficiency in Sweden. This seemed to make it acceptable to cooperate, also with customers, in the face of foreign competition, which was further strengthened by the successful neutrality policy during World War II. It might not have been very glorious at times but the policy kept the nation out of the war, which gave a head start to Swedish industry when the rebuilding of Europe started. But before that the state had grown strong.

A strong state in a corporatist society

In the early part of this century government was often based on a minority in parliament in Sweden. A struggling union movement was rather successful in organizing labour and its main political arm, the social democrats, grew steadily in strength. There was continuous political struggle through the 1920s and repeated invitations by minority governments to consult with the labour market activists on measures to achieve labour market peace. In the labour unions communist influence grew which resulted in militancy. There was police violence in the legendary 1 May demonstration in 1931. The years 1931 and 1932 were characterized by the world depression sweeping over the country, leaving about 25% of the labour force jobless, and the power struggle between unions and the employers seemed to subside.

The first years of the 1930s were dramatic in determining the subsequent institutional development. The international depression drove unemployment up towards 25%. There was a currency crisis in the summer of 1931 which included capital flight from Sweden (Lundberg, 1985) and which forced the Bank of Sweden to abandon the gold standard and left the Swedish crown to float once the pound sterling had fallen. The Bank of Sweden tried desperately to borrow abroad to keep the crown at its old parity; as Lundberg (1985) says "happily without success, although it employed Sweden's greatest expert on foreign borrowing, Ivar Krueger" (Lundberg, 1985, p. 9). In September 1931 Sweden devalued.

In March 1932 the Kreuger-crash broke. The Kreuger empire was a large conglomeration of companies, by any measure, centred around the core of International Match, and it was gigantic in relation to the Swedish industry. Kreuger was a highly visible industrialist with a reputation as a financial wizard. The holding company in the group was Kreuger and Toll which was listed on the New York Stock Exchange. It had the largest share in turnover at the time of the crash and had sailed through the 1929 crash without much damage. Kreuger was engaged by the League of Nations for peace-making missions, he helped several European nations with reconstructions of national debts after the World War I, was a frequent guest at the White House, etc. In return for his service to various countries he acquired monopoly rights for matches. He considered these rights very valuable and as he increased the value in the books for these rights he could show handsome profits which justified a high dividend, which, in turn kept the value of the shares high. This allowed him to issue debentures, which provided cash to pay the dividends that were justified by the artificial profits generated by the write up of the value of the monopoly rights. For Ivar Kreuger the difficulties in generating cash from issues in the international capital market grew. When there was not enough cash to keep his scheme going Kreuger committed suicide in March 1932. The fall of such an industrial giant had wide-ranging repercussions in the Swedish business world. The bankruptcy settlement realigned industrial power structures and legislation, for example the Bank Act, was reviewed. The number of industrial workers had grown continuously and the Swedes were clearly heading towards class-related voting. The unions organized for more centralized power and the employers had to devise a matching strategy.

The 1932 election lead to a social democratic victory and the party formed a government even though it did not have its own majority. It was soon obvious that a socialist revolution was not intended. Now the economic crisis had first priority. The social democrats struck a deal with the Farmers' party on labour market policies and farm subsidies, and thereby laid the basis for a long period of stable majority government. A group of young economists in Stockholm (with Myrdal, Lindahl and Ohlin as the most prominent names) wrote on stabilization policy and had an interested audience in the Minister of Finance. Myrdal was invited by the minister to work out a programme for an active fiscal policy to promote stabilization and growth. Scientific management and modernization, i.e. social engineering, was the banner under which the construction of the new welfare state was initiated. A period of export-lead growth started in 1933, with labour and the state working in mutual support and the weakened employers' federation adapting its strategy to new realities.

The rise of the 'Swedish model'

It was from this starting point that the outline of the 'Swedish model' was designed; a stable majority government applying a Keynesian economic policy supported by prominent economics professors, a union movement that had grown strong through the struggles in recent years, a currency that was recently devalued and an industrial establishment that was intent on strategy change. There was also underutilized capacity in industry which provided a good basis for positive effects from state intervention.

Liberal policies towards industry, instead of socialist experiments, included free depreciation, deductible for tax purposes, which was written into the tax laws in 1938 but which had already been the practice for many years. This favoured large companies which were stimulated to invest in new equipment and plants. Labour peace was institutionalized in the much celebrated 'Satsjöbad agreement' which stipulated that disputes would be settled by negotiations. The most important aspect, however, of the Swedish model is the centralization of wage negotiations.

After World War II industrial expansion continued as Swedish industrial capacity was undamaged by the war. A model welfare state was built with an ever-increasing proportion of national income allocated through the public sector. The policies of labour market mobility in conjunction with a solidaristic wage policy supported a transformation of Swedish industry towards better international competitive advantages. The solidaristic wage policy was built on the idea that central wage negotiations would push wages, across the board, towards the level which that part of the industry which met international competition could carry. This meant that low wage industries would be squeezed out by low-priced imports which were allowed by a liberal trade policy. The unemployment that resulted from inefficient firms being pushed out of their markets was counteracted by active labour market policies to increase mobility to advancing, competitive industries. Investment in new technology was stimulated through tax incentives.

The core factor in these policies, that must be considered as highly successful, was the centralized collective bargaining and disciplined local and employer organizations. A true expression of the modernist project of rational social engineering. Both sides would use a jointly developed economic model to determine the available room for wage increases compatible with stable prices.

The fall of the Swedish model

The long-term trends which tended to erode the operation of the economy and the shocks of the 1970s were the main causes for the fall of the Swedish model (Lundberg, 1985, p. 23). It is worth noting that this fall coincided with the rise of post-modernism.

The state weakened as social democratic domination was broken (after 44 years) and competitive disadvantages caused difficulties in financing the ambitious welfare state. The oil crisis demonstrated the impotence of the state to live up to its promises. Job security became a priority. The egalitarian spirit seemed to have been strengthened by the fact that the economy tended toward a zero-sum game as traditional industries like steel and shipyards encountered severe problems. Government policy was directed towards the dismantling of dying industries without too severe impacts on employment. The growth target came out of focus. The public sector became the solution as married women increasingly entered the labour market, and labour-intensive industries were liquidated. Industrial policy was transformed into regional policy.

Union and social democratic policy in the 1970s was economic democracy. Read positively it could be understood as a policy to bind the parties of corporatist society closer together to find solutions to emerging problems. By allowing union representatives access to company accounts, board rooms and, even, ownership in listed companies through the Wage Earners' Fund scheme, a rational plan for further development could have been be implemented. However, globalization had gone too far – no nation is an island – and larger institutional structures in the form of multinational corporations as well as supernational organizations like the European Community were already exerting their influence.

The logic of the Swedish model was broken because its assumptions were no longer valid. It is interesting to note that the main argument for the introduction of the Wage Earners' Fund was the history of the Swedish model itself rather than the development of the Swedish economy or democracy or similar. Instead a new confusion arose and there was a general search in the direction of decentralization, local solutions and teamwork. Smaller units surviving and prospering because they were smart, hard working and adaptive to local circumstances, became the model solution. The state was no longer the guarantor of the good life. This is, in a sketch, the larger context in which the case studies of the following chapters were set. Regulative, normative and cognitive aspects (Scott, 1995) of this context can be drawn upon to understand what went on. Of course, there is a choice of which aspect to emphasize.

Budget control

A further context in which the cases are set is the control of operations. In a sense the idea of controlling organizations through plans, translated into budgets, which are used in monitoring that the operations are carried out in accordance with intentions, is also a product of the modernist philosophy. Thought, translated into a plan, will provide for rational management of world affairs. Deviations from plans signify error. Our knowledge of how budget control works in real life, especially if participative moments are introduced, is however, limited.

We live by our images of how things are. Steering organizations by budget control is an activity that is overburdened with false images. This is especially true in the public sector where the dream of controlling through tough budget decisions survives in spite of repeated exposure to concrete evidence of failure. In the public sector there are opposition parties to scrutinize behaviour and publicize failures, but in large corporations there is no such opposition. Leadership and the impetus of decisions are assumed undercut by the opposition pointing out weaknesses in decisions. There are probably many leaders who believe that their authority would suffer from subordinates stating opinions that do not totally agree with their own. Hopwood (1972) found that managers who gave priority to budget discipline before profit opportunities tended to 'contaminate' subordinate units with the same propensity to 'live by the book' and avoid the risk of improvement initiatives. Zuboff (1988) found that improved access to operative data for operators uncovered power relations that were previously based in privileged information about operations, but now had to be defended with reference to hierarchy ('I am the boss').

If foremen and middle managers in general are considered to have access to superior information sources, it is quite natural to ask them for decisions on difficult problems. Hierarchy is built on this principle. Those who have better information should decide and those that have lesser information should do as they are told.

Similarly, if improvement of the competitive position of an organization is to be built on mobilization of the whole creative potential of the organization, participation is necessary. This statement has to be modified. There has been controversy among researchers for some time now on the relation between budget participation and performance. This debate has generated more sophisticated measures, and we can now be reasonably sure about the relationships.

It seems to have started with the study made by Hopwood (1972) who found that a high emphasis on budget discipline tended to be associated with subordinate job-related tension. Otley (1978) replicated Hopwood's study in another organization, but found no significant relation between the superior's style of evaluation and subordinate job-related tension or managerial performance. These results were contradictory, even if Hopwood did not actually measure the effect of job-related tension on managerial performance, and they inspired efforts to reconcile the findings. Otley suggested that one reason could be that both he and Hopwood studied behaviour in single organizations, i.e. the results might be due to specific cultures in the studied organizations. Others, for example, Brownall (1982) took an interest in measurement problems and found that high budget participation *and* high budget emphasis were associated with enhanced managerial performance (and vice versa). Hirst (1983) found that job-related tension was at its lowest when budget emphasis was high and task uncertainty low. This describes a situation where hierarchy rules and improvement efforts are low. Hereby task uncertainty was brought into the picture more definitely. The measurement of task uncertainty was problematic though. Most measures used in the literature are based on Perrow's two attributes; *task analysability*, which relates to the extent to which work is programmable, and *number of exceptions*, which refers to the frequency of unexpected or novel events. Even if those dimensions can be measured to represent analysability and variability quite faithfully, it is not evident how they could be combined into one measure for purposes of hypothesis testing regarding the effect of task uncertainty on other factors related to budgetary control.

Reviewing the Brownall (1982) study, with a view towards its validity under different conditions of task uncertainty, Brownall and Hirst (1986) suggested that Brownall's conclusions were based on situations with low task uncertainty because the organization where the data were collected had a relatively standardized production process. Under such conditions people do not have to focus attention on handling the job as such. That is, given low task uncertainty, high participation in combination with high budget emphasis will give good managerial performance. They also stated that Brownall's results should not be expected to hold in conditions of high task uncertainty. In their opinion the important effect of participation is that it "may provide an opportunity for managers to gain access to resources which can be used to buffer task performance from unanticipated effects of others, and to introduce new and better means to address tasks" (Brownall and Hirst, 1986, p. 242). The problem was that when they analysed their data Brownall and Hirst found that they could confirm that participation, budget emphasis and task uncertainty interacted as predicted to affect job-related tension, but they could not confirm any effect on managerial performance! Something was wrong.

In a new effort to explain the problems with earlier studies, Brownall and Dunk (1991) analysed further the measurement of task uncertainty and arrived at the conclusion that task difficulty (Perrow's task analysability) is more likely to give rise to a generally valid role for participation (whatever the level of budget emphasis) than task variability is. The key factor was considered to be the difficulty of specifying the relation between inputs and outputs. Task variability is less problematic. Many organizations have learnt to master customer driven production in small batches with the help of automation and information technology. Take, for instance, flexible manufacturing systems (FMS) where every piece of output may be unique. The machine has been programmed to perform a variety of operations in different sequences depending on the state of the piece being processed. A necessary precondition for the FMS to be programmed is obviously that the inputs and outputs of the various possible operations can be specified. Task variability is at its maximum while task difficulty is low, since the work to be done can be programmed.

Since the two dimensions – task difficulty and task variability – that constitute task uncertainty relate to work-unit rather than to the individual level, there is a risk that data gathered from individuals in a single organization may be biased. The more socially integrated an organization and the more work is team-based (individuals perform multiple tasks in a team that is responsible for a whole set of tasks) the greater the chance that organizational members will view matters in a similar way. This was an explanation, offered to Otley, of the difference in results between Hopwood and Otley. The common culture, as it were, dominates the other variables and the measurements come out distorted. Work is homogeneous within, but not between, organizations. Having taken seemingly adequate care to guard against these problems of measurement and sampling, Brownall and Dunk (1991) found that *participation has a significant positive effect on performance when task difficulty is high.* This is valid whether budget emphasis is high or low. Also when task difficulty was low there was a positive but weak and not significant correlation with performance. This finding explains why Brownall's (1982) results do not have general validity across levels of task difficulty. He proposed on behavioural grounds that matching high (low) budget participation with high (low) budget emphasis would have positive effects on performance.

Even if we may thus be fairly convinced that there is a correlation between participation and performance if task difficulty is high, we still do not know how motivation works. There is a mobilization of efforts towards shared goals. These goals must be accepted as relevant and possible to reach, it seems, and group members must see that colleagues in the group are sincere in their attempts to contribute in the common effort.

High motivation is sometimes thought of as synonymous with good performance. But it is not difficult to imagine (cf. Becker and Green, 1962) a situation where motivation is group oriented and manifests itself in group cohesion. With high group cohesion and low acceptance of budget targets, production slow-down is likely to occur. Stedry (1960) found that targets that were far above aspiration levels did not motivate, while a small gap between aspiration levels and targets was motivating. And there are the classical studies of Argyris (1952) and Hofstede (1967)!

Although the Argyris study did not include interviews with production workers on budgets, it formed enough impressions about the conditions of those who are engaged in the actual production to recommend measures of *improved communication* to achieve improved performance through budgets.

The Hofstede study included a questionnaire given to more than 100 managers on different levels in five manufacturing plants. It found that participation was an important factor positively associated with motivation to meet budget targets, but the results concerning first-level supervisors and workers were mixed. There was indirect budget participation for supervisors through participation in the setting of technical production standards, but this did not seem to affect motivation to meet these standards. On the other hand, in one of the Hofstede plants, the budget standards were based on data from another plant. Still they were seen as valid and relevant. In another plant, supervisors were included in the manager category and given cost centre budgets in a company that was highly cost conscious and included budget performance in job evaluation. In this plant foremen had positive attitudes towards budget participation.

The picture of the relationship between participation and motivation that emerges from these and other studies is indeed a mixed one. From the Brownall studies presented first it can be concluded that there is a crucial relation between task difficulty and the effect of participation that calls for further attention. From the Hofstede study comes an interesting concept that Hofstede calls "game spirit". Hofstede was persuaded by his data that the game spirit of the budget game was the key to understanding the mixed observations of attitudes towards budgets and participation. The idea is that people play games for the sake of the game itself. Games are highly motivating, partly because it is part of the game to follow the rules of the game, partly because the game is not threatening to the individual because when the game is over participants resume their ordinary lives. "A well-played budget game means involvement, cooperation, excitement, and a positive contribution" (Mackintosh, 1985, p. 16). If management could create an atmosphere where the budget process is seen as a game, and establish an attitude of game spirit, the problem of motivation and budgets might be solved. Participation in itself is not enough. There must be communication, proper targets and evaluations, and also adequate behaviour on superior levels of organization for the game spirit to survive. It may also be suggested that the focus of the budget game should be on the task of dealing with environmental conditions rather than control relations within the organization.

4

Controlling and communicating*

This case has been based on two studies that were done at the same time some years ago in a subcontractor to one of the major car manufacturers. One of the studies dealt with the budgetary communication between the plant, which specialized in producing one car component, and headquarters. The other study reported on an experiment with information support for operational self-management on the shop floor. Both studies observed anomalies that seemed difficult to explain when each study was seen in isolation, but if we see them together we might see a possible explanation to the perplexing phenomena.

Budgeting at the top

The multinational owner of this plant had negotiated with the Spanish government to set up a fairly large production facility in Spain. In that process the government exerted pressure for the plant to be built in a remote area in urgent need of reindustrialization. It was expected from

*This chapter is based on research by Luis Fernandez Perez reported in Fernandez Perez (1993), and by Salvador Carmona and German Perez-Casanova, reported in Carmona and Perez-Casanova (1993).

the start that the workforce would not be very skilled. The rationale for this location for the component production thus was to produce a standard product at low cost, but with acceptable quality. Local management could expect to be pressured to the limit by superior units. The unemployment rate in the area was extremely high, and the customer had alternative suppliers of the component. Still the new management team wanted to prove themselves. Production was performed in a high-technology environment in large batches.

The final decision on the location of the plant was to locate two plants together with some shared management functions. This had some disturbing effects as the two plants belonged to different divisions. Since the two plants were losing money during the first years of the 1980s, there were discussions and frequent redistributions of overhead costs including rebilling of expenses between the two in order to reflect the real expenses correctly in the two profit and loss accounts.

The plant we are interested in here employs about 650 people (in peak production up to 800), of which 150 are salaried. The plant was equipped with a rather inflexible production line which was specialized for high-volume production of one standardized component. The capacity was greater than the total component need for the European market. It would be costly to set production for new designs of the same product and, obviously, for other products.

The multinational owner was headquartered in the U.S.A. The components division had many subdivisions and was divided into North America and Overseas. The Overseas division had one office for each major part of the world. In our case the European office. The only customers were other parts of the car multinational.

Up to 1987 the new Spanish plant could not meet the sales forecast and heavy losses were inflicted. The European office decided to prepare a strategy change for the plant – it should seek outside customers.

After four years of implementation this new strategy had not achieved much. Some new customers had been captured through aggressive marketing. The trouble was that the orders had two characteristics in common; low price and low volume. The plant was less profitable than four years earlier. The main inside customer was not too much help since the price for the deliveries was fixed in an annual meeting, which the Spaniards saw as close to unilateral. Exchange of information or negotiation were not characteristics of these meetings. The low prices meant that the multinational was gradually taking back its equity investment by way of cheap components.

The plant had a functional organization. Finance and personnel were staff departments; and sales, product engineering and operations (with subdepartments) were the line departments. Originally all senior management positions were held by people that came from division headquarters in order to transfer its management culture to the Spanish employees. By the start of the budget process, which will be described later, all managerial positions, except that of managing director, were held by Spaniards.

The budget procedure

The budget procedure is regulated by a letter sent out by the European headquarters to the different units in June, specifying the steps in budget elaboration, who is responsible for what, and deadlines.

The first figures that arrive at the budget section of the finance department of our plant are units of sales and key indicators for the production process. On this basis the engineering department calculates the 'routings', that is the processing time needed in each process. By multiplying time per unit with the number of units expected to be sold one determines the total number of hours needed to produce the volume forecast. (The inventory is assumed to be zero.) The total hours figure is corrected for break-even efficiency, a factor that is determined in staff meetings, for absenteeism and structural overtime. This gives the exact total number of hours needed for next year. Dividing that number by the maximum number of hours a person can work in a year obtains the total number of direct manufacturing workers needed. The cost-driver of this subsidiary is labour. It also used to be the dominant cost item, but as technology changes it tends to come down. All indirect costs are allocated with labour as the base.

Now the finance department really goes to work on the budget. It receives information about the burden of all the departments. With requests on different items more or less well argued, they build the budget. It should be mentioned that the people involved have access to the base for each item; last year's budget, the actual budget and forecasted outcome for the current year, which has a disciplining effect.

The budget document consists of *ca.* 80 pages divided into eight chapters: profit and loss statement; head count; sales by product line; sales in monetary terms; materials and labour; burden; benefits; other. There is also a cash flow analysis and a funds statement.

Getting approval

It is not very easy to get budget approval from higher authority.

With the budget for 1990 the problem was that the resulting loss in the first draft budget was unacceptable. A staff meeting decided to take part of the 'slack' in overheads away which improved the profit figure. Then the budget was considered ready to send to the European office for approval. This was done in August as planned in the manual, in spite of the fact that the initiating letter from the European office had not arrived. The European office was a bit late. It was not until September that the Spanish plant got a fax with requested targets for the budget. These targets were not as easy as the figures used in the first budget version. So the budget document had to be redone to match the figures mandated by the European office. "All this work on the budget for nothing!" was the general feeling among staff who had participated in the original budget process. Overtime of a 100 hours that month for nothing! A budget was produced and the European office satisfied, but the figures in the final budget were not the ones planned when the engineering department calculated the processing time.

The 1991 the budget process had a better start in that the budget letter from the budget supervisor to all the departments was sent out early, in May. The reason was that the budget supervisor was newly appointed. This time the sales figures could be carefully calculated so that they would not have to be changed like previous years. Late changes in the volume figures would change everything else in the budget. It is best to get it right the first time. This time there was delay owing to the sales department taking care to provide good estimates. Still, late information, received after they had reported their estimates, made them want to adjust the figures somewhat. The controller would not let them because it would change the base for other budgets which were already out.

This year there was a change in the way the production department's overhead was calculated. Working groups had been set up with people from maintenance, engineering and finance together with the supervisors. These groups had meetings to work out their own expense budgets for their departments. (We shall hear more about this project later!)

While these processes were going on, the controller drew up a preliminary profit and loss budget that he thought could meet with approval from the European office. Everybody 'knew' that anything less than zero profit would not be accepted, and they also 'knew' that it was virtually impossible to obtain such an outcome.

The first compilation of the budget figures showed considerable loss on the operating profit level. Nobody in the finance department was surprised since the rules of the game had taught everybody that the estimates would be cut more than once in the review process.

In the first review meeting at the plant the plant manager and the sales manager were not present but all other managerial staff participated. Obviously there had to be cuts everywhere since profit was far from satisfactory. There was agreement that the main cuts had to be made in the burden and materials budgets. Every department took a small cut in its own budget and there was agreement that a larger slice could be taken out of the sales department's budget which seemed a little high (and the sales manager was out of town). Then there was the question of the expense budgets worked out by the groups in the production departments. Somebody said "They have not been planning for next year's budget, they are planning to close down the plant!". Everybody laughed and the controller was told to reduce the expense budgets of the production departments by a large amount.

The finance department had been represented on all the working groups in production and the controller told these group members from finance that the figures had to come down considerably. All the finance representatives disagreed pointing to the good work that had been done. "How are we going to tell them to modify the figures we have agreed are realistic and based on actual levels of expenses?", "They are not going to trust us again!", "Why are they asking us to make a budget if they then modify it arbitrarily?". Their choice was to convene the groups again and face them in the cutting exercise or to simply do the necessary cuts in the finance department. The latter option was chosen and the six working group members of the finance department sat down for a day's bargaining about which group could take the larger cuts. Finally the stipulated reduction was achieved. But they were all frustrated over how to explain to their working groups how and why the cuts had been made.

This was only the first review round! In the second one the plant manager presided and the sales manager was present. There was a higher operating profit now, but the budget was far from zero on net income. The plant manager worried about the inventory levels, that he believed had gone up, fixed expenses, and project expenses. The materials manager tried to defend his territory, but it was decided to make rather heavy reductions in materials, but a proportion of the reduction was left in the budget for the European office to take away when its representatives came for their review "so they won't leave us empty". As to the other items the plant manager wanted further studies before the final decision.

When the third review meeting started the adjustments had produced a higher operating profit, but there was still a long way to go before the targeted zero net income could be reached. The problem was that the plant, a limited company, had a large debt with the consequent interest costs. The adjustments to the budget achieved during the third meeting still did not suffice to meet the net income target, but it was decided to submit the budget to the European office anyway, after a final rush of review and revision of the budget document. The wait for the review meeting with the European staff was short.

The European review meeting started with presentations of the budgets, profit and loss, sales, materials, labour and expenses of the non-productive departments. The European controller took notes, and did not say much while the responsible managers defended their budgets. Then he spoke: "We all know that the European manager wants you to obtain a zero net income. Since you have not been able to do that there are two options; either we can forget all you have done and build the budget from the figures he wants, as we did last year, or we can make the following cuts that I consider possible to do after hearing your presentations and which would achieve zero net income".

His proposed cuts included cuts in materials (as expected), communication expenses, labour, administration and projects. With the acceptance of the proposed cuts the budget was completed by the end of July. Quick, intensive work! Once approved by the European office the budget was sent to corporate headquarters for consolidation with the budgets for the rest of the plants all over the world awaiting the approaching new year. However, this year something extraordinary happened. The European manager arrived at the plant late in December. His mission was to compel the plant staff to review the budget once more to make it more 'aggressive'. This final review was to be done internally. The official budget was not to be changed, but plans should be made on how to surpass it. The plant should be run on a more aggressive internal budget so that the plant could outperform the official budget. This was not in accordance with planning manuals of the company! There were hints that unless the plant was successful in this there were alternative sources of supply. An internally formalized aspiration level elevation!

Honoured by the visit by the European manager, but puzzled, the plant staff saw no opportunity to get clarification of the purpose of having two budgets. This would create uncertainty, surely. Organization members would not know what information to give to whom and what standards to compare with. We leave the plant management staff here with their imposed aspiration level elevation budget, their imposed budget and their new participative management style.

Improvement work at the bottom

As mentioned earlier the plant was originally set up to produce one car component for delivery inside the multinational group. By the middle of the 1980s this strategy was changed. Survival required the plant to seek customers outside the group. 'Customer satisfaction' became the catch-phrase for this strategy. Some outside customer orders were won but, as mentioned they were low on volume, and price. A more pressing concern, however, was that the plant found it difficult to comply with the product specifications of outside customers. This was owing to inflexible machine installations as well as inexperience in managing for flexible production.

There was general agreement that the four production departments were the key areas of necessary improvement. The plant manager decided to start a project based on teamwork in four working groups with the objectives of improving productivity, compliance with specification and quality standards, and working conditions. It should be noted that these four areas constituted only part of the production organization.

At this time teamwork was promoted as a basic principle in the management philosophy of corporate headquarters. Plants had to report periodically the number of teams that were operating. Production teams would have engineers, operators, maintenance people and somebody from personnel. If necessary other members of the organization were invited to join the team for specific problem solving. There were weekly meetings in a special meeting room away from the machines. The expected meeting time was set at one hour, but they could be extended to two hours and they usually were. Between meetings a foreman would call meetings on the shop floor to solve specific problems that could not wait until the next ordinary one. Participation was not compulsory, but there was compensation for overtime or stopped production without loss of pay, depending on whether the participant worked on the first or second shift. The teams were not recognized as part of the formal structure of the organization and there was no interaction for exchange of experience between the teams. The teams kept minutes from their meetings, which made it possible to reconstruct the history of the teams on the basis of minutes and interviews. This is the story of one of the four teams mentioned above.

The team was set up on an initiative from the production manager, who asked personnel to see whether a group could be started in this particular area. A preliminary meeting with operators and managers lead to a consensus among team members and top management to endorse the project formally. It was agreed that the team would meet monthly with the production manager to report on progress.

The team set its objectives as being to increase machine capacity, improve working conditions and production schedule compliance. The minutes show that these were the areas dealt with, although quality improvement was a frequent action area as well.

In the initial meeting the team listed problems that were under their control and related to the stated objectives. A list of some 70 problems were compiled and ranked, and the top 10 problems were selected for action. This took a couple of sessions. Despite the initial agreement that the team should confine themselves to activities that only involved their own department, it proved impossible to avoid problems that would involve coordination with other departments in the solution (flow and quality of raw materials, coordination with Maintenance). The personnel representative stressed that the discussion should be open and guaranteed that no discrimination would be directed towards any operators because of their opinions.

Group dynamics set in before long. After four months the team could report an increase in pieces produced per shift of 58% and in a memorandum to the production manager the team expressed satisfaction with the improved working conditions that teamwork had generated. These positive results prompted a meeting with top management where engineers and foremen made presentations about problems faced, actions taken and what they planned to do next. It is noteworthy that the presentations tended to focus on soft data, actions taken and procedures followed, rather than hard data on performance. In fact production had increased from an average of 3023 to 4805 pieces per shift. The team was encouraged to go on and undertook a number of actions of improvement in house-keeping, quality, set-up times, etc. Commitment was strong, for example operators took turns during coffee breaks and during the change of shifts to achieve an extra hour of daily production.

After 15 months, the following, impressive improvements had been achieved:

- in machine 1 the output per hour had increased from 485 to 955 pieces an hour;
- in machine 2 there was an increase from 612 to 1267 pieces per hour;
- a shift to preventive maintenance had reduced the number of maintenance hours by 33.5%, from 138.6 to 92.1 as a monthly average;
- the hours spent on set-ups had been reduced by 33.36%.

The corporate headquarters found reason to congratulate the team.

Decline!

As the project progressed problem solutions increasingly required coordination with other departments, and thereby the team lost some of its control over action. The minutes show initiatives that had to be taken in coordination with other departments such as quality control, production control, purchasing, security and a special task group charged with reduction of scrap. The activities involved thus grew more complex and demanded more resources from the organization. Managing these complexities required more time and the minutes tended to contain identical lists of problems to deal with meeting after meeting. Discussions

Table 4.1 Average production per hour in machine 1

Year	Average production: pieces per hour
1984	455
1985	580
1986	895
1987	752
1988	628

focused on different aspects of coordination and the participation of operators progressively decreased.

Having tackled the same problems for several months without seemingly getting ahead, the team decided to meet fortnightly instead of weekly. During the preceding meetings, minutes contained appeals for better punctuality and attendance. The minutes begin to mention problems which were previously resolved but now had reappeared. Most significantly, perhaps, the operators who used to rotate during coffee breaks and manage the handover between shifts to gain production time, refused to continue that procedure. Six months later the team decided to cancel meetings and hold informal meetings on the shop floor when needed instead. Four months after the last formal team meeting production in machine 1 was down to 669 pieces per hour. The average production per hour exhibits a kinked curve, as shown in Table 4.1.

The development of other performance measures was similar; a spectacular improvement followed by a rather steep decline. In addition, in the other three teams there were similar developments, except for team D that had never managed to solve the problems on their original list and was dissolved before it actually got started.

Analysis

In this case one might wonder what happened. What was the cause of the break in the promising improvement curve? If the improvement over a period of two years of nearly 100% is called organizational learning, should then the downturn over the following months be called organizational forgetting? Is the effect as a whole explained by a sharp decline in motivation owing to failure to solve problems that were more complex, and involved the cooperation of other departments as a precondition for success? Was there a lack of communication between departments? Does the downturn indicate a clash between the teamwork-based type of interactive communication about concrete problems and the hierarchical type of formal, abstract communication in budget concepts? Is this a question of leadership and commitment from the top or middle management levels? Are the Spanish or the American management culture(s) examples of cultures where forms of organization other than the hierarchical type cannot survive over longer periods? What is required for sustainable improvement and organizational learning that sticks? One should not generalize from the results of one case, and we do not know all the particular circumstances, but we are allowed to talk about the case and try to 'read' it.

The first part, describing the budget process in this company, shows convincingly that hierarchical control is very strong. At the same time there are efforts to introduce a more participatory form of management. Corporate headquarters promote team-based forms of organization, take an interest in experiments and praise good achievements. The local plant managers set up four working groups, partly to comply with the expressed policy of the corporation, but also to improve flexibility as part of the strategic change towards deliveries to outside customers. However, managerial behaviour was not consistent with the participative ideal. Budgets were imposed from the European office when targeted outcomes could not be met in the budget documents. The local managers decided they could not face the working group expense budgets after representatives of the finance department had participated in the discussions and were well informed about the details of the planned activities. The cuts in departments' expense budgets were made by the finance department without convening the working groups. This is hierarchy in action, and the people in the middle have the choice of losing face to the boss or to subordinates! And what on earth had come over the European manager to suggest that the plant should make a 'more aggressive budget' for their own private guidance? An aspiration level is set voluntarily by the actor, not imposed by the boss and formalized in a budget document. The will to surpass the budget is stimulated by positive deviations from the budget, not by setting a still tougher budget that one might not meet. The European manager was 'quacking' in motivation psychology!

These efforts to introduce a more participative form of organization were not consistent and forceful enough to break through the well-entrenched hierarchical pressures that dominate the budget process. It might be a generally valid conclusion that the budget process is not a very suitable medium for the introduction of participation. In the final analysis it will be dominated by the need to achieve corporate targets. The confrontation between budget requests based on the most well-intentioned plans for improvement will be settled in accordance with the corporate will. Plans have to be coordinated towards corporate objectives, unless there are unlimited resources available. A situation rarely experienced by large organizations!

Participation, with its motivating and cognitive effects, has a better chance of development in reference to current, concrete situations (given a budget that is seen as part of the given situation). The cognitive effect, learning, refers to the fact that participation provides opportunities to get access to job-related information and to clarification of role expectations. This makes it easier for the individual to use judgement and make efficient choices in the work process. The individual becomes more competent in his or her job, which could be called a cognitive effect of participation.

The motivating effects of participation is assumed to be related to self-management. It is also a traditional assumption in experimental psychology that there is a higher reinforcing value of work performed in a participatory setting (Milani, 1975). Empirical evidence to back up this assumption is still not as clear-cut as we would like it to be.

Why, then, did the participative effects of the shop-floor exercise in participative problem solving in the four teams not stabilize around progressive improvement? Why the 'kink' and downward turn in the productivity measure? (It should be noted that the budgeting study was made in 1991, while the shop-floor project reported here lasted from 1984 to 1987. The downturn thus could not be explained by disappointment with the outcome of that particular budget process.)

It seems that things went smoothly as long as the team restricted itself to problems and activities that were located within its own territory. When it went outside for cooperative solutions with other territories, proposals got stuck. It is only natural that people are sceptical towards ideas that are 'not initiated here'. Perhaps the problem presentations were understood as accusations of inefficiency and proposed solutions as attempts to take over. Perhaps the commendations from headquarters had made the team overconfident. Anyway it is reasonable to assume that the victories that the team had experienced made it look differently at problems. They saw them as opportunities for improvement, as something to act on, a stimulant. The neighbouring departments on the other hand were likely to see problems as constraints, as facts of life that were part of the organization and something for the 'higher-ups' to deal with if they felt like it.

In the old organization the role of a department is defined by the hierarchy, and part of that role definition is not to question the role. It is called discipline when it is referred to in a positive sense and it is necessary for the hierarchy to be controllable by plan. If departments do what is specified in the budget the outcome will be predictable and resources will be used effectively throughout the organization – given the assumptions on which the budget is built. Improvement, change and learning will reek havoc on carefully laid plans and specified responsibilities. "It might be a good idea, but not now!" is the likely answer from the head of the responsibility. "Why don't you take it up in the next budget process. That's when all improvements are considered at the same time and that is when they can all be coordinated to an effective plan. If you work with bits and pieces like this you lose the overview!"

In a sense he is right. It might be an economic disadvantage to increase the output per shift as team **A** did. The simplest case is the following scenario: before the project machine 1 was a bottleneck (that is why it was chosen for teamwork!) which means that in front of the machine, inventory waiting for processing was piling up. That inventory had a value in terms of raw material and costs expended on it up to the point in time when it entered the inventory state in front of machine 1. While in inventory it draws interest on the capital bound in it until it is delivered to the next responsibility centre. Now if team **A** and its machine 1 start to process the pieces quicker it is quite likely that an inventory will pile up after the machine 1 operation has added its costs to the product. That means that each product has a higher value after the operation than before. If everything else is unchanged the project will lead to a higher valued inventory waiting after machine 1 instead of a lower valued one waiting in front of it. The total cost for producing the product will have increased after the successful project! Strictly speaking the profit from shortened through-put time has not been realized until the product, of which the piece in machine 1 is a part, has been delivered and paid for by the customer (and paid for earlier than was common before the improvement!). So there are many good reasons for a neighbouring department to resist a lot of brilliant ideas from other departments and refer to the coordinating planning process of the hierarchy. It is difficult to assess the value of improvement, especially if it is in terms of shorter cycle time, and it is difficult to see the effects on other departments as a whole. This is the economic argument for resisting delegation of initiative to production teams. Improvements are of no value unless they are paid for by the customer or result in lower prices from suppliers (including labour). Furthermore, the likelihood of losing control and predictability in the production process increases, which means an increased risk.

There is also the decline in motivation and commitment when the improvement process is not moving ahead any more. It was frustrating to hear that nothing could be done about the problems listed and solutions suggested in the last meeting owing to resistance and the need for further talks with other departments. It does not seem meaningful to sit through meetings that do not result in progress. There is also the opportunity to consider the effects of improvement if it is constricted to shorter processing times. That would mean that the same job can be done by fewer people, an argument that might seem of doubtful value in a region with 20% or more in unemployment. Resistance also begets territorial instincts. If you are responsible for an organizational territory the first role expectation is not to yield to pressure from the outside. To do that without very good reasons would mean loss of face. According to Pascale (1990), 10 years of 'chimney-breaking' was part of Ford's efforts to respond to Japanese competition. Chimney-breaking meant promoting lateral communication and cooperation between organizational units that had used energy to fight each other rather than the Japanese. This problem is an almost natural consequence of relying strictly on hierarchical responsibility accounting structures to control large corporations. The problem is amplified if there is an economic incentive system to promote adherence to budget targets. This is likely to be the case in an American multinational.

There is probably not one single cause for the kink in the improvement curve for team A, but rather multiple causes, with the unwillingness of other departments to cooperate, which in turn caused a reduction in motivation even to maintain the achievements that had already been made, acting as a primary cause. The resistance also damaged the will to continue the regular problem solving sessions. The project died slowly during 1987. (Efforts have since been revived and improvement is again being achieved.)

No doubt middle management and top managers of the plant could have saved the situation, but it is not unreasonable to assume that they were turned off by the way American managers at the European office tried to extract improvement through the traditional budget-cutting behaviour. Asserting the will of the centre is not always the most rational way of solving management problems. Creativity and the will to improve are not promoted by a management through fear (of sanctions).

What could have been done? The case illustrates, even if it cannot prove anything, how dependent an improvement process is on the context in which it is placed. Both inter- and intra-group communication contribute. The managers sponsoring the improvement effort should ask themselves; what can we do to establish a working environment that makes the team enjoy problem solving and improvement? The team could ask themselves the same question. The two answers will be different in some dimensions, but then there is the possibility to talk to each other. If that is done with mutual respect and concern for the legitimacy of the other party's views much can be achieved.

Clearly problem solving and trial solutions will generate uncertainty and the tolerance of uncertainty – especially the risk of losing face – is different for different individuals or groups. With self-confidence and trust in the sincerity of others the tolerance of ambiguity increases and uncertainty avoidance is lower. There might also be cultural differences between countries relating to tolerance for ambiguity; Spain ranks high on uncertainty avoidance in Hofstede's (1980) study of international differences in work-related values. Therefore the project should have been accompanied by a programme to promote cooperation and communication between departments, and special efforts by senior managers to facilitate communication across organizational borders.

5

Controlling through problem solving*

Improvement work starts on the operational level

Industrial jobs have traditionally been designed to be simple and easy to learn. Now it seems that the trend has been reversed. We claim that learning to improve operations requires making jobs more complicated and demanding. In fact, improvement, by definition, makes it necessary for operators to be observant on more variables. This makes them more difficult to replace.

Earlier, under the influence of 'scientific management', the idea was to minimize training costs due to high personnel turnover by making jobs simple and repetitive – jobs should be designed so that someone off the street can be in full production in a matter of hours. Now, we have learned that the earlier approach alienates the holders of those simple jobs and that which was supposed to be a solution is the problem.

Still personnel turnover does occur and, consequently, learning should be organizational as well as personal. Experience should be encoded into

*The fieldwork in this study was carried out by Anders Grönlund and reported in Grönlund (1989). The case was also presented at a colloquim at Harvard Business School in January 1989 (Kaplan, 1990) and has benefited from comments by Chris Argyris, Anthony Atkinson and Robert Kaplan.

routines and this process should be built into the work organization. The encoding of improved operations into the work organization must be done by operations personnel to be sustainable. It could not usefully be done by the accounting staff, since the routines that relate to outcomes for a firm are located in local production units. Neither could learning be done by top management since it does not receive the data to be interpreted. Under scientific management top management, or rather its engineering staff, could do the encoding as it is the location where routines were designed. [In the old days management accounting systems also provided relevant information (Johnson and Kaplan, 1987) because organizational learning occurred centrally!] Manufacturing processes were, in fact, designed by engineers in staff offices and the production organization was structured to monitor compliance with the norm. When it comes to continuously improving existing operations the problem is different. Improvement has to start with things as they are (not with things as they should be). Therefore it has to be based on facts. This study illustrates how organizational learning and design of routines must be located in the same unit if a steeply sloped learning curve is to be achieved.

Improvement is not automatic!

As used in the 1970s (NASA, 1975) the learning curve referred to process improvement in a broad sense. The slope of the curve was generally specified in per cent resource use per unit with measures for every doubling of accumulated experience. The following factors were assumed to contribute to cost reduction.

- Operators learning to handle production.
- Engineers achieving improved methods, processes, tooling, and machines and improvements in design for manufacturability.
- Management learning to optimize batches and coordinate flows.
- Debugging of engineering data.
- Rate of production.
- Design of assembly or part, or modifications thereto.
- Specification or design of the process.
- Personnel factors such as fatigue, personal matters or employee morale.
- Material improvement or discount.

Several different 'theories' of learning evolved. They had one feature in common. Learning was assumed to be automatic! It occurred as a volume-dependent effect of production. The problem with experience curves was to estimate them! They were assumed to exist and be caused by underlying process mechanisms, governed, as it were, by 'laws of nature'!

The Boston Consulting Group (BCG) in the late 1960s considered the experience curve to be the result of the combined effect of learning, specialization, investment and scale. This combination of factors should permit a considerably steeper experience curve than is actually observed. However, to realize this steeper curve some additional overhead costs would need to be introduced in order to plan and coordinate the necessary changes. The curve was thus considered to be essentially a pattern of cash flow. Therefore accounting cost data were felt to be misleading due to arbitrary classifications between expense and capital.

Again the analysis was based on the assumption that learning curves are the same for companies in a given industry, as long as they use the same combination of the above-mentioned factors. But it is clearly wrong to assume that some mechanical learning function of experience exists that could be estimated once the appropriate changes in accounting systems have been implemented to provide the relevant information. Learning is not a matter of law at all! It is a matter of focusing attention, wanting to take the risk of changing habitual behaviour, and of having access to the relevant information.

It may be customary to write improvement requirements into contracts for large batch deliveries, and it might be viewed as a forecasting problem by the buyer, but for the organization that has to supply, learning is a long-term struggle!

Improvement must be made organizational!

It is sometimes maintained that only individuals can learn. The behavioural theory of the firm (Cyert and March, 1963), however, introduced the assumption that behaviour in organizations is based on routine. Routines have a logic of appropriateness rather than one of search for optimal consequences. Routines stabilize behaviour. Furthermore routines are largely developed and maintained through interpretations of the past more than anticipations of the future. Still organizations seek profitable outcomes. The complexity of judging whether a specific act contributes optimally to the joint outcome of organizational action can be so great, however, that humans resort to crude measures like success–failure or acceptable–unacceptable. Therefore organizational learning requires that ongoing discussions be maintained, involving organizational members, on what constitutes good performance and how it should be measured.

Levitt and March (1988) see organizations as learning by encoding inferences from history into routines that guide behaviour. These routines include rules and roles, habits and conventions, and in addition structures of beliefs, frameworks, strategies and the technologies in which they are embedded. In this way routines can be made sufficiently independent of the individual actors to survive when turnover occurs among organizational members.

An organization fortunate enough to have a steeper learning curve than competing organizations will have a competitive advantage in importing and implementing new technology. Better learning capacity will enable it to solve start-up problems and fine-tune equipment to its economic capacity more quickly than competitors. One precondition for successful local learning in relation to new technology is that good vertical (central–local) communication occurs within the larger organization. The 'theory' of new technology as well as the design of production systems are located with central engineering staff, while the actual observations of the process of production and anomalies that cause or contribute to breakdowns are made by operators on the 'shop floor'. These observations are particularly important in situations where new technology is introduced, because then no reliable historic process data are available for interpreting chains of events. The organization must learn *de novo* and start with experience found by facts.

If the engineering staff is competent and the competitive situation favours flexibility, the design of the production system will probably contain a team-oriented organization, with teams managing groups of automated machines performing multiple operations on small batches. Production will be controlled by the inflow of orders from the market rather than by fixed plans. When local improvement in an automated context is sought, an increased horizontal flow of process information is necessary at the expense of the vertical flow from the central management accounting system (MAS). Local learning will be the key factor in mature product areas, like the car industry, where competitive advantage (given the design of the product and the structure of the productions system) is based on flexibility, productivity and quality in small batch production. Flexibility and quality are largely a function of automated production technology, while productivity improvement depends on attention, a will to improve and relevant performance measurement.

This chapter will report on an experiment conducted over a four-year period on the role of information support for three teams in different plants of the Volvo Components corporation. Since the three teams chose to work differently, starting from different premises, it is not possible to give a complete account of all three processes. Experiences and results differ among the teams. Participants in the experiment, at a two-day seminar marking the end of the field study, unanimously declared that it was not possible to write a manual on how to manage performance improvement of production teams as circumstances are always different for different teams. However some results are generally applicable in some respects. It is advisable though, to pay attention to such a strong consensus among team members. Down there, on the shop floor, things are concrete, processual and different! Every problem is unique and demands its own solution. In this setting practices develop and the contexts of problems become complex and virtually indescribable. To relate the impact of these concrete events to, say, the cost consequences on accounts in a cost centre report is mind boggling. Anybody who does not agree with this opinion has not even begun to understand the problem!

Upstream a car production process

Volvo Components was formed some 15 years ago as a subcorporation of the Volvo Corporation. It consisted of eight production plants, formerly part of the parent company, delivering subassemblies and parts to the different assembly sites of Volvo. The main products are engines and gear-boxes, but there are many other components such as brake discs, brake drums, drive shafts, etc. During the period of our study, Volvo Components invested heavily in new production technology and operations were at full capacity except for some machine groups which were dependent upon a very large order from Iran which was cancelled.

Although Volvo Components is a complete, limited company it does not have all the normal functions of an independent company of its size. Product design, marketing, finance and some purchasing is done outside of the company (by the product companies).

Management control in the Volvo Group is organized in a matrix fashion with product companies (Cars, Trucks, etc.) having world-wide responsibility for products from design to post-sale services, and a return on capital employed criterion.

A production plant in Volvo Components is subject to pressures from two directions: from the product companies to deliver high quality parts, flexibly and promptly, at a low price without employing more capital than absolutely necessary; and from the Components headquarters to meet a strict cost budget, to be a reliable link in the materials flow and to maintain a high-quality index.

It is a policy of Volvo Components to be a leader in the application of new technology in its production process. The threat that the product companies will buy subassemblies elsewhere is always present. Consequently a balance must be struck between the installation of new technology and the avoidance of lost production owing to stoppages in the fine-tuning of such installations. In general new technology means a higher and more even quality, and an opportunity to produce smaller batches economically. But the investment cost, complexity and interdependence of installations make down-time costly.

The main site in this report is the Floby plant, a rather small establishment, built in 1957 and since expanded, with 185 employees with hourly pay and 24 salaried. The Floby plant produces brake discs for cars and hubs, brake drums and drive shafts for heavy vehicles. It has a fine productivity record. (Added value, or simpler, processing value is used in calculating the productivity index. Inputs as well as outputs are adjusted for price and volume differences, and the resulting processing value is related to the standard value. Then this year's index is divided by last year's index to get the improvement, as shown in Table 5.1.)

The latter three years constitute the experiment period. About half the Floby plant is devoted to car brake discs, our study deals with the responsibility centre of Börje, which consists of three production departments (hubs, brake drums and drive shafts) and constitutes the bulk of the rest.

Hubs and brake drums are produced in similar lines (turning, drilling, grinding, cleaning, painting, control and packing) with raw material coming from one of the foundries. The raw material for the drive shaft is not hardened when it comes from the forge. The shaft and its disc are first turned then splined and then hardened. After hardening the shaft is cooled, holes are drilled in the disc, and then it is ground, balanced and measured before it is packed and sent for subassembly into rear axles in another plant.

The machinery is mostly CNC-machines, that is numerically-controlled machines, coupled to a line with a controlling computer and one or more robots to handle materials. The machinery on the shaft and brake drum lines is about eight years old, a new hub-line was installed in 1986. All three lines are run at two shifts with two to three operators per line and shift. About 20 people were directly involved in our study. When we paid our first visit to the plant we were struck by the low noise level (academics being used to noisy offices and classrooms!). Most machines were light green. The place looked tidy.

Börje supervises the hub, drum and shaft lines. He is a friendly person with a keen interest in improving things. He used to be a rally mechanic for one of the national rally heroes in his younger days, which gives him prestige among operators. He has worked at the Floby plant since 1974

Table 5.1

1982	1983	1984	1985	1986	1987
+7.4%	+5.3%	+2.1%	+7.7%	+8.8%	+13.2%

and he had just finished a one-year full-time production management course given by Volvo Components when we started the project after the summer of 1984.

Magnus is Börje's partner in this project. He came to the Floby plant in 1981 as a production planner. His duties were extended in 1983, in a reorganization, to include the management accounting and information systems function of the plant. Magnus is an independent person with an analytic approach and a thorough knowledge of operations. He was willing to devote extra attention to the needs of this improvement project.

Getting started

The striking thing about the empirical evidence collected during the three years of this study is the unique, individualistic nature of the observations. They are difficult to describe in abstract terms. We could, of course, give statistics on outputs, productivity or cost curves, but since we are interested in organizational learning, we prefer to describe the dramatic events behind improved performance figures. Then, again, we cannot really describe what actually occurred during those events, because we were not there for most of the time when they happened. We have accounts of what occurred, in the form of stories, and we have been able to observe the outcomes of learning rather than learning itself. Situations and contingencies are unique and thus difficult to describe in a generalized fashion. In the following presentation of the empirical material we have therefore chosen to use these stories to illustrate what goes on when local managers (operators) identify and attack performance deficiencies and do something about them. In this way we believe we can contribute to a better understanding of what kind of information support best serves self-management in teams.

First it is important to realize the significance of getting started in the right way and with early victories. It is also important to realize that outcomes are often indirect and cumulative. This is how it went in Floby.

> The main idea of the project was learning by doing and we were anxious to get started without too much planning and meetings. Börje wanted to study the use of cutting tools in two lathes on the drive shaft line. Five different cutting tools can be attached to the rotating heads of these lathes. Each tool has a number of cutting edges and when an edge is worn quality declines so they have to be shifted. Cutting tools is account 631 on the cost centre report. Börje and Magnus had a feeling that the standard was too high on tool costs. The team decided to do a manual follow-up on these tools by just counting how many drive shafts had been processed for every cutting tool. Four weeks after the start of the project the first follow-up report was ready. During the 3 days that the counting took place 574 drive shafts had been produced in the machine group and 52 cutting tools had been used (the standard said 74.3).

Cutting tool:	Type 1	Type 2	Type 3	Type 4	Type 5	Total
Tools Standard	22.9	17.2	11.4	11.4	11.4	74.3
used: Actual	19	14	9	6	4	52
Price/tool	20:00	28:00	15:00	21:00	18:00	
Cost savings compared to standard (Skr)	78	90	36	113	133	450

Better than standard on all kinds of cutting tools! Not bad! But was it due to the follow-up or some change in procedures? Even the question as to whether it was better than it had been before or whether the standard was too high could not be answered with any certainty. But it was clear that the follow-up had generated an interest among operators. There was a motivating effect just from finding out prices and volumes. A side-effect was that people had cleaned out cupboards and reserves with tools that had been stashed away as buffers in case the materials department had run out of stock. An amazing number of half empty packages of cutting tools had appeared. People seemed to realize that it was difficult to follow-up tool consumption if stocks of unused tools were kept in reserve.

Nobody was really surprised by the findings of the first follow-up (30% lower cost than standard). People had felt that this standard was on the high side. They decided to go on like this with manual follow-ups as a warm-up before the PC, that was included in the project, was installed. "Keep it simple so that we know what we are doing" seemed to be the argument. A routine follow-up had been designed and people started to think about what more could be done in this way.

Börje and Magnus pointed out to us that sometimes cutting tools are changed, either because a new supplier is engaged or a new version of the tool is offered. This new procedure could be used to test new tools. The next time somebody from production technology came with a supplier to test some new tool, Börje would offer his testing routine and take responsibility for a possible new tool being phased-in properly into 'materials' supply.

The operators also decided to produce statistics on the consumption of all cutting tools during the autumn of 1984. These data could be used to set a new standard but chiefly they would come in handy in budget discussions to back up claims that they could meet, say, a 5% cost-cutting requirement for the next year, by a specified amount on account 631 (tools). This project, to collect a larger amount of operating statistics, provided a good argument for the instalment of the PC and for attending a course introducing the software they were going to use.

The outcome for 1983 on the 631 account had been close to budget and the cutting tool cost per shaft had been Skr4.69. Over the whole year of 1984 the cost reports from the central cost accounting system showed a decline to Skr3.67 per shaft in the last period. The budget on that account was Skr405,300 for 1984. Börje accepted a budget of Skr350,000 for 1985, with the same production volume, although the budget should have gone up owing to an expected price increase on those tools of 5.7%.

This was the start-up phase in the Floby plant. Nothing spectacular was done. No lectures and no speeches took place, just a follow-up on cutting tools. A simple manual counting exercise. The economic effects were astounding; the cutting tool cost had come down from Skr4.69 to Skr3.67. Was it that easy? What had really happened? Obviously, the outcome was a result of increased attention and motivation on the part of the operators. No routines had been changed but a large number of half empty tool packages had been cleared out of cupboards and shelves. No causal links between activity and costs had been clarified, but a continuing interest had emerged from operators in the consumption of cutting tools. Attention had been aroused just by collecting information, doing something and getting quick results.

Sustained improvement

Productivity has been the principal performance measure in Volvo for as long as most people can remember. It is based on value added, and adjusted for volume and price changes. The calculation of productivity improvement is rather complicated and when we confronted top management with the fact that the measure is difficult to understand for operators (or anybody), the answer was that it is not really that important to understand the calculations. As long as you realize that you improve productivity by producing more with the same resources or using less resources to produce the same output you are on the right track. Fair enough! That is how it is in theory!

If the cost centre report says that the budgeted productivity improvement was 4.1% and the outcome so far this year is 3.2%, what should be done? The answer under this interpretation is something like "Try harder!".

Towards the end of 1984 an educational programme in cost management for operators was initiated by Börje and Magnus. It consisted simply of going through the cost centre reports, explaining some cost concepts, and, where possible, breaking down the budget figures into concrete physical measures and discussing causes of changes. Training the shift teams in cost management was something new in Floby. The operators saw two new things in this: first, management in Floby was seriously interested in the follow-up of cutting tools; and second, the operators were asked what they thought about things. The troubles with the hub line was a case in point. During the latter part of 1984 a lot of stoppages and malfunction had occurred on the hub line (it was replaced in 1986). The maintenance account showed a large negative change in productivity. The account showed Skr110,400 for the last reporting period while the budget for the whole year was set at Skr60,000! In fact the whole Floby plant was in the negative on maintenance productivity and it was almost exclusively traceable to the hub line. The cost figures and the productivity decline could be related to the specific incidents of that period. These incidents could be discussed, and thereby be conceived as controllable. The new approach meant posing the question to operators: "What do *you* think?".

Episodes

Cutting tools continued

During a large part of 1985 statistics on the cutting tool consumption were collected. A couple of episodes contributed to attention being maintained on the turning operation of the shaft line. During the first tests in 1984 they found that they could do 33 shafts per cutting tool on average. The first reporting period of 1985 brought 46 shafts per tool, which was 13 better than standard. But towards the end of period 2 (week 12) something went wrong. The number of shafts done before the operator had to change tools went down to only 11. A couple of cutting tools were performing well below standard. The operator sounded the alarm. During the following weeks they worked on the problem. Was the raw material too hard? Too soft? The machine set right? Human error? Production technology was brought in, but they could not find an answer. Finally the team approached the supplier forge and asked what was going on. The supplier said: "Didn't you know? From now on the friction-welded joint between the shaft and the disc will be a little harder due to higher quality standards!".

The problem with cutting tool consumption had now turned into a question of whether a different tool could cut the joint better than the old ones. Normally the standard would have been adjusted to the new situation, now a period of testing other cutting tools began. During this period the division manager came down to the Floby plant to see how things were going, and the operators could demonstrate how they were working with this problem. And they solved it too! By the time the summer vacation started they had shifted to a somewhat more expensive tool but it cut an average of 66 shafts before it had to be replaced. (The earlier standard was 33!)

Production targets

From period 3 of 1985 a new wage system was introduced in the Floby plant. Operators could now decide themselves what production rate they estimated they could maintain during the coming six-month period. The rate is measured in MTM-terms, e.g. based on the piece rates used in production planning. The model is built on the precalculated production time (e.g. 0.166 hours per passed widget) according to the standard. Actual time is divided by the standard giving a ratio. The base ratio was 117% and they could go as high as 125% for the first six months. The outcome would set the base for the discussion for the next six-month period. The operators get a fixed salary per month but negotiate every six months to set a new target. Börje agreed with the three lines he supervised to go for 123% for hubs, 121% for shafts and 123% for drums. (The outcome six months later turned out to be 123, 123, and 126%, respectively.) On this occasion Börje had the opportunity to ask operators what they intended to do to meet the production target they had set. This focused attention on how to avoid lost production. Two factors were taken up, rejects and down-time. The drum line initiated a follow-up on rejects; these are classified as M-faults (materials) or P-faults (caused in processing inside the cost centre). They managed to reduce M-faults substantially by setting up communication with a supervisor at the supplying foundry and reporting immediately when, for example, sloppy sand blasting in the foundry caused processing problems in the drum line. P-faults remained largely the same (below budget) throughout the period.

The other factor, down-time, could be attacked by rationalizing production methods and by increasing flexibility. The latter was given the most attention. It was recognized that absence created problems owing to the small number of operators in a team. With one man absent the whole team had to produce at reduced speed. Operators were too specialized in their own section which made the teams vulnerable to absence. A programme was set up to enable all operators to run all sections. Breakdowns or set-ups would be used to teach each other how the machines operated. The drum line increased its average output from 5.0 drums per time unit in 1984 to 5.6 in 1985 mainly due to reduced down-time because of absence.

Consequences

The production target episode made operators more willing to take charge of production planning and to assume responsibility for meeting the target. Operators started to call in indirect personnel, such as maintenance people and fork lift drivers, without clearing these decisions with the foreman. They also started to sign for indirect material requested from the materials department. Towards the end of 1985 all three lines got an extra 1% in salary justified by the increased responsibility of operators.

In preparing the budget estimates for 1986 (early autumn, 1985) operators participated in setting budget estimates for the first time. Some operators were rather passive, others active. The discussion concerned, account by account, how costs could be controlled and what was a reasonable target figure for next year. Owing to the conceptual training initiated by Börje and Magnus a meaningful discussion could be held and causal chains explored. The amount to budget on account 606 (overtime and shift surcharges) was dependent on unplanned down-time, which sometimes had to be compensated for by extra shifts. By reviewing the outcomes from earlier years, operators could see that stoppages in machines caused cost increases on many accounts. It was easy to identify down-time as an important cost-driver, but relations were unclear. On the cutting tools account budgeting was very easy since the team had reliable statistics on cutting tools.

After the budget work was finished the team decided to stop collecting data on cutting tools consumption and go into an *ad hoc* mode, i.e. only start a follow-up if output figures showed that something was wrong.

No end in sight

The empirical evidence collected in this three-year project contains a large number of episodes. It is difficult to account for all the ensuing consequential changes that occurred. The actions form causal chains or, rather, spirals where one achievement constitutes the basis for a subsequent step. When we stopped observing the process, Börje's three lines were all better than budget on all indicators and Börje had two days a week off to design a course in local cost management at the request of the division head. Börje stated his philosophy in a closing interview: "I want the operators to be driving me instead of me driving them!". So, if any trouble on the hub, shaft or drum line arose that the operators couldn't handle themselves they telephoned Börje at home and they could usually agree on what should be done over the telephone. Börje has managed himself out of the supervisory job and is now becoming a teacher. The Floby experience will be transmitted to other units through 'contagion'. If other units want to know what worked in Floby, Börje is prepared to go there and tell his story with slides and case descriptions – a practice consistent with the promotion of good practices by storytelling in most cultures (cf. *The Bible, The Koran*, etc.). The audience are interested because Börje knows his business and his story is about how to be a little smarter and not to work harder than necessary.

Costs and quality

In the meantime headquarters had initiated a 'Quality 100' programme. 'Quality 100' means that a product is within tolerance limits on all measurements. Special inspectors take five random pieces from every week's production and do a number of measurements. On the hub line the products have 10 different measures to meet. 'Index 100' is when all five products are within tolerances on all 10 measures. (Measures that are essential for the function of the part are taken on every produced piece.)

Operators are sceptical about the wisdom of some of the quality requirements. ("Why this obsession with smoothness on the inside of the brake drum?", "After the brakes have been used 10 times the smoothness is gone anyway!", "One of the other teams in the study had a lot of rejects of cog wheels for gearboxes because normal air dust interfered with the measurements. Are we to start producing parts to heavy gearboxes in 'clean rooms' or even a vacuum?".) This scepticism seemed to increase with consciousness about the costs of rejects.

In one instance the sample from the hub line did not hold on measure 8 on three of the pieces. That measure had to do with the fixture of the piece in one of the machines. The measure deviated by 62 thousandths of a millimetre from the stipulated measure and the tolerance was 50 thousandths. After some deliberation the team decided that minuscule metal chips must have stuck on the hubs or the fixture. They decided to rinse all parts and the support plate of the fixture. A simple thing to do, and they could now keep within tolerances on measure 8. But was it the best possible solution?

Table 5.2   Pieces per man-hour

Year	1984	1985	1986	1987
Hubs	5.05	5.23	6.13	6.76
Shafts	3.66	4.03	4.30	4.71
Drums	5.02	5.60	5.92	5.82

For drums there was never any problem in keeping close to the index 100, but for the shaft and hub lines an extra effort during 1988 was required to surpass the index value 85 that had been reached in 1987. These higher quality requirements could seemingly be met without any significant effects on controllable costs in the teams that Börje manages.

Summing up experiences in Floby

The three lines in the study have all increased output while decreasing the number of man-hours used. (On the hub line new machinery was introduced in 1986, but the technological level was not significantly different.) The figures shown in Table 5.2 represent the pieces per man-hour that have been achieved. (On the drum line a standing night-shift had to be used in 1987, and some extra weekend shifts. This increased the man-hours more than the proportional increase in production.)

Although crude, these figures indicate a successful cost improvement operation. It is difficult to point out any specific cause or any single decision that brought the improvement about. This was a low key, everyday type of project, one that will continue and become a way of life in the Floby plant.

Short description of the two other teams

Team 1 (Lindesberg)

The Lindesberg plant, employing about 650 people, specializes in producing rear axles for heavy vehicles. It was set up in 1972 and in the first years of this decade it was very busy producing tandem axles with reduction gears for heavy trucks. These axles give extra power and the ability to move off roads (e.g. in desert sand). Reduction gears needed a large number of cog wheels. In a few years the demand for reduction gears declined rapidly mainly due to the cancelling of a large order by the new regime in Iran. When the project started in the summer of 1984, there was overcapacity in cog wheel processing in Lindesberg. This was one of the reasons why plant management wanted to include the cog wheel department in the study.

In Lindesberg some traditional Tayloristic views lingered. These views tended to be strengthened in the overcapacity situation that had emerged. Managers had mixed feelings about the wisdom of experimenting with self-management now that central coordination seemed required to overcome current problems. Also a strong centralist spirit was influencing the computer department serving Lindesberg.

Getting started

At the first meetings with our team in Lindesberg, the foreman and his second in command had no doubt as to what was the most pressing problem to attack – the piece count system. The current system was an old-fashioned clock system where you stamp production orders in and out and register the number of pieces produced on the order card.

The team produces straight and conical cog wheels. The wheels are processed in 12 cog-cutting machines (Coniflex) that are located in three groups of four machines each. The operator is surrounded by four machines and does the following operations.

- Load the machine with a turned blank. The machine cuts 10–15 cogs an hour depending on size. The process is cooled with oil, which makes the place a bit greasy.
- When a cog wheel is cut its identity number is stamped with a hammer and tool.
- Then the cog wheel is ground in a grinding machine.
- Finally the cog wheel is packed in Volvo crates.

Cutting tools are changed by specialists that are called in by the operators when needed, a process that takes about 20 minutes down-time. The main part of the operator's job is to load and unload machines, and since one operator serves four machines there is plenty of loading. The technology of these machine groups is not very advanced and they are rated in the lowest wage class. The Coniflex department has been looked upon, and used, as an introductory station to more advanced jobs in other machine groups. The machines are run in three six-hour shifts with one operator in charge of four machines. The standard is to have 52 minutes per hour in processing time (allowing eight minutes for loading and set-ups). There are about 15 different variants of cog wheels and the average production order is for 2000–3000 pieces. With every machine processing about 12 wheels an hour, every operator will produce (six hours, four machines) 288 pieces per shift. To get a good balance between the four machines an operator will normally run two to three different variants at the same time. That means that there are up to 27 production order cards at the Coniflex department at any one time (three shifts, three operators, three machine groups). These cards relate to production orders. Finished orders are reported in a special internal delivery routine. Only then does the wage clerk have a definitive basis for wages in the form of passed pieces and time used to produce them. A production order can last for several weeks and until it is accounted for the operator gets an advance payment. Several problems follow.

- Operators have difficulties checking their own wages.
- Operators have to stamp order cards several times during a shift.
- Supervisors have difficulties knowing the status of a specific production order.
- Cards disappear, time has to be spent chasing errors and correcting, and overproduction is common 'to be on the safe side'.

Everybody agreed that significant improvements could be realized by replacing the production order card system with a local PC-based system. To start this project, a plant controller would give a short course (five sessions of two hours each) in costing and relevant concepts and routines to each of the three shifts. The second step would be to set up a work party to specify what requirements a PC-based system should meet. A specialist from the computer department was a member of the work party, which generated quite a long list of information that the new system should be able to provide.

So far so good; although some operators found some of the concepts difficult to grasp, expectations ran high as to how much easier everything would be when the new PC system was operational. In discussions about the team, operators indicated repeatedly that they preferred to work as they had always done; every operator being in complete charge of his own machine group. They could not see any collective problems; nothing that concerned them as a group.

The PC arrived and operators went through a seven-lesson computer course. They expected that the new information system would be ready about a month later, but things started to go wrong. The computer expert, who was going to do the programming, recommended a new software package for the PC and in order to design the new system he had to learn the new software. The programmer was not located in Lindesberg, there were communication problems, the system requirements were changed after the programming had started. The first version of the system did not work properly. Errors occurred that were difficult to trace. The programmer was tightly controlled by his boss. A 'wait and see' attitude from all parties emerged. The system did erroneous summations and would mix up batches. Operators grew suspicious! This system generated more correcting work than the old card system! In addition, in order to substitute this system for the old, one personnel demanded that security measures be built into the system. Production planning had their demands and debates on the new system tended to involve more and more outside people. The programmer left his job and another had to be informed about the ideas. The new system project came to a virtual standstill.

In early 1988, the team was running two systems in parallel. Owing to personnel turnover the team was completely new, nobody knew how to use the software with which the new system had been programmed, and any increase in productivity that may have been registered must have resulted from factors other than the local systems project!

Team 2 (Köping)

The Köping plant is large, devoted to production of manual gearboxes. Our study included three lines producing cog wheels and shafts for heavy boxes. The shaft line, A5, processes eight varieties of gearbox shafts, weighing 5–15 kilogrammes.

It produces 15–30 shafts per shift in two shifts, every shift having two operators. The line consisted of 11 machines positioned along a transfer line and the technology was fairly recent with computerized process control and automated transfers between machines. During the latter part of the study period a new shaft line, A6, using FMS-technology was installed. So the attention of the people involved was divided between:

- producing shafts for the old gearbox models;
- installing new production technology;
- starting to produce shafts for the new models of gearboxes using new technology.

These three activities competed for attention and resources throughout the period. The average batch size on A5 was about 500 shafts which would take 25–50 hours depending on the variety of shaft. The set-up for the next batch would take about 20 hours.

Since the trend was towards increased flexibility and smaller batches, set-up times were a significant problem, but other down-times needed to be reduced because of the capital costs the lines had to carry.

Getting started

In Köping the atmosphere of the starting phase was different to Floby. There was no open conflict, but there was an undercurrent of negotiation. It more or less boiled down to the demand: "If we are going to increase productivity we want half of the gain". The issue obviously was present in the other plants but it was never stated so bluntly as in Köping. (To explain this difference one should probably refer to different union traditions, Köping being more used to solving problems by confronting arguments from either side.) The will to improve was present, but there seemed to be less trust between parties.

In a sense it was a good start because the next issue automatically became: "How will you know that you have caused the improvement rather than the planners, or maintenance, etc.?". The answer was that the team needs a local system to keep track of operational factors that influence productivity. Even if the discussion on how the productivity gain should be split between the parties caused some turbulence, we do not believe that it had any significant effect on the course of events. Still it was part of the context in which the experiment was conducted.

Rejects

The team decided to start producing statistics on rejects (causes) and real processing time (in relation to precalculated). Initially, they focused just on collecting the information. During the last 6 weeks of 1984 the number of rejects was recorded. It amounted to about 2%, and the team had noted where in the machine line the error had occurred and what had caused it. During that period there had been 20 set-ups of the line and, on average, 1.5 rejected shafts could be directly attributed to the set-up. Set-up problems were bound to increase, since the product companies were pressing for greater flexibility and smaller batches.

Processing time

During the last reporting period of 1984 the team found that they had used 368 hours for the 20 set-ups (against a standard time of 291) and this in spite of a drive to decrease set-up times during the last 6 months (initiated by a visit by a Japanese expert). They had first reasoned about what could be done to reduce set-up times (which took the focused machine down from 195 minutes to 66.4) and then used video filming and further analysis (which peeled off another 32.4 minutes). Still, setting the whole line in normal, everyday, operational conditions seemed to be different from the laboratory-like conditions of the focused study! But at least they had a record of the most important delays and their causes.

Processing time was also above the precalculated time (497 hours against a standard of 411 hours). This meant that customers had paid for 702 hours during the period, while the team had worked 866, an efficiency of 81%!

Although the initial data collection showed that the team did not get budgeted processing time out of their machines, the start-up of the project seemed to have gone quite well. The team had set up routines to collect operational data that they wanted. Now it was time to install the PC and to have some training in management accounting.

The team set up a computer group (which included the department manager), acquired help from the computer department and even used a consultant. Perhaps the fascination with the ongoing installation of the gigantic new FMS line in the same department influenced the group to look for too sophisticated a solution with high level language software and as a consequence it was a very long time before the PC was operational. Once the FMS line (and PC) was in operation the team started to do follow-ups and improve operations, but there was not enough time to achieve the same kind of success story as the Floby plant.

One interesting episode, that illustrates how learning can be interpreted differently from different perspectives, was an experiment with a designated maintenance man for the three lines involved in our project. It went on for a little more than a year. The maintenance man taught the operators how to tend to the machines to avoid breakdowns and what signals and noises indicated imminent problems. The outcome was encouraging. The maintenance costs decreased by Skr150,000 between 1985 and 1986 and added to that was less down-time owing to faster service. However, this experiment had to be abandoned. Our maintenance man worked only day shifts while his colleagues in the maintenance department worked two shifts. His colleagues were jealous, especially of his socially satisfying work relations with the team. They complained and after union pressure our maintenance man had to go back to the traditional form of maintenance job. (It was also said that a maintenance man that works only with the trivialities of one machine group will lose competence, but we are not convinced that this is a valid argument, at least not if one man can help a department cut its maintenance cost so significantly.)

Summing up

In Köping the team was delayed in getting started because of the interference from the FMS installation and the overambitious PC-installation process. But once they got started they seemed to be moving in the right direction. The limits to team self-management are illustrated by the maintenance incident.

Analysis

The experiences from this field experiment illustrate the potential and the limitations of self-management approaches in teams. The Floby (drums, hubs and shafts) success shows a step-by-step development where the team has a firm grip of what they are doing, which generates chains, or rather spirals, of motivation and action that spreads outside the team. In Lindesberg (cog wheels) we see how an old technology, which ties operators to the manual handling of inputs and outputs from the process, preserves a Tayloristic view of work, and consequently a lack of perception of group problems. Instead of a team we have a group of individual piece-rate workers that are dissatisfied with the production order system. The lack of automation seems to get in the way of team problem solving. It should be noted that the problem that was attacked by the Lindesberg team – allocating the right amount of production output to the right period (shift) and person in a situation where there is interaction between periods – is a classical accounting problem with no solution.

In Köping (gearbox shafts), the experiment was distracted by the installation of a fascinating FMS-complex and by the choice of a too advanced software package for the PC. The team was doing the right thing in collecting data on its own operations, but did not get around to much action as a result of these distractions.

In analysing the experiences of these three-year experiments one should be aware that all kinds of interventions have occurred in this case, even though special care has been taken to place the initiative firmly in the hands of the teams and their foremen. Nonetheless special attention has been given to these groups, and even if Volvo has a long tradition of experiments with group-oriented production structures, Hawthorne-effects cannot be excluded. There is really no basis for generalization. Still some tentative conclusions worthy of further investigation can be drawn.

Control

It should be noted that it was not the variable or direct costs which came into focus in the successful case, but the semi-fixed costs like rejects or cutting tools. These costs are the key to cost control since they are controllable to a larger extent than materials and labour. Labour is controllable in the sense that operators can manage to get more output per effort hour.

The main advantage of automated machinery, however, seems to be that operators have time to conduct projects while they oversee the producing machines. To the extent that when operators are bound, as in Lindesberg, by manual operations (like loading and unloading several machines) to the production process, it is more difficult to conduct self-management. Projects in environments of a low level of automation seem to be possible only with outside help, in which case the self-management properties of the project tend to become dominated by expert views, which in turn diminishes responsibility and motivation.

Material costs can also be influenced in an indirect way by reducing rejects, etc., since purchasing is centralized to staff departments. It is, however, interesting to notice how great the differences are between different batches of steel from a cutting tool point of view. The team in Floby decided from the beginning that materials costs were largely out of their reach.

A striking feature, throughout our observations, is the pre-eminence of action over analysis and planning. Even if the teams in all three plants indicated that the statistics on operations that were collected would be useful in forthcoming budget negotiations, it seems that the driving factor behind the projects was the will to know more about the effects of action. Knowing is owning; and owning is, by definition, having control.

The crucial importance of ownership of the data and of the projects was obvious in the successful Floby team where all projects were initiated and largely carried out by the team itself (or on its terms). The Floby team chose to work with problems they thought they could handle. When they asked for outside help they were able to specify what the problem was and thus the criteria for an acceptable solution.

In Köping and Lindesberg the teams were not given a proper chance to take ownership of their team projects, perhaps because support was too intrusive from higher levels in the organization. In setting up their first projects both teams involved other departments, conspicuously the computer department, which blocked the formation of a team identity that could serve as the platform for action.

In the Floby case actions also occurred with other departments, but only after the team had established itself and learnt how to cooperate in order to solve common problems. In Köping and Lindesberg the teams became dependent on other departments for the success of their main project which demonstrated the dependence of the team members on the outside. When the project drags on, it is easy for team members to attribute the lack of success on the environment and to shun responsibility. Furthermore it is obviously demoralizing if the team believes it has improved operations, but the cost centre reports show no improvement or deterioration.

The opposite development – to do something, have success and realize that you have control – is, as we all know, a potent motivating force.

Our foremen agreed that team spirit is central to success. Team spirit can be destroyed almost instantaneously, but takes a long time to build. We believe that it relates to the feeling of being in control, but this is something that cannot be observed properly in this kind of study.

Attention

We see the world through our concepts! Academics tend to see the world through models where processes are treated as black boxes, described with the help of relations between inputs and outputs. These teams are inside the boxes! The closer one gets to the process the more difficult it is to achieve enough distance from the process itself to get an overview. To compensate for the lack of distance from the ongoing process one has to focus attention on a few things at a time and to work with standard procedures in areas where attention is down-scaled at the moment. Attention is a limited commodity to be applied with wisdom. Learning is a useful tool in establishing standard procedures that do not require much attention once they are established. But learning requires attention! The teams have a strategic choice as to what factor is judged to be critical for success at a given instance. Part of the process deserves an interactive approach at the moment, and other parts must be delegated to programmed control (cf. Simons *et al.*, 1987).

Interactive control of operations and changes in those processes, within the limits set by the context, requires information not normally accessible by operators. True that a lot of data are displayed on screens in the machine group, about the depth of holes currently being drilled, etc., but those measures are 'physical' and directly coupled to the machines. Data relating to the performance of the group in economic and strategic terms require an interpretational leap to become meaningful and thus worthy of attention. Interpretation means a translation between operational activities and financial measures in both directions so that a reversible figure-ground situation (one set of measures providing the explanatory background for the other set, and vice versa) is established. Engaging interactively in constructing interpretational schema means that the team builds these translations into their work routines. Once a new routine has been confirmed as reasonable it may be delegated to programmed control as part of normal procedures until it is brought to the fore again on another interpretative occasion. It should be pointed out here that the relevance of data *emerges* in such interactive episodes, where attention is heightened temporarily. Consequently the local need for data on operations is also *temporary*. Hardly any local performance data are needed or wanted all the time. 'Physical' measures such as temperatures, etc., are another matter, but performance in terms of costs or quality is learnt by organizations by being built into routine behaviour.

If this claim is valid it follows that data for organizational learning are needed only temporarily, for example, in these episodes of high attention when problem searching and solving is occurring. When things are normal, the relevant information is contained in standards such as how many rejects per shift correspond to the cost centre budget, or how many shafts should normally be turned before a tool needs to be changed. Deviations from normality may arouse attention and subsequent problem solving if the deviation is put on the agenda. One of our interviewees said that a foreman receives a large number of signals every shift. Operators tend to report observations and complaints to the foreman as he or she passes by. Most of the time these signals are ignored. A good foreman, however, has the ability to register those signals and detect patterns. When a pattern is interpreted to be a problem, the foreman should publicize the problem to the group; "We have a problem!". Once the problem is put on the agenda operators will start to think about it, and if the foreman communicates continuously with the group, it will generate most of the pieces of the puzzle that constitutes the solution. Attention generates problem solving in the group and the will to know – to be in control of your own operation – drives the members of the group to provide tentative solutions to parts of the problem. The foreman's task is to integrate and to gather the holders of pieces of a solution in a joint session when the time is right. The resulting solution will be the property and responsibility of the group and it will be implemented.

The will to know

To assume responsibility for performance and to take action for improvement are acts of will. The mobilization of that will in the team is largely the task of the foreman. In this study we have seen different styles of foremen. One of our foremen was primarily interested in technology, and tended to search for solutions by adjusting machines. Another had a philosophy that told him that if operators are happy with their work conditions and the social environment, they will keep machines going even if technical indicators tell us that there should have been a stoppage. Finally there is the problem-oriented foreman that works in sequences such as:

* find out what is wrong (follow-ups);
* analyse what could be done (problem solving);

- act and see whether there is improvement (test solution);
- end sequence (implement routine).

Such cycles are repeated preferably in a sequence of rising difficulty. There are longer or shorter periods of normal operation between the projects of improvement, which gives the process of improvement a discontinuous character. There is no smooth learning curve but a stepwise development in terms of projects. Leadership in improvement work means focusing group attention and declaring the problem solved. It seems to be important to end a project and secure a victory, by fixing the new routine, before the project turns into a bore.

Operators, like top managers, have limited attention to pay to different aspects of work. Since attention is a scarce resource it should be focused on one problem that could be expected to be solved in a reasonable time. Problems that require lengthy investigations and complex design cannot be dealt with successfully on the part-time basis that an operator can afford. Such larger projects should be delegated to project groups organized differently to the production team.

Börje, the foreman in the Floby plant, was according to our judgement, a good example of problem-oriented leadership. He was so successful in establishing his production teams as problem solvers that he soon was more or less dispensable in the daily operations. His statement: "I want the operators to drive me, instead of me driving them", stands for a role where he mainly represents the team in its dealings with the outside. He does play an active role in initiating follow-ups, but a large part of the decision-making under normal conditions is delegated to operators.

To a large extent, we believe, the leader of the team establishes the identity of the team. Having an identity as a responsible unit, that can act as a partner in cooperative problem solving with other units, is quite important for the motivation of the team. Especially, when the team interacts with expert staff units (like the computer department), the relation between the two very easily turns into a subservient relation where the team has difficulties in articulating its problem and where the expert imposes his or her favourite models on the team, taking away any sense of responsibility it might have had. Partnership in cooperative problem solving presumes an identity as a responsible, knowledgeable unit. The team thus needs a track record of successes (demonstrated competence), a leader to represent them in negotiations and some attention from top management.

The importance of identity was highlighted by the response of participants from the teams in a final seminar about how a manual on teamwork (the way the teams had done) should look. The answer was, unanimously, that such a manual cannot be written. Circumstances are so different, the task so complicated and teams so unique that one could not pronounce any general rules on how to go about teamwork. Possibly this strong signal of uniqueness is part of each team's desire to be in control and to protect its identity. "No other team would (could?) have done it the way we did it!". But there surely are some common conclusions to draw from these experiences.

Contracting

There seems to be a natural progression in improvement work, in that a team will start with establishing itself as a competent problem solving agent first and then develop cooperative problem solving with other departments. The first step in demonstrating to the team itself and to its environment that it is a competent agent is done in an inner dialogue, where team members participate in the articulation of what is the problem and what could be done about it. It is not necessary for all members to be actively influencing the process. Participation through active listening is fully adequate. What seems to happen in the inner dialogue is that intuitive knowledge about the production process becomes articulated and thereby available for action. There is also a process of role development and commitment to action. Here contracting is implicit in the sense that the responsibilities of a team member are not explicitly articulated, even if everyone knows what work membership requires.

In a later stage when problem-solving attention is directed towards the environment, like the foundry or the forge, contracting is more explicit. Communication between teams is largely through representatives, who have the authority to make binding agreements, or to exert the rights of a customer. The arms-length communication provides for articulation of terms even if initial discussions are based on socially established relations.

This social dimension of communication in problem solving casts a different light on information and information use in improvement work. It seems like an intuitive kind of knowledge based on thorough knowledge of the details at work. This knowledge is articulated through the follow-ups which serve as a reminder (updating, as it were). Such knowledge is soon discovered to be valuable in negotiations with the environment. First it is a good base for arguments in the budget process (provided that teams are allowed to participate), because then the team has to have documented evidence when they want to challenge biased standards. Secondly, it is a good factual basis for customer complaints. It is probably not very difficult to make the foreman at the foundry see that sloppy sandblasting of the brake drum blanks will cause cutting tools to be worn more quickly than they should, but there may be more subtle or counterintuitive effects that need documentation to be convincing. Once the other party admits to being convinced that there is a causal link a contracting situation has been established.

Concluding words

This study, as it has been conducted, does not allow any safe conclusions in a scientific sense, since we have not had all independent variables under control (and since we do not really know what our dependent variable is). We have studied a three-year process of organizational learning in three locations with similar, but differently aged, technology, and we are trying to make sense of what we have seen. Further research will provide a more sound basis for conclusions.

This report may seem to contain no spectacular conclusions or few new ideas but this is precisely the point! Cost improvement is much easier to talk about than to do.

6

Controlling through dialogue*

In the previous chapter the inner and outer dialogues of improvement work were not the centre of attention from the start, and observations in the field of the actual discussions were virtually non-existent. In the case presented in this chapter, again dialogue was not central to the study, but this time the design of the study happened to place the fieldworker in a position to observe the outer dialogue. It was found to be important.

Imagine an orchestra!

Imagine an orchestra and its conductor. In it there are units, for example, the brass section, of professional instrumentalists who are very good at hearing what they themselves play and adapt what they play to what they are supposed to play. They also have collaborative skills in that they are able to listen and adapt to how their colleagues are playing so that the joint product is harmonious. Then there is the conductor who tries to impose his will on the orchestra (by waving a baton). When, in practice, the joint product does not match the ideal he will stop the orchestra playing and

*The fieldwork in this case was carried out by Rolf Solli and is reported in more detail in Solli (1991).

use verbal and bodily expressions to illustrate how the deviation could be corrected. Orchestra and conductor will listen again, correct and, when they are satisfied, move on to the next section of the piece at hand.

These are professionals. There is individual skill that has to be maintained through regular practice. There is the ability to adapt mutually inside the ensemble, and the ability to translate the gestures and other expressions of the conductor into a specific profile of the performance. Call all of the ingredients of this professional 'competence' and the kind of control exhibited by the conductor 'orchestration'.

Like all professionals, musicians have to maintain their skills through practice, but this is probably done more through performing ('doing their thing') than by taking courses or participating in seminars. There are, of course, interesting opportunities to participate in new combinations of skills that will extend the experience and, thereby, the scope of the professional competence of the individual musician. But, by and large, the violinist's profession is defined by his or her membership in the philharmonic orchestra. Beside the daily individual practice the job is done by members of the orchestra adapting to colleagues' playing and to the conductor's intentions.

Now consider conductors. Their job is to bring out the best in the collectivity of the orchestra, by choice of repertoire and by coaching. Guest conductors will be brought in and tours organized, but it is all in the pursuit of excellence. The conductor is supposed to push the orchestra – and its finances – to the limit. No conductor wants to be recognized as an expert on keeping budgets. It is remarkable performances and memorable moments of perfection that they are after. To hear possibilities in the orchestra, to innovate, to think of new interpretations, to recruit new members, but above all to perform; these are the means towards excellence. But to engage in cost cutting or to debase the orchestra by playing popular music to earn money, never! Cost cutting can only be justified as an experiment to achieve better performance and playing popular music can only be justified as an effort to bring music to the masses.

Any conductor would resign in a dramatic gesture when facing a serious decision to cut the budget by a significant amount. Finances do not mix well with professionalism. A real professional is supposed to ignore financial information. Finances normally do not enter the professional discourse, other than as complaints about their inadequacy. This is the problem area this chapter is trying to deal with, the apparent incompatibility between professional discourse and financial calculation. The professional area is social services performed in the public sector, and the location is a small town somewhere in Sweden.

Before the musical area is left, please turn again to p. 5 in Chapter 1 to refresh your memory of what happens when a nationalization expert interferes with music!

Joking aside, there is obviously a serious problem of communication between the financial calculative lifeworld of accountants and the professional discourse of those who do the job of, for example, a social services department or a clinic.

Finances, in a way, have to do with not primary, but secondary effects of activities. In terms of revenues they represent the evaluations of clients expressed in concrete payment of money for services. In terms of grants they represent evaluations of plans, promises or programmes expressed in concrete authorization to spend a certain amount of money for that purpose. In terms of costs they report values in concrete money of the inputs to the activities that produce the desired output. Here the valuation in money may be dependent upon rules and regulations concerning, for example, allocation.

These secondary effects, characteristic of finances, cause a time lag, forwards and backwards, that makes it difficult to couple finance and activities. Either finances concern plans about activities that are contemplated for the future (budget) but are not yet immediately at hand, or they concern reports about the financial effects of activities that have already been carried out some time ago. Bridging these time lags and establishing links between activities and finances, in such a way that they enter everyday thinking about what to do now, is not easy under normal conditions of industrial production. It is still more difficult in the professional production of services, or applications of knowledge to unstructured problems, where links between activity and secondary outcomes are still not wholly understood. The time lag causes difficulties in learning from experience (Kolb, 1984). Difficulties may be the wrong expression since they are experienced only by those who want to learn – it might be more appropriate to propose that the time lags favour ignorance of the links. For the professional there are strong incentives to relate professional competence to primary effects of activities, for example, if the therapy shows an improvement in the client. Attention is drawn to them by traditional patterns of professional training and by the concrete visibility of primary effects.

The problem

This chapter is based on the assumption that there are specific communication problems between discourses. In the case of a professional area of activity like a laboratory, school or clinic the difficulties in translating primary effects into secondary financial effects are considerable. The competence profile of the professionals and the assumed immediacy of primary effects initiate learning cycles that more or less block learning to link the financial and professional spheres, at least so far as these links are of any complexity. Therefore special efforts are necessary to enhance the use of financial information in activity-oriented professional decision-making.

If a field study with modest intervention indicates that this general working hypothesis is justified then further studies into the use of financial information in professional problem-solving discourse are warranted.

An action research approach

An action research study was made of six social service units in a medium-sized municipality in Sweden. The intervention was modest in the sense that there was some training in economic–financial concepts and relations, managers were also allowed to design their own financial reports after instruction and, finally, attention to financial aspects of activities was maintained through 'monthly chats' on the financial situation. The study lasted for one year (Solli, 1991).

To be able to observe the use of financial information in a professional setting one has to resort to field studies. It is not likely that professional discourse could be simulated in a laboratory-type experimental setting. Neither would interviews after the fact reveal much about the content and impact of professional reasoning on the spot. To set up instrumentation to register the actual use of financial information in professional problem-solving discourse might create such unnatural working conditions for the professionals that the validity of the observations could be questioned.

Therefore an approach with modest intervention and observation of secondary effects was chosen. It was not a primary task at this stage of the research programme to observe how financial information was integrated into the professional language or how the professional problem-solving process was constituted. We wanted indications only of the fact that financial information had been taken into consideration and that the financial performance of the units had improved without a decline in professional performance or quality of services. In addition, we did not want to make such a conspicuous intervention that the ordinary conduct of professional work would be distorted.

Social services is a professional area where it is also possible to communicate with non-professionals. Everyday language is used and it is possible for a layman to judge performance reasonably well, even though it obviously is not possible to know what the situation would have been if activities had been focused differently. Such a choice of research site allowed us to discover whether integration between the languages of professional work and finance had occurred. However, this does not mean to say that the work in social services is easy.

The unit of observation is a cost centre. In large organizations professional services are usually organized into discretionary cost centres, controlled by a budget, restrictions on personnel policies and some quality standards. We have reasons to believe that in social services there are strong inclinations towards teamwork even though there are some aspects of the work that require strictly confidential relations between the client and professional. The professional dialogue, that is seeking and giving advice, recounts of 'cases', current professional evaluation of colleagues, etc., will create an inner network of relations between members, making them a team with an inner dialogue on, for example, criteria of performance, problem solving and resolution of conflicts. The leader of the team will be its spokesperson in the outer dialogue, e.g. on budget or personnel issues.

Hopefully the intervention of the action research project could be focused on the outer dialogue and the effects on the inner dialogue would be observed through changes in performance indices and in the development of new activities.

The research site

A research project like the one about to be reported on requires active participation from the study object. We wanted to study an organization that was undertaking a decentralization of authority and responsibility and was ready to invest the necessary resources in training and redesign of financial reports to meet the individual needs of participants in the project. In the spring of 1987 the small mid-Swedish town of Hillside volunteered to participate. Six operations managers in the social services department were chosen to form the S-group which is the focal group of this report. (Other studies have been made of other groups in Hillside and in other communities.) It consisted of two managers of full-time day-care centres for small children, one old-age home manager, one manager of home services for a district, one manager of a family-based day-care for children and one manager of a part-time day-care centre for small children.

The town is located in a scenic, rural area with a good supply of recreational facilities, good communications, a small airport and some 30,000 inhabitants. During the study period there was an under supply of labour, especially to the manufacturing industry in the area (unemployment was reported to be around 1.5% for the whole country). The public sector accounts for about 35% of the employment in Hillside including a fairly large hospital (15% of the 35%). The city council has a non-socialist majority and the finances of the municipality are fairly good. The municipality had investigated the pros and cons of reorganizing from a sector-based (school department, social services department, etc.) to a district-based organization with local councils responsible for all municipal services in their districts but decided to focus on decentralization inside the existing functional structure.

The intervention

First a mapping of the initial situation through structured interviews with the participants (the S-group) in the project was made. In these interviews questions were asked about the professional training and experience of the respondents, their work role and the most difficult problems they had encountered. Respondents were also asked to describe the activities of their unit, what kind of reports they received and how these were read, about their opinion of the budget as a control instrument, and to what extent they felt they could control costs and performance. This first round of interviews gave a reading of the starting point for the process for later comparison.

The intervention was three-fold:

- an introduction to accounting systems and concepts used by the town;
- an introduction to report design, and participants' individual design of own report;
- regular 'talks' on the financial situation on the basis of reports.

The accounting course consisted of a two-day and one evening intensive exercise in the concepts and structures of the financial system of the municipality, accounts and budgets, aggregations and disaggragations of financial reports. This part of the intervention was later judged to have been too intensive and overloaded with information that was, to a large extent, alien to the participants. On the same occasion, and after the accounting exercise, participants were introduced to the possibilities of designing financial reports to suit diverse information needs and individual styles in using them. This session ended in the participants designing their own cost centre reports as they wanted them. This report design was then used during the year of observation. In the 'talks' that ensued monthly during the year of observation participants were asked whether they wanted to change their reports. Few changes were made and they were marginal in the sense that one or two rows or columns were added. They were thus expansive (no-one wanted to reduce the report format). The exception was that the interest in including activity indicators in the report declined over the period. The explanation was simple; those measures were easily available elsewhere and could be excluded without loss of information.

The third intervention was designed to maintain attention on financial matters, but it was intended to be unobtrusive in the sense that it was not intended to dominate the participants, for example, by telling them what should be done. Instead the talks were intentionally started with a question "What is your economic situation?". (Translation not quite to the point here, maybe "How are you doing, financially?" better catches the mood of the question.) This question, being an open invitation to conversation with a slight direction towards financial matters, started conversations that touched upon a large number of subjects and grew in length over the observation periods. The field researcher (Solli) and the controller of the social services department, sometimes jointly and sometimes alone, visited the participants every month in connection with their understanding of cost reports. The intention was originally that these conversations would give information on how participants used the individualized cost reports, but they could also help the participants to pay attention to financial matters. This latter intention was realized as the cost figures in Table 6.1 show, but there was an added feature that we will explore more fully later. Talks tended to grow in scope and time over the period of observation. From approximately 20 minutes in the first visit to several hours of strategic discussion towards the end.

Results

Economic effects

The economic effects of the intervention are difficult to measure because there were structural changes occurring at the same time, in particular, a decentralization of the responsibility for personnel costs. This meant that the budget of all the participating units had increased significantly. For a couple of the units there were also changes in the definition of the cost centre which made comparisons with the previous year impossible. For three units it was possible to determine comparable cost figures for the two years.

Inflation during the period was about 7%. No adjustment for inflation has been made in Table 6.1. For the three other units it was not possible to secure comparable figures for the period before the intervention, but the economic results have been positive and of a similar magnitude. It

Table 6.1   Financial outcome for three of the six participating units (Skr thousands)

	Budget outcome 1987*	1988	Cost growth 1987–1988†	Budget 1988
Kindergarten 1	+20	+150	0.0%	3100
Kindergarten 2	+30	+300	+2.9%	2800
Old-age home	−600	0	+3.5%	7200

*'+' means better than budget.

†The average cost increase for kindergarten units in the municipality was +5.7%, and for old-age homes it was +7.1%.

should be noted that a large proportion of the costs for this kind of service units is personnel and that salaries increased during this period. The 'savings' are probably best described as lower cost increases than other comparable units in the municipality, and surpluses in the budget add up to a considerable 'profit' for the intervention.

Conceptual training

The training in accounting and financial concepts and the structure of the accounting system of the municipality took the form of an out-of-town two-day seminar at a luxury hotel in a city some distance away. The fact that the municipality accepted the cost was a clearly audible signal that this was important. The participants valued the course as interesting, useful and difficult, with the average figure on a five-grade Likert-scale (5 being the best value) at around 4 for all three dimensions. The most 'interesting' part of the course was listed "report layout". The most 'useful' was judged to be "accounting principles". The most difficult one was the "finances of the municipality". There were some comments about the course being too intense. More time should have been allotted to some of the topics. However, the course must be said to have been successful overall.

Reports

The six participants designed reports that were different in complexity, but there were some cross-influence between them (see Table 6.2). One of the kindergarten managers chose to more or less copy the layout of a colleague. There was a strong relation between the size of the operations and the number of rows and columns used in the reports. One might assume that the more complex the activities of the unit the greater the need would be for abstraction and thus aggregated measurements, but such an assumption was not borne out in this case.

Table 6.2   Characteristics of the reports designed by participants

Unit	No. of rows	No. of columns	No. of employees
Kindergarten 1	10	5	18
Kindergarten 2	9	7	20
Part-time kindergarten	8	4	3
Day-care district	7	6	16
Home service	8	5	25
Old-age home	21	9	46

Even if the difference in number of cells (rows × columns) is increased by the multiplication effect of the number of rows and columns one should probably not read too much into the differences in 'complexity' of the reports – except the correlation between size and complexity. The participants designed the reports themselves and therefore 'knew' it.

Two of the participants were convinced from the start that their report was relevant to them and that it would be a support for them in analysing their activities. Two were doubtful of the usefulness and described their commitment by talking about 'looking at' the report. One of these had an overall doubt about the usefulness of financial information. She knew her activities and provided a good service as she had always done. Financial information seemed to be beside the point. She was a likeable woman, approaching retirement age and twice the size of our fieldworker. Responsibility was with the task not with the 'accounts'. Not to waste resources is part of the task. The other doubtful manager was responsible for the smallest unit and she grew more convinced over the observation period that she really did not have any use for the report. This was a rational conclusion since the small number of transactions could easily be checked in the current accounts or notebooks. The transparency of the small unit activity makes accounting reports superfluous.

With one exception the participants did not experience any surprises during the period. The reports said what they were expected to say. The exception was the manager of Kindergarten 1. She was shocked by the financial size of the operations (personnel had been budgeted on a higher organizational level before) and by the financial outlook for the rest of the year according to the first reports. Those participants who had expressed distrust in the figures claimed that the budget had been miscalculated. On no occasion were accounting figures questioned. It seemed as if the participants had at all times an intuitive feeling for how the 'finances were', and that the primary function of the reports was not to inform but to confirm. One should not, however underestimate the value of the confirmation that reports give. It adds to the security in one's work role the feeling of being in control – and thereby the propensity to take initiatives and, possibly, to learn. The shock felt in Kindergarten 1, on the other hand, gave an illustration that uncertainty in the work role (this manager was fairly new to her job) may be amplified by a report saying that things are larger, more complex and worse than expected. A further indication of this tendency of uncertainty to accumulate is that this manager had in fact copied the report layout of her colleague in the other kindergarten. It is not justified to make generalizations based on one case, of course, but we have made similar observations in several other studies of this kind, and found that there is a risk of vicious circles emerging in learning situations involving financial and operational information. This is an illustration of the decrease in the capacity to integrate complexity, described in the cognitive complexity theory formulated by Schroder *et al.* (1967; see also Ims, 1987; Hedberg and Jönsson, 1977a, b).

On each occasion when there were talks on the monthly reports participants were asked whether they thought the layout was good. They were usually satisfied. Few changes were made and in those cases the change was always expansion in the form of adding another row or column in the report. No one wanted less accounting information.

Talks

The most interesting part of the observation period turned out to be the talks on reports. They were structured so that our fieldworker and/or the controller of the social services department visited the participants shortly after they had received their monthly cost reports. The opening question was "How are you doing, financially?". As mentioned previously, this opening question was intended to give the ensuing conversation an open character. On the other hand, the talks were also intended to focus on action – what would the participant do next. They were imposing in the sense that they could not be avoided since it was part of the deal with the participants that they would set aside the time needed for the talks. Some of the monthly meetings were in fact cancelled for *force majeure* reasons like illness or trouble with the production of the reports.

The content of the talks changed over the observation period. First, the main topic was what was included and not included in reports and the effort seemed to be directed towards the formulation of a joint image (true and fair, as it were) of the financial situation, what had happened and what was going to happen. After some months, however, one could notice a shift in focus towards impediments to the conduct of good and/or effective operations. There was never any expression of desire to achieve cheap operations, but nobody had anything against better and cheaper as a proper objective. This shift in focus to impediments meant a challenge to the higher organizational level. All hierarchies are built on rules and regulations. It is in general quite difficult to eliminate old sedimented routines and procedures that have petrified since the days when they were functional. Such non-functional rules were made visible to the central level in the talks. Quite often the arguments made sense and there was agreement that the central level would see what they could do to eliminate these identified blockages to efficiency. Action on such issues confirmed that the talks were meant seriously.

Another topic that appeared, and may be classified in the same category as removal of bureaucratic anomalies, is the clarification of territorial boundaries, like who is responsible for what and what the proper charge for inter-unit services is.

A third focus in the talks appeared more strongly towards the end of the period and concerned reflection and articulation of ideas and latent projects. Participants would take up preliminary ideas related to a problem, test "what if?" questions and articulate, in dialogue, the first sketches of new initiatives. Our fieldworker could see that towards the end of the period scribbling and calculations in the margins of the report form were more frequent than in the beginning. It would seem that an important use of reports is to think about "what if?", "could this be done otherwise?", to reflect on the conduct of operations while reading the reports. The dialogue form seemed to provide an outside partner in conversation who could serve as a preliminary scrutinizer of 'crazy ideas', if they were not rejected in these first probings they might deserve further development. The act of articulation, however tentatively, may serve as a beginning to initiation of action.

The rapport between local and central levels is obviously a sensitive issue in this respect. One of the participants (the manager of the old-age home) reflected on his working relationship to the social services controller in an interview some years after the observation period:

> When I started this job Peter was controller. I don't think I ever met him. I remember calling him about a broken TV-set once. He saw to it that we got a new one. Otherwise we never heard from him. There were definitely no discussions about finances with us. That was handled centrally in those days. Peter left in 1981, two years after I started.
>
> The new controller was Ellie. She had completely different ideas about finances. She gave us a budget and that was it. Not much of a budget really because it included only materials – personnel and the rents and costs for keeping the house in shape were still centralized and never revealed to us. She had ideas about how we should run things. For example, we couldn't buy the quality of sheets that we wanted. She sent directives about that. We knew that the poorer quality wouldn't last long enough to justify the advantage in price but we could do nothing about

it. If she thought a unit wasted money she would call. Once the cost of food for the clients had increased and she called. She cared about the costs – the fact that the increase had been caused by more out-patients coming in to eat and the fact that they had paid for it was beside the point to her. I remember she said once "Are you still alive?! I thought you had eaten yourself to death!". Well, there was never any real cooperation with Ellie. One thing was good with her though, I had to learn how to side-step rules and regulations without the central level noticing anything. Ellie left in 1986.

Then, after a period of vacancy, came Ylva. She arrived at about the same time as this pilot project got under way. She saw to it that all of us in the project got the economic reports we wanted, in the way we wanted them. Budgets and accounting reports contained all costs and revenues. The big achievement was that we could use the revenues from, for example, sales of meals the way we wanted to, for example, to buy food. Ylva and I had long discussions about how we should charge for the services we delivered to the outside. We calculated all kinds of things to see what it meant to do or not do things. Actually I didn't work that long with Ylva, about two years, then these researchers came and took away the time she spent with me. Then she became pregnant and there was a substitute, Britt.

Britt worked for a couple of months and we got the reports we wanted but there was not much more. There wasn't time to establish contact other than occasionally. Then she got another job and moved on. Then we had no controller for months. That period was strange. Suddenly there was almost no information again. It was frustrating to be back to where we were in 1979. Even Ellie was better than that.

Last year Bertie was hired as controller. He had to show his mettle! He was fresh from university and had a lot to learn at the same time as there was a lot of catching up to do. There wasn't even a proper budget. He is getting to know how things work now and what our problems are.

It seems like the outer dialogue is meaningful as well as habit-forming. Turnover among central managers seems to effect relations between central and local units. It is not only a matter of systems and routines, or even a dialogue between professions or different knowledge bases, and it is not just a matter of (personal) chemistry. It is all of these in a specific mixture for the individual case. It is a matter of functionality as well as trust and responsibility. At first glance dialogue seems so complex that it could not be done on a large scale throughout an organization, which would mean that the standardized and formalized form of reporting is the only reasonable solution to the problem of information sharing between levels in organizations.

Analysis

Still the effects of the improvements in costs and qualities of the services that these six participants delivered during the period of observation are so encouraging that it is necessary to pursue the possibilities of this dialogue form of management control further. The practical justification for the effort clearly rests with the improvement of services that the participants achieved. The theoretical one is the improved insight into the processes of management that field studies of this kind can provide.

What actually happened in terms of improvement of the daily management of activities was beyond the reach of direct observation in the research design we chose. Descriptions came in the shape of anecdotes. Typically our participants would use a concrete example to make a point. Some of these stories were followed up in our interviewing. Thus our documentation of the effects of the intervention is largely in the form of stories, more or less corroborated by factual observations or documents (plus our measures of cost improvement). Often these stories have a moral, and they are used as persuasive tools in the professional or semi-professional dialogue. They seem to become a constitutive part of the organizational culture expressing exemplars of behaviour in the organization. These surviving stories have to be awarded more attention if we are to understand how managerial techniques and changes in information flows influence managerial behaviour. It seems reasonable to assume that managerial or trust relations between groups or individuals in an organizational setting are only changed gradually (unless relations are rent abruptly, for example through structural changes in the organization, in which case new relations will be built gradually). Changes will be caused by events that are given narrative meaning in organizational storytelling. Some stories become legendary milestones in the history of the organization. The following story is our favourite one from this project. It seems to have all the ingredients to give it impetus in the development of an organizational culture.

> The manager of the old-age home, Olle, had decided that the home needed a set of new chairs for the outside patio. The finances allowed it, which had been sorted out in one of the talks. Ten chairs were needed, and a suitable type was available in one of the shops in town, but there were several possible vendors. Olle compared prices for comparable offers. The local store offered a price of Skr113, but there was another shop some distance away from the town centre that offered Skr98 including transport. A difference of Skr15 which could not be ignored. On the other hand Olle had a bond with the local store which managed the kiosk service at the old-age home. This was not a profitable operation for the local store. The shop owner saw it as a communal service he provided to society. Olle realized this and offered to accept a price of Skr105 in a deal with the local shop. The local shop owner was a man of principles who stood by his word – Skr113 or no kiosk.
>
> Olle, also being a man of principles, scouted around for an alternative provider of the kiosk service and when he found another local shop that was willing to take over the kiosk service, he closed the deal on the chairs at 98 with the outside shop.

The existing kiosk service was terminated at once, but for some reason the new arrangement did not work, possibly because the kiosk service in fact was not a profitable one. A solution had to be found. People wanted to be able to buy sweets and other small things in the kiosk. A local solution had to be designed. Olle found it in the "Everything club", which is a club run by the pensioners in the home and from the outside with picnics, theatre, bingo and dance evenings on its programme. There was an active couple in that club who needed a challenge. Olle arranged the purchase of necessary supplies for an ambulating kiosk and the couple took care of the sales.

Our fieldworker had heard about the chair event and the kiosk business before but had not made the connection until one of the talks with Ingrid, the manager of the home services of that district. She had her office in the old-age home and when the researcher and the controller were conducting one of their talks with her an elderly gentleman came in with a pile of money in his hand which he gave to Ingrid saying "Here is some money. It is Skr1152". Ingrid went on talking about her (fairly uninteresting) monthly report, took out a small cash box, made a single entry note in the cash book of the amount, put the money into the box where the researcher could see a bank book.

Ingrid, who was the participant with the most explicit disinterest in financial matters, had caught the attention of her visitors, not by what she was saying but by what she was doing. What was all that money? The explanation was quite natural. There was the "Everything club" at the home which had, through an initiative of Olle's, taken over the kiosk service. Ingrid was the treasurer of the club and this was the revenue since the last time the elderly gentleman had reported in. But what about vouchers, receipts, VAT and things like that? Well they did not bother so much about that. This operation was run on trust. A simple, correct and rational bookkeeping system kept track of 'revenue' and 'expenditure' and the difference was deposited in the bank account. That money was used for bus trips and other pleasures the "Everything club" fancied. It was this incident with the elderly moneyman that alerted the fieldworker to the activities of this extra-organizational unit.

Olle liked to see the club expand and since this event we have seen it take over the management of the inventory of materials used in the hobby activities at the home (also for outside clients). The seniors did not like to tie up as much money as was required in stocks, so Olle arranged a five-year loan from the municipality so the club could buy the stock of materials from the municipality and manage the purchasing and distribution from then on. That loan was probably illegal but it was for a good cause. There are more projects run by the club! A year after our observation period the club opened its own pub in the basement of the home. Mobilizing local retired carpenters, getting the leading brewery to donate beer glasses and a fieldworker to provide the dart board the club is now running a regular pub (only members and friendly visitors). The last thing we heard was that they were planning to set up a subsidiary operation in a day care centre in a neighbouring part of town. A garden café they say.

We cannot claim that there is a direct causal link between our intervention with accounting concepts and report layouts and this expansion of client-managed activities at the home, but we like what we see and it is a nice story to tell. Certainly these activities are an indication of improved quality of the services provided at this old-age home! And costs have, if anything, come down. We have observed that the talks have given participants opportunities to articulate projects that have later been implemented. Our intuitive feeling is that this early stage of project articulation may be crucial in the generation of improvement initiatives. An overview of the financial situation that is not coupled with unnecessary uncertainty and has an outside partner that will listen and contribute in a relationship that is based on trust built from signals of sincerity, such as removing obstacles to efficient operations, are powerful action generators (Starbuck, 1983).

The relationship between an inner (in-group) and an outer (between groups) dialogue may hold the key to a better understanding of the mechanism of organizational learning (Levitt and March, 1988). This will be the focus of our reasoning in the following text.

Meaning and explanation

Bruner (1986) distinguishes between the narrative mode of understanding and the more abstract scientific mode which he calls paradigmatic. The paradigmatic mode is suited to making sense of principles abstract from context. Describing the old-age home in terms of accounting concepts would give financial, paradigmatic meaning to its activities. The narrative mode of understanding includes the weight of the context and is therefore better suited as a medium for relating human experience with the contradictions and inconsistencies that it entails. Encapsulating experience in the form of a story makes it possible to make interpersonal sense of it. The story makes experience available to those who did not directly observe the event and its context.

It seems useful to distinguish in this way between paradigmatic and narrative meaning. A professional field may be described as a field of experience where the conceptual development has gone far enough to allow extensive use of paradigmatic interpretations. Learning includes conceptualization from narrative meaning to paradigmatic through encoding inferences from narrative history into routines that guide behaviour (Levitt and March, 1988). Possibly a professional field stands in relation to finance as paradigmatic does to narrative. The translation and implantation of concepts across this relation have to be done through dialogue.

According to Wittgenstein (1953) and Winch (1958) meaningful behaviour must meet two criteria:

1. the actor must be able to give a reason for an action; and

2. the actor must be bound by the act now to do something consistent with the act in the future.

When these two criteria are met the actor's behaviour may be said to have a sense.

The first criterion means that the actor must be capable of providing a justification or account for the act. The actor will usually not have to specify all the alternative acts that were at hand, but it is obviously necessary to show that there was a choice (at least to abstain from action) and the reason for the actual choice. The reason does not have to be true but must be recognizable as a reason and not incompatible with other information about the situation.

The second criterion establishes the rule-following or commitment aspect of action. As the actor makes public the reason for the act, he or she also announces an intention to behave accordingly in the future. A principle has been applied that is elevated to be a rule in the repertoire of rules which generates a behavioural pattern which, in turn, constitutes identity. Hereby accountability is established. The actor declares a willingness to be held accountable for this and consequent acts.

This giving of reasons for acts constitutes explanation to the environment. As such it has to be geared to the conceptual framework (paradigmatic meaning) or constitute a self-contained story (narrative meaning). The environment will signal its exceptance of the explanation by holding the actor responsible for this and future acts. Competent rule-following will lead to increased trust and a granting of a status of self-management, i.e. to be allowed to handle sensitive matters and warranty relations without interference from other members of the group. This is akin to being considered 'Mündig', which means having the right to sign binding contracts.

This line of reasoning will be used below to further develop the difference between inner and outer dialogue.

Trust

When a person understands the reasons for the acts of others and expects them to be bound by their commitment to behave consistently in the future he or she may act confidently and effectively because of the trust in the rules of the game. Garfinkel (1963) illustrates a conception of trust via a description of games. The basic rules of a game frame a set:

- which the player has to chose from;
- which the player expects to be binding for him as well as other players; and
- which the player expects other players to expect the same thing in return.

In this way they give rise to the constitutive expectancies of the game. Trust is then defined as constituting a situation where individuals in their interpersonal relations are governed by constitutive expectancies.

When trust is broken, for example by an actor making moves that violate the rules of the game, Garfinkel found that individuals engaged in vigorous efforts to 'normalize' the situation, that is return it to the original constituent expectancies. He also found that people who tried to retain the original rules of the game were more frustrated in their normalizing efforts than persons who were willing to redefine the game. Some of the experiments referred to by Garfinkel were designed to explicitly disallow redefinition of the game in order to register expressions of distrust, but these may not concern us here since the topic is dialogue between professions in social services and finance. In this dialogue redefinitions of the game may be what is desired.

With these sketches of the concepts meaning, explanation and trust we can make sense of the case.

Making sense of the case

The empirical material in this case consists of notes from the talks, i.e. dialogue between representatives of the central and local levels in the social services sector in a municipality, and stories about which intra-unit events caused a measurable improvement in costs as well as quality of services in the participating units. We have, as it were, observed the outer dialogue directly and the inner dialogue only indirectly through the stories. The research design was to let the inner processes of the units go on undisturbed (except for the effects that the three interventions might have).

We propose that the inner dialogue of a unit is chiefly concerned with a translation from narrative meanings to paradigmatic ones, i.e. from stories to principles. This translation work gives members of the unit opportunities to reflect upon experience, build trust and improve professional competence in experiential learning cycles (Kolb, 1974). The vehicle in this reflection is the story and the appended question: "Do you see what I see?". Confirming that the story makes sense – that it works in my experience, to use an expression from pragmatism – prepares participants for action and provides an explanation. The ability to focus the attention of members on common problems seems to be an important aspect of leadership. When action is sensible and explanation shared action serves to enhance loyalty to the unit norms. This loyalty is akin to trust and is largely implicit. Once stories are translated into principles, signals will have implicit meanings for group members. Representatives of a team seem to be forced to use narrative meaning to a large extent when communicating with the outside.

The outer dialogue, between the representatives of central and local points of view, served clarifying and contracting purposes. Clarifying, what the reports did and did not say, and what the area of responsibility was, played a greater role in the beginning of the observation year than in the latter part. Eliminating bureaucratic rules that impeded effective operations served as a signalling function. By taking the local problems seriously (doing something about them) the central level could show that rules of the game applied both ways. This allowed trust to be built on a situational basis which, in turn, made contracting possible. Most of the time contracting was implicit, but there was a distance between the local and central levels that had to do with non-interference in operations.

The relation between operational units and the centre is illustrated in its personal, as well as general, aspects by Olle's reflections on his contacts with the different controllers. There is a need to keep the relation from becoming too intimate, since the interruption of personal relations can have consequences that are far-reaching. Possibly it is necessary to distinguish between trust among persons and trust among offices. The latter will require articulation of rules of the game.

Since personal interaction is less frequent in the outer dialogue it is not possible to develop practices in the sense of Bourdieu (1977), i.e. as practices that can be transferred between situations "independent of individual consciousness and wills" (Bourdieu, 1977, p. 4). Trust among offices then becomes a relationship of seriousness and rule-following (which, it might be added, does not preclude the occasional 'rule-bending' exercise that may serve as an exemplar story to illustrate how a 'principle' may override the rules). Such trust is formal in nature and includes accountability.

In situations where the institutional trust (between offices) has for some reason (reorganization, budget cut-backs, policy-change, uncertainty) diminished, new institutional trust will have to be built by way of personal trust. Central representatives will have to participate in establishing relations across institutional boundaries that are personal and which express and focus attention (Simons, 1990) to matters of importance to the organization. Once such interactive relations have become routine they might become part of a formalized system or expressions of practice (in Bourdieu's sense). Such a translation of personal to institutional trust is probably dependent upon access and frequency or valence, and the face-to-face establishment of trustworthiness on both sides. Part of that institutionalization process is that individuals construct their roles and identities. When the identity as a competent unit is established explicit contracting is possible.

Afterthought on the role of personnel turnover

As can be read from Olle's reflections on his controller counterparts it seems safe to assume that the role a controller takes in relation to operative unit matters, significantly affects the form that accountability will take. For success there has to be professional competence, respect for roles, and attention to quality and efficiency. It seems, if Olle's account is representative, that some (most?) operational units never have a real chance to establish proper accountability and trust relations with the centre because of personnel turnover in significant communicative roles. The formal system of budgeting and accounting allows such a diversity of roles that adapting to new holders of positions may take too long for efficient communication to appear before there is a change.

Some organizations use the transfer of people between jobs in the organization as a training device to let future managers get to know many aspects of the organization. In organizations where formal roles are important, like in a modern army, there is also systematic rotation of officers between posts. In the first case the policy might be to get to know 'the culture' in the second case the main objective seems to be to maintain the formal hierarchical structure and the chain of command (to make the organization robust against losses of personnel).

This issue of the effects of personnel turnover on organizational l earning is a puzzling one. On the one hand, organizational learning seems to be enhanced by stability and trust in relations between organizational levels (and in a turbulent environment internal stability may be considered a favourable condition for learning). On the other hand, transfer of personnel is sometimes seen as a suitable instrument for dissemination of competencies throughout the organization. But, certainly, personnel turnover may accelerate organizational forgetting. Possibly, we have to deal with two types of effects, one that has to do with restructuring of myths (Hedberg and Jönsson, 1977a, b) which might require structural change in the form of a change of people in leading roles, and another concerned with experiential learning which requires stability and trust.

7

Controlling through local planning*

When we were contacted by the Road Authority about participation in a gigantic project to decentralize the management of the agency we saw it as a golden opportunity to test our ideas in the most demanding circumstances. We knew the Road Authority to be a state agency covering the whole of Sweden, controlled by a large planning staff at the centre, but with operational units scattered all over the country.

The history of the organization is important for the understanding of current problems.

A first overview of what was going on told us that we were dealing with one of the older state agencies of Sweden. It was set up in 1841 as 'The Royal Committee for Public Roads and Waterways' lately the Road Authority. In those days the waterways were an important transport route and the building of canals was the main task. In time roads gained in importance. In 1891 Sweden got its first Road Act. It divided the country into 368 road districts, placed responsibility for keeping roads in trim with municipalities and expected farmers to provide labour. As motoring grew in the beginning of the century the idea of basing the organization on

*The fieldwork in this case was carried out by Olle Westin and reported in Westin (1993).

labour provided in kind by people in the road district was gradually abandoned. Road taxes and road maintenance were managed by municipal road treasurer's offices. A road master was employed and, in time, workers.

Today the organization is not very different except that there has been a number of reforms to the superstructure. By 1934 the number of districts was reduced to 170 and the state took overall responsibility for the road network. This meant that the local state administration (in 24 counties) had a road engineer to deal with road issues. In 1944 parliament (Riksdag) decided to nationalize the road maintenance organization since municipal management delivered uneven road quality. Now matters could be handled rationally and could be financed via the state budget. Road work also became an important means of providing jobs in times of unemployment.

This large organization in charge of building and maintaining national roads, with a large number of districts in the base and a planning staff at the top, remained for a long time. An organization that became used to the management of large projects, partly building with its own resources and partly by contracting, gained experience in the management of countercyclical measures via the state budget, its only source of revenue. It also, gradually, got used to negotiations; with municipalities that wanted to dump municipal streets in its lap, and with landowners and politicians about the positions of new roads. Everybody knows that roads affect the value of property, location of industries and jobs, and even who wins the next election. In such an environment the Road Authority had to uphold an image of rationality and impartiality as it is surrounded by individuals and organizations that want to take advantage of its projects. It must be seen to be a master of planning, in the sense that it must have projects ready when the state wants to boost employment in different parts of the country, as well as be able to deflect local propositions by reference to soil characteristics, wildlife, economics, climate, etc. It is only natural that the Road Authority assembled an impressive staff of experts on almost every aspect of road maintenance. In 1990 the number of employees was 8000 and 4000 of them were white collar employees!

The management structure of the Road Authority was redesigned in 1986, and in 1991 there was a more thorough reorganization of the whole Road Authority in preparation for a probable privatization. The planning organization was expected to become a service organization. The budget for 1989 was Skr9.5 billion out of which Skr5.0 billion was to be used for road maintenance, Skr2.7 billion for investment in roads, and the rest for contributions to municipal roads and miscellaneous expenditure. In the budget request for 1992 the Road Authority asked for Skr20 billion, up almost 100% from the previous year. Unemployment was very high, and the newly elected government was expected to favour investment in roads to fight unemployment and to prepare for entry into the EEC. Part of the argument in the budget request was that road surfaces had been worn to below acceptable standards owing to inadequate budgets during the 1980s. Now was the time to correct that and provide jobs as a bonus. But television news reporters were quick in criticizing the Road Authority for using up a lot of money on new roads without creating more than 700 new jobs. Much of the increased volume of road building was taken care of using expensive machines instead of labour. Even road maintenance is now carried out in a mechanized fashion.

Reorganizations

The 1986 reform was mainly a gigantic information technology project with attending organizational adjustments. An organization built on planning and starting from a very centralized structure would choose to base decentralization in information technology.

The new IT policy was to replace a UNISYS–CPM and HP environment with a minicomputer-based VAX system. Up until 1989 vast amounts had been invested in hardware (see Table 7.1).

A number of applications had been installed including the accounting system and PLUS (Planning and Local monitoring system).

PLUS was a planning system intended for the regional level, but the input of data was supposed to be done on the local level and then forwarded to central systems. It was said to be a tool at the disposal of local operations as well. The advantage was the instant access to information. The main problem was that it was unwieldy to manage the interface. The manual lists 84 different registers in nine pages. Our region chose to install the operations monitoring module of PLUS, which was compulsory, but not the planning module which was considered too complicated to use.

Table 7.1

No. of minicomputers	36 (incl. six at head office)
No. of terminals	1900
Printers	800
Personal computers	300
No. of users	3000
Days of training	54,000
Cost/user	Skr150,000
Investment/user	Skr70,000

Life with PLUS

The reader will notice that we are approaching the action from above. Next it is necessary to know how PLUS works in order to understand the local level of the Road Authority. As with most advanced information systems the only way to learn what PLUS is like is to have it demonstrated. A knowledgeable assistant road master in one of the districts of the western region took us through the system commenting on the pros and cons of the system.

If I want to look at a specific activity I have a choice between two things: (i) object with text; or (ii) subaccount without text, the accounts sum up to an activity group (like paving?) ... .

Usually we monitor by object (e.g. a road) in order to see what we have done so far. It is a strength of this system that we can get relatively detailed reports. You just order a cost and resource specification for the cost centre. ... Of course you have to predetermine the layout of the reports you want. In this case we have the paving work for the ... . You can't see which road it is directly. You have to know which road has what object number. In this report you can see actual costs split up into workers (different kinds), own and rented machines (kind and hours), materials (kind and volume), and miscellaneous. You have to know the number for the respective cost item, e.g. No. 11 is 'trucks'. If you look at this cost item, No. 16, 'macadam', we can't get it split up into the different fractions, which have different prices, so it is averaged which means that it is not exact ... .

In a cost centre report you get a specification of all the accounts related to your activities. In this case it is somebody responsible for paving activities in one of the districts who wants to see the jobs he is in charge of ... uh-oh this is an example of a not too unusual situation. This is typical, he hasn't done as he should have – well there aren't very many who do things as they should have. Discipline is required, to feed the system, to give input. Otherwise you get the output you deserve ... Charlie hasn't put in the budget and forecast for activity groups 18 and 19 even though it is September. And there are errors! Those 25,000 that are located during the winter shouldn't be there! And there is some other garbage waltzing around in activity groups 15 and 16. I am not sure whether activity group 18 belongs here at all. Errors like this are caused by people making input errors. And then they shovel errors between each other, errors waltz around in the system ... . This is a scary aspect of PLUS today, anybody can look into the other's cost centre and even change the figures. It didn't use to be like that, but because responsibilities are changing now when we are reorganizing anybody could wreak havoc for the others. They have tried to clear this mess up, but they aren't done yet... .

Here in the district we got our budget in November, the plans were ready in December and the final allocations are made in February. You can't close the books on the previous year until you have reconciled the activities, i.e. the standard prices that are used in the budget must be translated into real prices. They do that in the regional office, calculate prices per whatever the base is (á-prices), reconcile, and suggest new á-prices.

The budget is followed up quarterly. After the first four months we see how the winter has been. Then we review priorities. With a mild winter we see where we could put the surplus, with a tough winter we decide where to cut costs to cover up for the deficit. A forecast for the rest of the year is made, and when it is accepted by the district manager and the road director (regional manager) it is substituted for the annual budget. The same procedure is repeated after eight months.

Before we became PLUS users we were given extensive training which included word processing and data communication. For those who were new to computers it must have been a bit much, but you had to learn how to input data to the system. Immediately after this training programme four of our people were sent to headquarters to learn how to use the planning module of PLUS. They were supposed to teach us. But after that training programme they thought it was too demanding to teach it all to us. So it was decided to put it on the back burner for a while. So we have a dormant planning module in PLUS. One of the guys thinks it is feasible and has used it a little … .

You have to be really good with this system! If you aren't good with it you can't take advantage of its potential. It covers everything. It is big, so it is kind of difficult to find what you need. You know 'every man' isn't that interested in pushing keys and he finds it awkward to find his way around.

The summary of this session with a good guide to the PLUS system might be that its main advantage is that one can access almost any economic data at any time. In the old system you got the standard, hard-copy periodic report sent to you. They also used to punch in the input data at the regional office. Now it has to be done locally. It obviously is awkward to make good use of the potential of PLUS because there are so many options and thus many keys to push. There are input errors that 'waltz around'.

There seems to be a threshold effect! People find it too demanding to break through as users in one push and choose to leave, for example, the planning module, for later. Therefore they are likely to shut themselves off from future use, because they will probably not be able to mobilize the necessary effort to take the next step once they have let go the first time. The PLUS system is probably as good a system as is possible to design with limited resources, but our impression was that it was overambitious and that it did not respond to the needs of people in charge of day-to-day operations. It had too much of a central perspective and prescriptive planning in it for our taste. But it really is impressive!

What is going on here?

Our local management project was disturbed throughout the three-year period by large-scale reorganization, actual or rumoured. Still the project had a significant impact on the work organization at least in the western region. In August 1991 the final decision on the total organization for the

Road Authority was taken. The main principles were to manage by objectives, decentralize responsibility and decision-making authority, and to establish targets for every activity. The Road Authority would be more business-like.

The agency was divided into three divisions, road holding, production, and business development. 'Road holding' 'owns' the road network and buys jobs from production or external vendors. It is organized into seven regions. Each region has local units close to the customer, for certain governmental decisions relating to roads, and for the monitoring of performance. 'Production' does the job, i.e. design and project management, building of roads, operations, and maintenance, etc. The division has five production regions and is supposed to contract out a considerable part of the projects even if its own efficient operations provide a powerful bargaining chip. What the 'business development' division was supposed to do can be imagined, but is, by definition, more diffuse.

The orientation in this reorganization is towards better market orientation through a distinct buyer–seller relationship between units in competition with external entrepreneurs. It is the heads of regions or the local organization that will buy new roads or services from outside. On the local level the earlier units (there were about 250 'work areas' in the Road Authority) were merged into districts for more efficient use of resources. The earlier local manager, the road master, was eliminated and the new districts were functionally organized according to tasks, 'activity groups', to achieve specialization and shorter set-up times.

The western region, where our project was located, had been selected as a trial area for the new district organization. Seven work areas had recently been merged into three districts. As the region was redefined in the 1991 reorganization, the districts had to be rearranged into still larger districts again that year. This fairly long introduction to the context is intended to remind the reader that the local management project was carried out in a period of organizational instability.

It is to be expected that the middle managers were preoccupied with organizational issues during the period and had to pay lip service only to the improvement of operations. It also affected participants in the teams since part of the implementation of the new district organization was to dismiss everybody from their jobs and invite them to apply for positions in the new organizations. To take on added tasks in the construction of models for the local planning of jobs was a burden for some participants. However, the continuous support of the head of the region, the commitment of many team members and the anchorage of the project in the concrete activities of the district carried the project through. This latter factor made the project relatively immune to changes in the hierarchy even if the application of activity models was sometimes hampered by changes in functional authority. The following account is based on the situation and activities before the reorganization in 1991.

The district – flexibility and many jobs

The district is the operational unit of the Road Authority. At the time of the study a district was responsible for keeping *ca*. 500 km of road in trim and traffic flowing. That meant a number of different jobs, some of which could be planned ahead.

The district has one road master, three foremen, 15 workers, three trucks, four pick-ups, one road grader, one jeep, three loaders and an assortment of small machines. In the winter some 10 trucks will be hired for the snowploughing jobs and, when necessary, excavators, bulldozers or extra trucks are hired. The budget was about Skr12 million in 1988 and added to that was asphalt and oil gravel surfacing for about Skr8 million. The budget allocation was based on road class indicators, traffic load statistics and special directives that might have been given. Inside this economic framework the road master controlled activities and was responsible for reporting variations on allocations. His immediate superior was the operations manager of the region, who was in charge of seven districts.

The jobs could be divided into three activity groups.

Service jobs like
- snowploughing and reducing slipperiness (spreading gravel and salt)
- patching up potholes and cracks
- cleaning and maintenance of pull-ups
- putting up and maintaining road signs and sign posts.

Maintenance jobs to uphold an adequate standard of road facilities like
- repairing road surfaces which is one of the most resource consuming activities (together with keeping winter roads open)
- ditching and drain pipes
- bridges and road railings
- moving road banks and clearing bushes.

Improvement work to achieve higher road standard or safety, like
- redesigning a crossing or straightening a curve, building bicycle paths
- strengthening surfaces (like asphalt instead of gravel)
- new roads in the district, bus-stops, new pull-ups, etc.

District 1, which will be in focus here, had 384 km of road of which 94% had asphalt surface, and traffic was heavy owing to the fact that a major city was close by and that an international main road cut across the district. There were 64 bridges. Gösta was road master and he had not delegated any of the economic responsibility to his foremen, even though there was some functional specialization among them. Ivar did most of the service jobs and could 'fix' things, Bo did strengthening jobs, while Bert, who was fairly green, was a Jack-of-all-trades and knew about geotechnology.

The management of daily operations was largely teamwork between the four managers. They had adjoining 'offices' and talked daily about what was going on. There were problems, though, owing to different views on control. The road master, Gösta, saw control in a wider perspective than the foremen who related control to getting the specific job done and controlling the activities entailed by the job. The road master also had the operations manager of the region breathing down his neck. The conflicting views would become visible when the road master put a higher priority on getting a new job started, while the foremen wanted to finish a job before jumping to the next. They thought that starting a job that had been broken off earlier was a waste of time and money because of the planning and transfer of men and equipment needed. Many set-ups and short cycles are costly for the team, and who would reap the benefit of all this flexibility anyway?

The road master saw flexibility as the strength of the district. In this way he could offer deals to the regional office and do business with them – stretch the budget a bit. He had been told by the bosses higher up and in the printed material department about the reorganization, and that decentralization was the solution. Local managers were supposed to run their shop like a business.

The three foremen usually discussed the following week on Friday afternoons, and the next day on the afternoon before. There was a meeting with the workers 6.30–7.00 every morning. Even if the intention was to plan ahead, the workers were usually only told in the morning what to do that day. It was also common to lend people to other districts. During the summer several districts set up joint patrols, for example, for paint or asphalt across districts. Half the workforce might be engaged in such activities, which sometimes resulted in a bureaucratic muddle with billing occurring between districts.

For the individual road worker we found the average number of jobs per week was two to three when the work done in district 1 was monitored over a 10-week period, January–March 1990. The maximum number of jobs in one week was five. The group of workers (14 people) as a whole did on average seven different jobs every day, mostly at different locations. Two workers were hired out to work with drilling/blasting – their specialty – on road 122 during the whole period. Workers and foremen alike complained over the 'jerkiness' of their work.

One of the road masters involved in the project said:

Activities are controlled chiefly by the rear view mirror, which is based on practical experience and coupled to money. Standards, the allocation model and five-year averages are still ruling today. We look in the rear mirror and allocate the money. We shouldn't go by allocation models, but by where the need for action is today! ... and our directives! They say that a 1/15th of our total road mileage should be 'ditched' this year. And the manual says "thou shalt not ditch with a steeper inner slope than 1 in 3". Pure folly! Why our ditching money wouldn't last more than 20 km if we followed that commandment!

The situation for the foremen can be illustrated by the following exchange in an interview that took place in December 1989.
The interviewer had asked "how do you plan your work?"

Foreman 1: For the daily operations, not the larger projects, it is mostly routine. Traditionally we do the jobs as we are used to doing them, there is hardly any planning and no follow-ups. We go by experiences from previous years.
Foreman 2: We foremen talk to each other during the spring about what to do. ... You know, the Monday meetings, which are not always held, when we talk about what should be done, who should do it and who is to be responsible.
Foreman 1: For bigger jobs we try to plan ahead, and as for building jobs we are pretty good planners. We don't have to budget jobs like ditching. The objects we chose to work with we chose on our own judgement ... where action is needed, well, we are influenced by different parties in that choice of course. More money would of course allow us to do more ditching jobs which are really needed. In that area we are behind because of lack of money. We have a map where we mark things we haven't done.
Interviewer: Which do you consider the greatest problems today?
Foreman 1: Surfaces are the greatest problem. Wear, deformation [tracks] of the surface, cracks, potholes increase year after year. Draining and ditching comes next. If you don't take care of that the roads will be destroyed sooner or later. Bridges are also a great problem, because it is so costly whatever you do with bridges.

Here is an intercepted conversation between a worker and the road master:

Worker: Look ... [name] ... yesterday in the morning we were down in the south end of the district fixing railings, and in the afternoon we were sent north to fix another rail. Today we had to go down south to finish the first job on that rail, and now we are on our way to go north again. We are going up and down like a yo-yo. Don't you guys have any planning?
Road master: [caught off guard] ... Well, yeah we have ... but this case was an emergency.

Variety in a job may be a blessing but here the problem seemed to be that nobody felt in control of their situation. Workers were not given time

to finish before moving to the next job. Foremen had to manage a fragmented workforce engaged in different jobs. The road master tried to keep
himself informed about the budget situation through the central system,
and broaden the budget base by selling the services of the district to others.
Nobody felt in control and the notion of responsibility seemed ambiguous.
A context of organizational learning was missing.

There were ideas about how to improve the situation. One road master
had an idea about zoning the road maintenance work to keep activities
more concentrated. There were complaints about the accounting system
giving too aggregated information to make monitoring of the individual
job possible. One should be able to pick an activity group, build an information model to see and monitor how a type of job changes in costs and time
over the seasons of the year and learn from that. There are always new
conditions. One should be able to change models to give a correct view
of activities: flexible modelling that rolls with the changing conditions.
Attention was directed towards describing and modelling work rather than
budgeting or planning systems. To be able to do a good job of budgeting
and planning it was necessary to make an inventory of the state of the
district in different respects. [If you have an inventory of the road signs
describing the state of every sign you can plan a sign maintenance tour,
pack the signs that will replace old ones (bent poles, reflex paint that has
come off, etc.) in the right order and quantity on the truck, and the chances
of using the day effectively will increase.] An inventory will also provide
the facts necessary to persuade higher levels in the organization of the real
needs in the budget process.

Summary of the problem

The analysis of the work situation of a district that we carried out, together
with the teams, arrived at an agreement on the following characteristic.

There was no adequate information support for the control of
operational activities. The central system was sluggish and inflexible. It was
necessary to change the attitude of team members towards taking a more
active part in planning and follow-up of activities. There was a gap between
objectives and resources that had to be closed. The solution was to create
clarity (or transparency) and to change behaviour.

Getting started. There were considerable difficulties in getting the project
started. The first contact between us and the Road Authority was when a
member of the central staff attended a seminar where the author presented
the approach to local management support applied in the Floby plant.
There was support at the very top of the Road Authority for the project,

but some people at headquarters saw the project as competing with the PLUS system. The project was finally labelled as a regional personnel development project.

There were local problems as well. The foremen saw a lot of extra work before them, learning to use PCs and building models of activities. They asked for compensation and after some frustration there was agreement on that issue as well, and the project could start formally in the beginning of 1989. There had been a head start, though, because district 1 had bought a PC the year before and people had started to get acquainted with it. It seemed natural for our fieldworker to discuss 'jobs' and how they were constituted. Gradually the PC became the instrument to use while modelling small things. A sequence of 'models' were developed. In the summer of 1989 about 70 applications of different sizes and complexity could be logged. Some of these are presented below.

Road salt. Salt is used to remove ice or prevent freezing on surfaces. When forecasts predict slippery roads, preventive salting is undertaken which saves money because acute situations require massive increases in capacity which is very costly. Salt is bought by the Region once or a few times during the season and stocked in huge heaps in the districts. Keeping track of the salt was one of the first models that was dealt with on the new PC support system. A simple monitoring model, with deliveries in and out and stock, was built and updated every day. "You look at the report (on the screen) and then you can look out the window and see the salt stack to confirm that it is there – and in the process we found a form we could eliminate." Simple, understandable and it worked. Initiatives could be taken to adapt the salt stock to the actual use of salt.

Better budget control. In district 1 the road master wanted an improved check on the budget. He was not satisfied with the reports he got from the central system. It was too slow for adequate monitoring. He put the chart of accounts into his spreadsheet program and made summations of resource consumption on a daily basis updating the model himself. He designed a routine so that he could take out daily, monthly and quarterly reports during 1989. The road master felt more in control of his area of responsibility.

Planning overtime. The timing of some personnel administration routines is essential for the economic use of overtime and compensating time off.

From the daily reports we take out 'overtime I' and 'overtime II' for every guy, then the model calculates how much compensation time off or pay that gives, and how much each guy has taken out. It is interesting to see how much overtime they have accumulated. A heck of a lot of money. ... It is quite easy to do and when you have the overview you can influence things. If there is a peak because we start the Mabo-vägen project in early February, people cannot take their compensation time off during those weeks, so we can tell them to take the time off before February or take the money. Those are the facts and the guys accept it.

Just having an overview makes it easier to plan ahead. If the group talks about their plans over a list they have produced themselves it is very easy to agree on what is the best way to deal with things.

Tank-patching. In spring, when the frost on the soil breaks up, it is a good time to take an asphalt tank, heat the asphalt, mix it with different gravel fractions and patch up cracks, potholes and worn patches.

Tank-patching is a big thing. It costs a lot of money to fix potholes. It is an important activity. We knew what money we had in the budget and what it could cost, but we did not know where we put the stuff. ... If we knew which roads we put the patching money in, we would know when it was better to stop patching and redo the whole surface. So we built this model, first the road number, than the kinds of damage [holes, cracks, etc.] and the resources we put into it. We designed simple input data forms for the guys to bring with them when they go out on a job. It only takes a couple of minutes, nobody complained, they are interested in keeping track of what goes on. ... Look, this year [1989] 119,000, all the money allocated for this, was already spent by March. But we see what we are doing, how much money we have spent on each road. We can calculate indicators like Skr/metres. We get facts for our discussions with the Region. We know we are behind with preventive maintenance and that we are filling potholes at capacity. Look, this road, 933, is costing us around Skr4.60 per metre in tank-patching. We could save a lot of money by putting a new surface on. It is uneconomical to go on like this! ... Look, by March we have already used 13,482 litres of asphalt! It's crazy! Before the winter is even over! We have spent all that we got for this year, but we have some money for oil gravel left!

As it could be calculated that it was uneconomical, the team had a good case and during 1989 a new surface for road 933 was laid and the Road Authority saved some money. This episode provided the team with an experience of how arguments could be reinforced with facts in the form of ratios and key indicators.

Bus-stops. To gain some extra revenue and use available capacity the district takes on small building jobs on and off during the year by building bus-stops, bicycle lanes, crossings, etc. During November and December of 1989 district 1 built bus-stops for the municipality generating a revenue of some Skr250,000. To plan and follow up these projects a simple model was built. Going through this bus-stop model the following remarks by a foreman were registered.

Small jobs cost money too! You know the talk is that this is small change, that it does not matter. Well we want to show the guys that it does! ... We trace the costs for every bus-stop; how many hours of different resources we put into it and the price. Our own machines and excavators. Should we have our own excavator? Some people think so. ... We have set the prices ourselves. The computer picks up the prices and calculates every object separately. We use it for invoicing. We do that ourselves. We don't send it to the Region for invoicing any more. We just add our 9% for administration and then we deduct that from our budget. There is no reason why money should disappear in there [at the Region] as it used to ... The idea is that the buyer gets an estimate. We did that manually before. We saw that the PC could do that for us. We could get a better structure, better layout and precision. Not a minute more work for us – on the contrary! ... and we can go in and change the estimate if they want to change the specification or we can change prices. ... You know the guys used to grumble about this before. You hire too much they said; you don't use our own resources efficiently; what you say does not check with reality! By putting the bus-stop model in the PC we could show them. In November we put 400 hours into those bus-stops for the municipality! That's a lot for building a few bus-stops! ... We used to invoice a lump sum "Bus-stops for *X* municipality". Now the buyer can see what resources we have used and what we have done. He gets a copy of our report ... Yeah, we are more interested in seeing every job separately now, we want to see everything and we want to see it directly. ... It is fun to build these models with prices and volumes for each object. This kind of activity takes this time and costs that much. Too low or too high. If you are allowed to dig into it you realize that different jobs look different [financially]. ... When you provide good service you get trust and respect in return!

This model provides an illustration of the benefits of being able to see the details in what you do. Every job was treated separately to give both detail and overview. Actual resource use was input continuously to allow current control of the projects. Summations for each object (job) were used for reporting to the region. The buyer got better information and the 'guys' were convinced that it was necessary to hire machines and people from the outside occasionally.

Roadside poles and snow stakes. These are safety measures. Roadside poles are reflecting 1-m poles that are fastened to plinths that are drilled and hammered into the roadside. Snow stakes also mark the roadside, but are set out only during the winter, and are probably most helpful for the snowploughing trucks during dark winter mornings. The roadside poles are one-time investments, but have to be replaced when they are run-down and washed a couple of times a year. A special unit, attached to a pick-up truck, is used for that purpose. Snow stakes are collected in the spring. Then a small truck with two or three people drives along the road at a slow pace. Setting them out in late autumn requires a drilling aggregate to be attached to the truck.

To a certain extent the two substitute for each other. The debate can be heated about the benefits of putting up permanent but expensive reflecting poles or temporary, cheap stakes. It should be noted that both types become run-down now and then, and there is always a stretch of road near country dancehalls where every pole is down on Friday nights. The matter seems to have been resolved in district 1.

Ivan, one of the foremen, illustrates this on the PC.

> Well, they called from Region and asked how much it would cost to put up poles along the motorway. They are in a hurry up there and often take decisions which are not that well founded. If you do it like this ... [shows his model on the screen] ... you have the basis for a decision, costs and capacities. It took me half an hour to provide an answer. It [the model] calculates how much setting up the poles costs, adjustments, and how long it takes. You put up 27 an hour or you can adjust 24. All machines have a cost per hour, I enter the cost per hour. The cost of setting up warning signs – people often ignore that cost ... The whole job costs 300,000. ... I had no idea it cost so much earlier. Now it is all in there. The Region has given us the job now. The next thing is to plan it ... . The guys say they can do 20 poles an hour, I say 32 and give them a rebate of 5. They can do 27 an hour. It is a matter of planning the job and carrying it out efficiently according to plan – that's the challenge now. You can use the model to see the consequences of what you plan to do. Look, if I enter 23 poles an hour and push the 'F3' button I get the answer in kronor and hours. I can easily change the prices, etc., and see the consequences.
>
> An amateur can see the point of putting up permanent poles along the motorway. But what about smaller roads. The smaller the roads the more factors speak for snow stakes, isn't that true?
>
> Well, to decide between poles and snow stakes we built this model ... I have specified all the necessary data for that; materials, resources, time and prices. It is the work that is expensive with the poles, and material is cheap for snow stakes. But when you look at the annual cost spread over three years you see that the snow stake is twice as expensive; 94,000 against 43,000 for the poles. The point with this model is that I can go in and change anything and see the consequences. I get the details and the bottom line, black on white.

There is pride in Ivan's voice when he shows how he manages his job. The road master joins in:

> The result was that the Region 'bought' Ivan's model and decided to put up poles along the whole motorway. ... Now we enter the budget dialogue with the support of our models. We have experienced that we gain trust and goodwill with the Region when we show them printouts like this. There is no way they can decide against stuff like this.

Building the Mabo road. The Mabo road project was a project to build a new road and rebuild two joining roads. It was a big project for the district, estimated to cost Skr3.5 million. It put a strain on district management since resources had to be used efficiently and coordinated to cope with ordinary operations as well as the Mabo project. It was decided to plan this project carefully and follow it up. Bo, one of the foremen, was put in charge. He explains:

When we started this a year ago, we had the traditional premises. Traditional paperwork means that you work with these forms, you end up with a bunch of paper, and you accumulate the 'sum costs' as we call them. Should you then want to change anything you have to erase and recalculate, erase and recalculate on eight copies. You tend to find yourself in that situation every time. You have to 'forget' about this higher price and that lower price. You try to unload the forms somewhere and end up with not one trustworthy figure anywhere. You can't use it and the 'unforeseen expense' account grows larger and larger. We said never again and decided to use the PC to plan and follow up this one.

You plan ahead and have an idea about how you want to do the job and what capacities are to be involved. But you are never in real agreement with yourself about how it is going to be when you do the planning. I calculated the big job [the new Mabo road] at Skr2.6 million and then the small joining roads. ... Well, we landed the job [in competition with outside contractors] at Skr3.5 million, and then the question was how to follow up and see to it that we live up to our commitments. You have to meet the contract 100%. We have these meetings where it is very important to be clear about what is and isn't in the contract and what you can charge extra for. I have been to so many of these meetings that I know what is going on there. You had better have your data in order.

This job is organized in three files; one for the levelling work, one for ducts and cables, and ... we have always been poor on follow-up. With this we learn and improve. When you see the details you learn. It is fun and concrete with building projects. You can be effective.

The guys report where they are, what object they are working on and at what time. I update and enter the figures every day. It takes me half an hour and I do it before I go home. I [pre]book all machines, material, and men on the accounts myself. I don't wait until the [official] day reports and hired machine bills drop in. I enter them directly and I have a diary for the [pre]bookings. When the lists arrive I check them against my diary. This is the point with this system. I don't wait for the [official] day reports. In that way I have a 100% complete system. I capture all the costs myself and I can do something about a problem before it is out of hand. If an excavator just sits on a job and draws hours and costs you see how the taximeter is running and you can do something about it. If you wait for the day reports it can take days before you see what is going on. I have the economic outcome the same day.

We haven't included the costs for management in this. If we run it properly there will be a surplus to cover management, travel, and overtime and a handsome profit for the district. ... You can see that we have finished the ducts. We are below projected costs. We can see the profit. We were able to work rationally. When we laid the drainage pipes we used three excavators ... it is great fun. In the old system we could only get lump sums. Now we can get the costs day by day. During my 15 years as foreman we have always had only those lump sums ... .

The Mabo project was a big one for the district. Skr3.5 million is a lot of money and when the books were closed on the project and all bills paid it showed a profit of more than Skr300,000. It is probably safe now to be indiscreet and say that the district team thought it was a bit much to show officially, so they used some of the money for investing in equipment. The key to success in this case was the detailed, and almost real time, follow-up of plans built on experience.

Summary of the case

There are many more episodes to report, but the ones mentioned give a flavour of the complexity and variety of work on the operational level of the Road Authority. Life is a sequence of projects which all differ in some respects. Being in control and learning from experience is a matter of:

- taking stock to know the situation one is entering;
- planning the expected activities necessary to do the job;
- follow-up, real time to adapt to surprises and deviations from plan.

The team effects are different here than in other cases. The central theme here is planning. You keep a project together by planning it and you gain respect by adapting to the fact that you hit rock where clay was expected. Two kinds of leadership are involved: being able to think through a set of activities that forms a project; and being able to reformulate plans in the face of surprises that occur now and again.

Motivation and growth, leading to improvement initiatives, come from delegation of responsibility to manage a project, and successful completion of such projects. A project does not have to be large and complex to be motivating. It has to be a project, i.e. a set of activities with a beginning and an end, under someone's control.

A large part of the frustration exhibited in the first round of interviews with the men in the three districts in our region related to the feeling of not being able to finish a job before being sent to another one. The modelling of projects on the PC mainly helped the foremen to build projects, which were then acted out in real life. This enabled closure of work processes and made learning possible.

Knowing the details and being able to stand up to superior levels in budget dialogues brought respect and self-respect. Once you achieve self-respect you have to behave responsibly and preserve respect by taking initiatives and by delivering on promises.

It is very difficult to prove that the local management initiative produced economic results of a certain magnitude since this would require comparison with what would have been the case with the old organization of work.

Work flows in a sequence of overlapping projects, every one with its specific difficulties, in a road district. There are indicators which can be provided with goal statements, of course, like how fast the snow was removed from the main roads after the first snow fall of the winter, or how many traffic accidents the district had. But then again the weather is not always the same. Sometimes the snow is wet and heavy to work with, and also the number of accidents is affected by the weather. The indicators often get their meaning in context. Furthermore, the flow of work is influenced by the changes in approach. That Mabo road project was won in competition and it generated a profit that was invested in equipment that made the next job easier, etc.

Epilogue

Unfortunately district 1 was unable to follow through and harvest all the benefits from the very promising start of the project. The team was shocked by the information that the road master had been seriously injured in a traffic accident. He never returned to work. Soon after that, towards the end of the summer of 1990, two of the foremen in the district left their jobs for better offers elsewhere. These three were the leading enthusiasts in the district for the new way of tackling the organization of work.

It was the road master who took the initiative and bought the PC on his own budget instead of squabbling with Region or Central about who would pay for the PCs needed in the three districts. He took an active part in the development of models and used them too. He experienced the advantage of having his own detailed data in budget discussions with the Region. The two foremen that left had done a large part of the modelling.

Analysis

One might wonder why it was not an easy task to spread the word to other districts and overcome the setback caused by the loss of those who carried the project in district 1. The main explanation is that the Road Authority was initiating a major reorganization at the time. A reorganization that caught the attention of everyone. The number of districts would be reduced sharply, which everybody knew. The number of road masters would be reduced as a consequence. The top of the organization was preoccupied with its super solution for the information technology problem and, in principle, intolerant to experiments with alternative solutions. The Region did not quite understand what was underway in district 1 except that there seemed to be excellent leadership. The head of the Region was a supporter of the project all along and argued for the approach in meetings with the Centre.

The Road Authority also fostered a rather conservative culture. The people on the road have to be able to cope with contingencies often by themselves. A kind of cowboy attitude develops. It is experience and knowing the ropes that enables you to cope. The road masters are middle managers that run their districts on a budget and if nobody complains they are left alone. The exception are the specialists (here understood symbolically) at the Region or headquarters who provide the manuals for how to make road banks with a slope of 1 in 3 (a standard that the budget does not allow road masters to follow anyway).

The effect of that culture was that district 1 did not get the encouragement it deserved and the attention required to spread the news to other districts. Meetings were arranged with line managers from other districts but the presentations seem to have been met with passive listening. As far as we can judge the district was very successful. It achieved a mixture of expansion of the budget and was also able to do more for the money. It was a very active district which was visible in its region. It built a number of bus-stops, bicycle lanes, etc., and took on the largest road building project undertaken by a district in the region. And made a handsome profit.

This resistance to learning from the experience of others is probably a product of the project-wise life of Road Authority districts. It is natural to assume that things are different in our district and that it is individual capabilities that make the difference when it comes to coping with contingencies or, for that matter, performing dull routine jobs. This activity orientation makes it all the more important to build organizational renewal and improvement bottom–up. We found valuable support from Kolb's (1984) ideas about experiential learning in understanding events in this case.

Experiential learning according to Kolb

Organizational learning might be thought of as an organization developing its ability to discover and correct deficiencies in its structures and processes. This learning obviously takes place through its individual members. It is to a large extent stored in its routines and propensities to act in certain ways on certain cues. One way of learning is by copying the behaviour of others. What concerns us here however, is learning from experience.

Kolb (1984) describes experiential learning using a circle, as shown in Fig. 7.1.

Kolb recognizes heritage from Dewey, Lewin and Piaget. Dewey's pragmatism with experience as the organizing focus of learning, Lewin's action research concept and his model of a feedback-based, circular

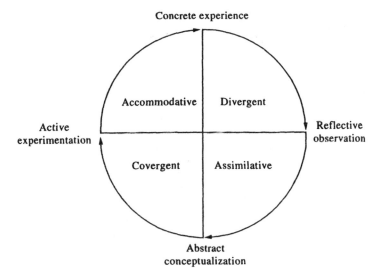

Figure 7.1   Kolb's (1984) model of experiential learning (see also Fig. 1.1).

learning model, and, finally, Piaget's ideas about dialectics in learning from experience are examples. The most important aspect of Kolb's learning model for the cases reported in this book is the circularity of the model. The working hypothesis has been that organizational learning is best served if the individual is given the opportunity to participate in, and act out, the whole circle.

Concrete experience – a person must be in concrete contact with the process which is in focus. It is essential to check designed solutions in real processes in order to learn. It is also necessary to design experiments to discover problems. (Consider the image of lowering the water in the river to discover dangers of running aground.)

Reflective observation – it is necessary to collect data on the process in focus and discuss what they mean. Data are given meaning in reflection.

Abstract conceptualization – by reflection and debate organizational members can build models of the processes they are engaged in. The concepts that are formed become part of the language used by the organization.

Active experimentation – when a conceptualization is reached and the team considers it, or the model, true it is ready to act on that basis. This action provides a public commitment to the truth of the conceptualization and confirms learning (or disconfirms in the case of a dissatisfying outcome of the experiment). The experiment also gives concrete experience for further reflection.

We have been able to influence the design of the experiments – the cases are all set in organizations that are conducting their ordinary daily business – the most important aspect has been to provide a context that allows participants to complete whole cycles of learning.

Time and again we have found destructive effects of breaks in the cycles. Even delays have been found to cause strong effects on motivation. Delays that might be caused by, for example, rules and regulations that specify that certain decisions have to be made by superordinate levels, or by territorial competition and defence of administrative boundaries. When projects have been successful we like to think that it was because people had the opportunity to complete the experiential learning cycle. But, again, how can we prove it?

The main cause of frustration reported by informants in the preliminary interviews about work and organization in the road districts was the problem of not being allowed to finish a job before being sent to the next one. It was described as a wasteful stop-and-go way of organizing jobs, but it should be interpreted as frustration with the fact that learning cycles were not completed. One might go as far as to claim that the joy of doing work well – when work itself is a motivating factor – requires learning cycles to be completed.

In a type of activity like that in the Road Authority district, where work comes in projects, the completion of a learning cycle means participating in the planning (thinking through what has to be done to do the job), executing plans, getting confirmation that the job was done according to plan, and having some time to reflect on the project as compared to other projects and what could be learned from it.

The technology is different from, for example, the automated context of the shaft line in the Volvo plant. This provides for a different group structure as far as problem solving is concerned. There is a more visible division of labour in the road district. The foremen do a lot of planning and are, to a certain extent functionally specialized. Since work is dispersed group members do not work as a group in the same fashion. Things have to be kept together by planning, and that is delegated to the foremen. The foremen, in turn, must put the members in the larger picture so that they know how their part fits the whole picture; members should also be able to check plans against reality. That is why foremen are preoccupied with detail and being able to adapt models to new premises. This flexibility in models also comes in handy in discussions with customers and budget people. The point seems to be the job of packing activities together into projects which can be monitored and talked about. Talk is conducted with outsiders as well as insiders, constituting two contexts of discourse which have to be dealt with convincingly to win the respect necessary to be allowed self-management.

In this particular case the study was disturbed by the ongoing reorganization projects and rumours in connection with them. It also suffered as a result of the car accident that took the road master of district 1 away from the group and the subsequent loss of two of the foremen to other companies. Still there was an impressive accumulation of models that gave the district self-confidence and a greater say in the dialogue on budgets. It was also possible to show that the models worked in practical applications which were much more difficult for the leaders of centrally sponsored development projects. The approach to organizational development and continuous improvement demonstrated in this project has gained credibility and acceptance in wider circles of the Road Authority.

8

Controlling through competence*

Complexity as environment

It is virtually impossible to avoid being utterly impressed by the sight of 'high-tech' machinery at work, be it an FMS installation, a laboratory or a computer centre. The structures of a well-functioning team, top management or an operational team running and improving the performance of an automated production line, are less visible but no less complex. Our attention is attracted by the moving parts of the machine, we do not even mind if some of the parts are not moving, but idle members of a team are seen as signs of inefficiency. We also tend to forget that in all probability the idle machine costs more per hour than the idle operator.

In a recent pilot study of maintenance (Halldin and Schiller, 1992) it was found that the estimated cost per hour of stoppage was about equal for process industry (refineries, nuclear plants) and advanced manufacturing. However, while process industry had its machinery running 95% of the time, critical machines in manufacturing industry were idle close to 50% of the time. This indicates that the attitude towards technology varies as well as consciousness of the costs involved.

---

*The fieldwork for this project was carried out by Stefan Schiller; part of it was reported in Schiller and Jönsson (1992).

Our ability to grasp and master the complexity of modern industrial production of goods and services is further handicapped by the differentiation of competitive strategies. While earlier there was rather straightforward thinking in terms of economies of scale and market shares, today there may be differentiation, niches and upgrading (Porter, 1990). The governing structure of large multinationals may have shifted from hierarchies with headquarters firmly in control from the top of a diffusion of core strategic activities and coordinating roles, to several competence centres in an organizational structure that could be described as "heterarchy" (Hedlund and Rolander, 1990). Sophisticated customers and vendors make it necessary for the company not only to develop its own individual strategy but to be on the same wavelength with its partially chosen environment. This has occasioned a new customer orientation in production management discourse. Having the customer in mind all along the production flow with on-time delivery given the shortest possible lead-time makes the flow vulnerable to disturbances. Since lean-production drives have eliminated many buffers the shocks will have to be absorbed by skilful operators and maintenance crew. Time is money, stoppage is waste. Furthermore institutional structures vary, as well as management cultures, in the different nations in which a large company is active. In global competition, and due to European integration, coordinating structures tend to become more closely product (product family) oriented with time-dependent flows crossing national and cultural boundaries. This adds to the complexity of managing industrial production processes.

Against this background of multilevel change a rapidly growing literature of competitiveness, strategic change and management of technology tries to depict and analyse the processes that are implicated in this *panta-rhei* (Heraclitus). Maintenance cannot escape being affected by this development and it is not just a matter of cost-drivers, overhead allocation or technological development. The question is "what role can maintenance management play in support of organizational learning, improvement and upgrading?".

The answer to that question is likely to be conditioned by culture. Under the 'rational' assumptions of hierarchical control of standardized production it is reasonable to claim general validity of conclusions concerning the effects of information provision. But in a learning setting a specific understanding of the situation is developed through interaction between concrete experience, reflection, conceptualization and active experimentation (Kolb, 1984). Data are rendered meaningful, becoming information, in that context. The challenge for the maintenance function in large complex companies seems to be to support local learning in day-to-day management of maintenance, while at the same time coping with the introduction of new technologies, new customers and products.

The nature of maintenance

The economic potential of maintenance in automated production cannot be overestimated. Not only does the maintenance function of modern manufacturing industry employ a considerable number of people, but the economic effects of stoppages increase with the leanness of production. Even if stoppages have been reduced to close to zero, as in many process production plants, the maintenance function can participate in improvement work of many kinds, for example in product design. An especially challenging task is to participate in training operators to take over a growing part of their job! Perhaps future manufacturing plants will have the maintenance function, as we know it today, performed by operators in the production departments or by outside vendors. Then the maintenance department might take on the more challenging task of upgrading the competitive ability of the plant and assisting operators in problem solving.

There are many rules of thumb in maintenance, and adequate measures of performance are rare because the objectives of maintenance and the focus of attention of the maintenance department has not been properly specified. This ambiguity is also a hindrance to organizational learning since it instils in maintenance a sense of irregularity and acute urgency which are not the best conditions for organized learning.

"If it ain't broke, don't fix it" is a classic saying that might be attributed to someone in the American car industry a long time ago. It represents a time, long since gone, where ample buffer inventories made continued production possible and costs of stoppages in individual machines affordable. Now the question of what is the proper balance between preventive and acute maintenance urgently needs an answer which is contingent upon technology, position in the value-adding chain, organization of the maintenance function and costs of stoppages. The organization of maintenance work includes the division of labour between the specialists of the maintenance department and the operators in the production departments. It also includes how the cooperative structures between production and maintenance are set up and how maintenance performance is monitored. The maintenance task should also include assistance in the upgrading of the plant through modifying maintenance, whereby the capabilities of machinery are improved. The problems which this entails and the ways in which solutions could be sought can be illustrated by the case of how the Volvo Components plant we visited earlier (Chapter 5) introduced preventive maintenance. First I will try to give an impression of the enormous number of factors and actors which have a potential influence on a plant-wide programme like the one on preventive maintenance in this case. There are very many things that can go wrong. The situation of a person in charge of implementation calls forth the image of the Chinese juggler who is able, with difficulty, to keep 20 dinner plates spinning on bamboo sticks by running back and forth speeding up again the ones that are about to fall down. Given all these factors and the situation, it is obviously almost impossible to isolate the effects of the implementation from the noise generated by all the other factors. Still, we only have one world and that is where we have to test our ideas.

A reform in context

The Floby plant had excelled in production management innovation and won prizes and recognition. In August 1992 the leading daily business newspaper had a small item announcing that the Floby plant was about to start production of brake discs for Renault. In passing the plant was presented as "Volvo's model plant: Volvo's Floby plant is known as the most efficient Volvo plant and the employees are sometimes referred to as Volvo's Swedish Japanese. Personnel turnover is ... " (DI 19.8.1992). Part of the explanation for the success is that the plant specialized in machining hard metal products like brake discs, drums, shafts, etc. (cutting spinning steel, as it were) and had developed a good capacity to improve operations. A legendary plant manager (long since promoted) had started the process and then the local management support (Chapter 5) had generated further success in the middle of the 1980s. This had in turn given Volvo occasion to locate a new line for mass production of connecting rods (not a spinning steel product) to the Floby plant. Then in the beginning of the 1990s the alliance with Renault had effects on production as well as the fact that SAAB, in its concentration on fewer vendors as part of their cost-cutting efforts, had awarded production of all its brake discs to the Floby plant. Increasingly the environment of the Floby plant grew in complexity and dynamism.

   The reform which we focus on concerns a plant-wide effort to increase 'availability' (eliminate stoppages) through gradually increasing the proportion of preventive maintenance, i.e. when maintenance is done according to plan and when the production line is at a standstill for several hours (as opposed to acute maintenance when something is broken). This reform in itself is fairly complex. A list of goals for the maintenance department used in presentations of the reform to personnel and their necessary underpinnings in terms of information systems and training may serve to illustrate the following.

1. Increased availability will lead to lower production costs, which will in turn generate more demand which will give larger batches, etc.

2. Self-managed maintenance by machine operators.
   - Operators are responsible for their machines. Machine managers see to the welfare of the machines. The status of the machines will be improved by improved knowledge among those responsible for machines and through them among all personnel.
3. The ambition is to maximize machine efficiency by avoiding:
   - Losses due to stoppages;
   - Losses due to slow downs;
   - Losses in quality.
4. This will be achieved by the following.
   (a) Meeting the service demands of production.
   (b) More effective control of preventive maintenance in view of machine efficiency.
   (c) Cost-efficiency.
   (d) Meeting quality targets.
   (e) Delegation of responsibility.
   (f) Actively increasing preventive maintenance to decrease acute maintenance.
   (g) Involving designers in preventive maintenance.
   (h) Better use of specialist knowledge.
   (i) Better exchange of knowledge concerning production line technology.
   (j) Training of production personnel.
   (k) Meeting environmental requirements.
   (l) Effective purchasing and sales.
   (m) Better opportunities to participate.
   (n) Better service with spare parts, tools and handling equipment.

The leading idea from the start of this project was that preventive maintenance is the key activity. Preventive maintenance is a planned activity where professional competence is applied. If it is done well, acute maintenance will reduce. Daily machine care carried out by the operators and, of course, running the machines properly can increase the availability by 10% units over the 3-year period of the project. This and the incidence of mechanical and electrical errors were issues which were discussed on the first meeting of the project group held in December 1989. The next meeting was to be held after the first production stop for preventive maintenance in February 1990.

From the field notes:

On that first occasion the brake-disc line stood still for 24 hours while it was attended by maintenance. That start could have been better. There was not enough time to clean everything up. In the meeting with the project group a week later the project leader (from maintenance) complained that there was not a clear enough division of responsibilities between the brake-disc department and maintenance. He did not feel that he had full responsibility. They did not really know what preventive maintenance was in the department. Who is supposed to do what? On top of that, availability went down drastically in the weeks to follow. There were acute mechanical failures in a machine in the middle of the line and they had to wait hours for maintenance to start repairs. There were electrical failures as well and both kinds of errors continued to appear for several weeks. Then there was a shortage of blanks for several weeks owing to some foundry failure. Sometimes there was an oversupply when the Danish and the Swedish foundry did the same article.

In connection with the May meeting of the group, Stefan, our field researcher, thought that there was not enough 'stability' in the preventive maintenance project. There should be local responsibility in the department. Somebody to participate and follow-up to ensure that things are done and not just talked about. One of the qualified operators, Tord, took the job. The project leader from maintenance had the theory that preventive maintenance is a new way of thinking and that it takes time to get used to it. Lately the Mingarti line has run better. Whether this is because of preventive maintenance or something else is hard to tell. But there is improvement.

As Tord started to take initiatives and sometimes do a little extra to keep the machines fit, he noted that territory was at stake. When he went to maintenance to get a replacement sheet of steel that he thought best to replace for preventive reasons he was told that he was doing maintenance work. Maintenance people on their part referred to the new regular maintenance activities listed for the operators as 'cleaning', which was not appreciated by the operators. In another episode Tord went along with a repairman to learn how to fix a certain failure. He was turned away by the repairman with the words: "This is a trade secret!". Tord and the plant engineer responsible for the line made an inspection-round in connection with the last preventive maintenance stop, in May, and found some deficiencies. It was obviously wrong to start from the outside and work inwards in cleaning the machines. There were also problems owing to the use of water in cleaning and something needed to be done about steel chips 'splashing' from some of the machines. It would be a good idea to involve operators in the project group meetings, perhaps on a rotation basis.

Nineteen-ninety was a bad year in terms of volume. Deliveries of brake discs were more than 10% lower. Deliveries to SAAB and Spare Parts went down still further. There were redundancies. The people in the brake-disc department got a full bonus for quality that year and some, but not full bonus, for availability. When the maintenance manager analysed the year (in an interview) he could see that the per cent time spent on preventive maintenance accounted for a little less than half the stoppage time, but at the same time acute maintenance had gone up from 2.3% to 4.0% of total time, when it should have gone down. Something is wrong here. Acute maintenance must come down during 1991. On the other hand, the new drilling machine which will be installed in the brake-disc department will take at least half a year to trim. There is bound to be above normal maintenance next year ... . In this interview the head of the maintenance department argued that half of the stoppages were caused by the

operators not keeping the machines clean. Cleaning also allows the operator to
see if some part is worn and in need of replacement. Cleaning is the critical
activity. It is also desirable to have preventive maintenance groups in all departments as soon as possible. As for the maintenance department it is a priority to
improve competence especially on the electrical side. Perhaps the consequence
of this project will be that maintenance loses up to 20% of its personnel. In the
production department improved competence will allow operators to put more
distinct demands on maintenance. Economic responsibility should rest with the
foremen of the production departments. It is somewhat of a problem that the
success of maintenance is measured in terms of its effect on the production
departments, but this is the way it is. The monitoring should be related to the
value-added produced by the department. We do not know what is the optimal
allocation between preventive and acute maintenance, but the hypothesis is that
it is somewhere around 80/20 (80% of the time devoted to preventive and 20%
to acute maintenance). The indicator value added/maintenance cost has to be
related to a number of supporting measures like 'availability' and the listing of
causes of stoppages. (It was, of course, necessary to go through the cost accounts
to determine which accounts to use for preventive maintenance costs and which
for acute.) In fact people from the central accounting department participated
in a detailed review of the costing system and the budgeting calculations for
maintenance towards the end of 1990. This discussion continued well into 1991
and interest in the management of maintenance is picking up. The head of the
maintenance department starts an initiative to implement the same procedures
in other production departments from the beginning of 1991.

Most of the meeting time in the brake-disc department group during the
autumn of the first year was spent on discussion of a 'competence ladder' for
production departments. Operators will be able to improve their salaries by what
they can do rather than what they actually do. For this purpose it is necessary to
devise the list of activities by degree of difficulty in each of six categories
(production, quality, materials, personnel, economy, maintenance, and
program handling). A slight problem in connection with this was that a production
planner earns less than most operators and the difference is likely to increase as
operators take on more tasks.

An interview with Tord, the brake-disc man in charge of the availability project,
in April is focused on the need to document the lines better. In particular the
log on stoppages is not specific enough, the causes have to be interpreted. There
are still communication problems with the repairmen from maintenance. "If you
tell the electrician that we had a similar problem last week and that it might be
the same failure they will tell you: 'This is none of your business' and they bring
their oscilloscopes and measure and test run. It often is the same failures. Like
when the motor on operation 20 burned several times over a couple of weeks."

An interview with Helge, the foreman of the brake-disc department, at about
the same time indicated that he was preoccupied with training a new 'fixer' who
would take over when Tord gets promoted. There was also satisfaction with the
installation of the new drilling machine and the relief of having the opportunity
to run the old equipment in parallel for a while. The new drilling equipment is
being adjusted; too many borers have been burnt lately. This is probably not only

a borer angle error but also a matter of finding the right number of revolutions and the right feeding speed. The same kind of trimming is going on with the new balancing machine. Plans are being finalized to increase operator competence by a job rotation schedule. Not all operators want to participate though. The target for this year is to increase availability by 3%, chiefly through less waiting time but also through preventive maintenance. Money has been granted for a new packaging machine (robot). There will be a rush in the coming months!

Part of the rush was due to SAAB awarding the production of all its car brake discs to the (Volvo) plant. That created six jobs which were welcome in a situation where there were 20–25 redundancies in the plant. The SAAB order also implied that a whole production line would have to be moved from its previous place in a Finnish SAAB factory to Floby. This, in turn, meant another trimming exercise. If the bid to GM-Europe to produce brake discs comes through there is no limit to how big the operation could become. In the meantime, volumes are still too low owing to low car sales. People agreed to take vacation days when production was stopped at the assembly plants to balance production.

End of summary of field notes.

A relentless pace

The project went on amidst a large number of disturbances. In April 1992 the Floby plant reached quality Index 99 (of 100) which is an indicator they have struggled with since 1984. In June of the same year Index 100 was reached for the first time. The number of suggestions filed by personnel increased rapidly in 1992 as a result of a campaign. In January 1992 a tender for brake discs was sent to Renault, and in June of the same year Renault decided to take the offer with production starting at the end of 1992. In June the plant applied for certification with Lloyd's, and the certificate according to ISO 9002 was awarded in April the following year. In August 1993 the plant was awarded the production of yet another Renault brake disc. This occasioned a business development project. There were more opportunities out there. The Floby plant had to be marketed. One of the leading enthusiasts in the preventive maintenance project was given the task.

One might wonder what are reasonable expectations concerning improvement in maintenance under such conditions. Since the Floby plant was discovered as an effective plant and a learning organization, it has been driven at a relentless pace with changes in production and investments in new machinery all the time. What are the effects expected from an experiment with preventive maintenance when the situation is basically unstable? What is the point of increasing availability of machinery when production is below capacity? There is possibly the basic idea that increased capacity use will result in savings in personnel. There was also the expectation that volumes would increase shortly. During the latter half of the period the Floby plant increasingly delivered to customers other than Volvo. This increased volumes, and allowed a lower full cost, however it meant more frequent set-ups which affected availability negatively. The wider assortment of products meant not only a variety in products but also that newer products were more complex and thus demanded more complex operations. Finally the slack in car sales during the period of study caused Volvo to lay-off personnel. This naturally had effects on upstream production such as that in Floby. Part of the austerity programme that this resulted in was a reduction in inventory to free capital. This in turn resulted in smaller batches, which meant more set-ups and other stoppages. As we said initially; maintenance is a complex activity in a complex setting. It is not very easy to detect causal links between, for example, increased proportion of preventive maintenance and efficiency in production.

Results

Owing to the dynamics of the period when the implementation of systematic preventive maintenance took place at the Floby plant one has to be careful with conclusions. Clearly any discussion of the effects of maintenance has to start with availability – the extent to which machines are available for production (P). Stoppages may be due to maintenance (M) (acute plus preventive) or other causes (O) (like operator induced stoppages for set-up, lack of material, lack of personnel, reduced speed, etc.). Table 8.1 shows the availability achieved by the brake-disc department between weeks 2–12 over the four-year study period.

Table 8.1 Availability – brake-disc department (weeks 2–12, 1990–3)

| Week | 1990 | | | 1991 | | | 1992 | | | 1993 | | |
	P	O	M	P	O	M	P	O	M	P	O	M
2	74	6	20	80	7	13	77	11	12	74	14	12
3	68	9	23	86	10	4	82	11	7	65	9	26
4	81	8	21	69	16	15	81	11	8	66	21	13
5	86	7	7	72	10	18	68	16	16	84	12	4
6	68	6	26	60	19	21	67	16	17	80	9	11
7	69	9	22	69	9	22	64	14	22	84	9	5
8	66	12	22	47	36	17	81	9	10	83	11	6
9	62	10	28	64	28	8	78	8	14	76	12	12
10	80	10	10	80	15	5	68	19	13	67	7	26
11	84	9	7	72	13	15	67	17	16	77	10	13
12	75	13	12	72	10	18	78	7	15	83	10	7
	73.9	–	17.1	70.1	–	15.0	73.7	–	13.7	76.2	–	12.5

The last line of the table illustrates a steady decrease in the infringement of maintenance on production time. The variety of other stoppages is due to installation of new machinery, test runs, set-ups, new products, etc.

Even if the availability figures do not show an improvement it is possible to deduce from the figures on stoppages, owing to causes other than maintenance-related ones, that the implementation of preventive maintenance has had a beneficial effect on availability. The extraordinary increase in stoppage in February 1991 is connected with the changeover to the new brake discs (900 series), and the related installation of the new drilling machine (advanced enough to be reported in one of the national technical magazines). Similarly, the high figures in March 1992 may be assumed to reflect the installation of the new line for the SAAB discs. In the beginning of 1993 the brake-disc line was disturbed by the rearrangements necessary as a consequence of the introduction of a water-based anti-corrosion liquid (and preparations for the Renault order). We can see that, in spite of these outer circumstances, an improvement in the proportion of time used for maintenance can be discerned. Time used for maintenance of total time has decreased from 17% in 1990 to 12.5% in 1993. In the meantime preventive maintenance has increased from less than 20% in 1989 to about 60% in 1993. In the final analysis it is the economics of maintenance that decides where the optimal balance between preventive and acute maintenance is. Throughout the project period production and maintenance managers have discussed what is the best indicator of maintenance efficiency. Obviously maintenance costs have to be related to the value produced by the production departments and this is reflected in the indicator which is used currently – maintenance costs/added value. That indicator has oscillated in the region of 5–10%. The objective for 1993 was to bring it to below 6.5%, and by the middle of the year that target was achieved. Again the increase in volume owing to improved sales of Volvo as well as SAAB cars helped.

Implementation through a portfolio of activities

The case of preventive maintenance implementation was in a sense top-down, because the initiative came from plant management. An inter-departmental group was set up between maintenance and brake discs. This group decided to launch the project by carrying out preventive maintenance in the brake-disc department. Preparations were carried out by going through a check list of activities and then the whole department was stopped for a day and a night. The first time they tried it they did not have time enough to do everything on the check list. In the follow-up meetings it became clear that responsibilities were not specified enough. Who should do what? The first experience also lead to the conclusion that it was essential to improve anchorage for the project in the production department. Therefore Tord was appointed as locally responsible. Organizational work, on anchorage and motivation in both departments, was on the mind of most participants. This lead to work on a system of competence-related pay, to plans for a training programme, and to increased attention on existing information sources. In the autumn of the first year Tord started to go through the stoppage list with operators to discuss causes. After the first year's experience with the brake-disc department the plant management group decided to introduce the system of preventive maintenance in all departments. This made some specifications of accounts in the cost-accounting system necessary and it affected budgeting for the next year.

During 1991 two overall characteristics could be detected: first the increased rate of change in the machinery (drilling machine, new line for the SAAB discs, packaging); and second, the organizational work in the maintenance department. During the first part of the year there were heated discussions about how the electrical repairmen should be organized and improve their specialist competence. It seemed as if (monthly) pay related to a competence ladder would be a suitable instrument to confirm the new preventive maintenance regime. Specifying responsibility and pay based on competence seems the right mix of motivation. A large number of activities relate to maintenance and 'availability'.

By the beginning of 1992 the project team noted that all departments participated, that all departments had developed checklists for preventive maintenance. Intervals differed. There were daily activities, weekly, monthly, etc. Every production line had a log with a reliable entry of causes of stoppages. Operators were given a total of one week's training in preventive maintenance. Sceptics were still found in the maintenance department. (Stress was caused by the production departments who were more sensitive to what maintenance charged and to waiting time.) It seemed like some repairmen preferred the excitement of acute stops above the planned drudgery of preventive maintenance. There was still, however, some anxiety owing to the threatened redundancies in 1992, changes in equipment and the increased number of products. By 1992 the standard team for a preventive maintenance job was five operators, one qualified operator, one electrician and one mechanical repairman. The latter two came from the maintenance department.

In the beginning of 1993 stability seemed within reach. Volumes increased and a new bonus system for maintenance had been developed (it was possible to increase pay by 5% on the basis of department performance). During 1993 the preventive group meetings and interviews indicated a tendency to integrate the preventive maintenance project with quality improvement activities, and also the principles of local economy, developed in the drive shaft and brake drum lines in Börje's department (Chapter 5). Incidents that came up in interviews dealt with remaining clashes of priorities between departments. A problem which was taken up in the brake-disc department was what to do about the fact that the electrician and the repairman who were assigned to preventive maintenance in the brake-disc department had been redirected to another department where they had had an acute stop due to some breakdown. It is maintenance policy to attend to acute problems before preventive work. What should be done? Maintenance had an obligation and they were not delivering according to the contract. Both departments were standing still and costing money, and maintenance attended to the breakdown before the planned work. It was the electricians in particular who distanced themselves from the operators. Perhaps it has to do with the fact that electricity is more difficult to learn than mechanics. It has more theory as it were. One can see how the electricians feel 'on stage' when they are analysing and testing what the cause of the breakdown might be, and how they are a bit 'backstage' in preventive maintenance. One respondent remembers a recent discussion in the preventive maintenance group where the maintenance representative said, on the issue of balancing preventive and acute maintenance, that fault-detection is the best way of learning the trade. "If there is too much preventive maintenance we might have to send our electricians on courses to train them in fault-detection – like they do with pilots ... ."

Otherwise the last year of our maintenance project was noted for its activities in integrating the project into other routines. The final version of the bonus system for maintenance was implemented. The bonus was based on four variables: availability; the proportion of preventive maintenance; value added; and maintenance costs. There were also adjustments in the cost-accounting system to allow for monitoring of operators' maintenance work, integration with quality work and further training. A directive came from the group headquarters to work on cutting inventory and lead times. In Floby they calculated the cost effects of reducing buffers further and found that the effects were quite small. Finally there was an experiment with job rotation among production managers in the plant. It was deemed to be worthwhile even if there was a temporary loss of organizational competence when people moved to jobs they were not well acquainted with. This could no doubt be seen as part of Floby's new customer orientation. The plant could be less vulnerable to variations in volume if it had more customers. A project, hailed by the local community, was started to find more customers.

Analysis

This case illustrates the complexities of improvement work across teams and the difficulties encountered when the positive effects of activities can only be registered indirectly. In such a situation the process seems best lead by enthusiasts and conducted by design. This means that the enthusiasts have a 'theory' about the beneficial effects of working in a certain manner. They are granted permission to try out their design in real-life departments and if successful a change in practices is implemented plant-wide. Inter-departmental groups have 'cultural' difficulties and communication across cultures will improve only gradually as practical interaction improves the understanding of the other side. They do not interact frequently as a team and commitments made in a group meeting tend to become less binding when the participant is back in his ordinary environment. Departments with a strong team spirit are reluctant participants in this kind of integrative project and need persuasion that relates to their ethos.

There is also the glory of problem solving ('on stage') for maintenance men when there is a breakdown as compared to the unglamorous 'cleaning' job of planned maintenance. The differences in status between maintenance and operations are clearly noticeable, and exhibited by people wearing different coloured overalls in most workplaces. Project leadership has to be geared towards the ideas of the project rather than towards the benefits of the project to the group. Once the project has demonstrated its benefits it starts to lose its identity in a general integration with other current practices. It seems reasonable not to try to uphold the project organization any longer than is necessary and to start working with the establishment of ordinary network practices which serve the integration purpose as soon as the idea of the project is accepted by the host organization.

9

Controlling by words

Introduction

The cases presented so far have demonstrated one thing that has not been dealt with properly yet: communication is essential in improvement work. Gradually as the cases unfold it seems as if accounting reports become less prominent and communication becomes more focused. This is no coincidence. Even if the cases are presented in the same sequence as they were carried out in our use of accounting information study, they mark a shift in emphasis in our enquiry. The series of studies has taught us something – that management, as well as control and organizational learning, is virtually a verbal process. Managers do things with words. This means that not only do the accounts in a financial sense play a role in improvement work in organizations, but 'accounts' in a narrative sense seem to play a more central part, which has largely been neglected by organizational researchers. This chapter aims to suggest how this negligence could be rectified by close-up studies of how managers work with words. We have to start by reviewing some of the classical studies of managerial work.

Research on management

Much of the literature on management control takes the authority of the top of the *hierarchy* and the *stability* of environmental conditions as given. As far as there is problematization it usually deals with analysis for the purpose of setting the rules of the game, like in agency theory or in transaction cost analysis. Also a significant part of the contributions to organization theory during the last few decades is based on empirical observations of university hierarchies – a place most academics will be familiar with – where anarchy might be a better descriptive term than hierarchy. We have been entertaining ideas about organizations in changing environments (Hedberg and Jönsson, 1977a, b) being better off in terms of flexibility if they have organic structures (Lawrence and Lorsch, 1967) provided that suitable integrating mechanisms are in place. Argyris and Schön (1978) argued that double-loop learning had specific characteristics, including the questioning of basic assumptions. In this connection the difficulties of unlearning should be and have been noticed to a certain extent (Hedberg, 1981).

I would describe the direction management research has taken during recent years as change oriented. It is not the rational production of large batches taking advantage of economies of scale in stable environments that comes to mind in contemplating managerial problems, but small batches in lean production and customized services. There is a dynamic development in the area of strategy and strategic change. No doubt this has been significantly influenced by the fact that Japanese companies have proven themselves to be very competitive in spite of the fact that they may break many, if not all, of the orthodox rules of management contained in our well-established textbooks. 'Community', or network, has been added to the traditional dichotomy of market versus hierarchy. Virtues such as loyalty and trust pose challenges to opportunism and individual maximization of utility in our conception of rational behaviour. There are also considerable advances in our thinking in terms of organizational learning and communication. Even if information technology has not assumed the position as a learning medium that many had hoped, it has stimulated our imagination as to what is capable of being achieved.

In a broader sense, technology has become more differentiated. Products, as well as processes, contain more varied technologies than before. Organizations therefore become more knowledge-intensive and management has to cope with cooperation between groups of specialists – knowledge communities, as it were – attending to the different technologies. All this calls for reflection on the role of management accounting as an instrument of control and, more worryingly perhaps, the future of management accounting research.

The discussion in this chapter aims to develop an alternative way of approaching management accounting research in order to align it more

closely to the current developments in management or strategic management research focusing on the communicative aspects of managerial work.
Hopefully, the cases presented earlier provide ample illustrations of the
need to conceive of accounting and improvement in new ways. We will
develop the argument by first pointing out that cost accounting (or
management accounting for that matter) assumed its present form as part
of the scientific management movement, that is, as part of an engineering
or systems approach to the information problem related to the planning
of production. Then we will review a few of the best-known studies of
managerial work. The notable aspect of these studies that has not been
taken much notice of is that they point out that managerial work is verbal.
This is so much taken for granted that its implications have not been
spelt out. Managers work with words and it seems that much could be
gained in terms of theory development and practical application if studies
of how managers work with words when they do their jobs could be carried
out.

"What would it mean to relate management accounting to managerial
work?" is the question which guides the bulk of this chapter.

Finally, an example is given of how the work of a managerial group can
be studied with the help of videotaped meetings which are played back to
participants for comments and interpretation. What goes on in these
managerial conversations? How are commitments made, and how do
participants evaluate candidates for new rules of the game?

Management accounting developed out of a 'systemic' perspective

In Sweden as in many other countries (Garner, 1954) management
accounting (or rather, cost accounting) developed rapidly in the inter-war
period (Jönsson, 1991). This was due to the institutionalization of the
scientific management movement and the increased strength of state
authority as a consequence of the introduction of Keynesian economic
policy and a stable parliamentary majority. The most intensive debate in
Sweden on cost accounting was carried out by engineers and concerned
the conceptual structure of full cost calculation. Only when the major issues
were settled did accounting experts enter centre stage. A standard term-
inology and a preliminary standard for full cost calculation were established. As the economic crisis of the 1930s remained and World War II
approached, the calculation of a fair price based on incurred cost was
politically desirable. The standards, set through extensive committee work
and after public debate, were later used in university courses in accounting. When, following the German tradition, charts of accounts for cost

accounting adapted to various industries were introduced in the 1940s, they were readily adopted and also used in education. In this way a conceptual, systems-based framework for management accounting was firmly established in practice as well as in academic circles. It was securely anchored in the modernist project of scientific management and the calculation of cost-based prices.

The next phase in the development of management accounting was initiated by the introduction of computers. Even if computers had limited capacity for handling data, the possibilities of storing information items in several dimensions and to design report generators which could produce reports to order, provided further opportunities for system design studies (Samuelson, 1989, 1990). The practical experiences of academics working together with practitioners on projects to introduce more dimensions and more flexible reporting in industry and the public sector provided opportunities to discover organizational and behavioural aspects of accounting. The academic research interest largely turned towards these aspects while reforms in practice to a large extent meant moving existing systems over to more powerful computers.

As the oil crisis and merger and acquisition strategies took their course, the attention of accountants in practice focused increasingly on governance structures with strategic and financial control. Product costing has hardly changed in its basic structures (Ask *et al.*, in press) even if the ABC approach, with its analytical and decision-making focus, provoked a lot of attention. (Interestingly the thrust of the ABC project is to bring back the old engineering and analytical approach to cost accounting, with its detailed studies of cost-drivers and causal links between activities and costs. This is done by statistical analysis much like in the old days when engineers were in charge of cost accounting developing in Swedish and continental Europe. The approach may seem more revolutionary in the U.S.A. where accountants with a tendency towards financial accounting had put their stamp on cost accounting practice.)

Managerial reformers turned to lean production ideas and global competition issues took over. Responsibility accounting along governance structures has moved interest away from the nitty gritty of detailed cost accounting. 'Relevance' may have been lost somewhere in this latter-day process, and management accounting must regain its former status by rediscovering its alignment with management work. It is a 'clinical' subject and it should be tuned to what goes on at the clinic to prosper. If this is accepted as a reasonable point of departure, the not so simple task of maintaining the systematic/conceptual basis, while developing the communicative aspects of management accounting, lies before us.

What, then, is the nature of managerial work?

Perspectives on managerial work

The first systematic, empirical study of managerial work was probably carried out by Carlsson (1951). Mintzberg (1973) was inspired by Carlsson, but applied a more intensive observation method (participant observation) than Carlsson who used a diary method in combination with interviews. Mintzberg observed his managers for five days each, while Carlsson collected data for one month for each manager. Kotter (1982) used a combination of interviews and participant observations over two periods for each participant.

Carlsson structured his observations on incidents where the following data were recorded: where was the work done? How long did it take? Who participated? What manner of communication was used? What was the nature of the business? What kind of action did it imply (decision, inquiry, command, etc.)?

Carlsson complained when reporting the results that top managers spent too much time away from the company for non-commercial contacts. When they were not away they spent a large part of their time in inefficient meetings. Meetings were too long and were not properly coordinated with other forms of control. Far too little time was devoted to analysis and planning. Why not use subordinates in all these meetings? They could devote their full attention to the matters dealt with by the committees and work parties! Managers also seemed to systematically overestimate the time they spent 'managing-by-walking-around'.

Carlsson found that over a one-month period the typical top manager (CEO) worked undisturbed in his office for more than 28 minutes on only nine occasions. The average time alone in the office before being interrupted again was eight minutes.

Carlsson used a contact diagram to map patterns and found that functional business dominated the agenda. On average about 15% of the time was spent on corporate matters and the rest was spent with representatives of functional areas.

An interesting finding from Carlsson's study was that decisions play a minimal role in the work of top managers. Only 6.3% of the incidents were classified as ending in a decision. The most frequent activity was 'getting information' (39.6%) followed by 'give advice, explain' (14.6%).

Mintzberg (1973) worked with a chronology, postal protocol and a contact protocol that was coded for a week for each of the observed managers.

Mintzberg provides an excellent review of earlier research on managerial work and summarizes his observations on the nature of managerial work in terms such as "relentless pace" and "brevity, variety and fragmentation".

It seems as if managers prefer activities that are current, specific and well defined before the abstract and non-routine ones. They work verbally with fresh information rather than analytically with systematic information.

Mintzberg's study is probably best known for its typology of leader roles: relational, informational and decisional roles. The empirical bases for these role descriptions must be considered rather thin. If one considers the fact that roles are developed over time and in interaction with others, the one-week observation period is not sufficient. Still the criterion question in Mintzberg's classification of activities into roles: "Why did the managers do this?" indicates the multitude of tasks managers are obliged to carry out. Mintzberg refers to Katz and Kahn (1966) who stated that leadership is related to incompleteness and uncertainties inside and outside the organization, which means that management could be described as unprogrammed activity since it is mostly concerned with solving unique problems. Barnard (1966) claims that the most important task for the manager is to 'maintain' organizational activities. All this adds up to a description of management's main task as being to assure that the organization is effective, stable and has an ability to adapt. This requires continuous vigilance concerning environmental, task, person and situation variables. "Emergencies are normal" (Walker *et al.*, 1956, p. 76). Nonetheless, there are routines and recipes for certain types of problems (acquisitions, turn-rounds). Mintzberg discusses the possibilities of programming these recipes; whether or not this could be done in cooperation with analytics who could distance themselves better than the manager. Mintzberg is thinking about academics here, but the task of extracting patterns in managerial behaviour and 'programming' could be done equally well by staff departments. When he gives advice on how the situation could be improved, it points in the direction of more teamwork in top management.

One cannot help wondering if, perhaps, all these intelligent, successful managers indulge in managerial work characterized by brevity, variety and fragmentation because it is an efficient way of running a company!

Kotter (1982) began his study in the complexity of managerial work. It is not so much the analytical task that is difficult but the intensity of the competitive pressure which provides for variety and change. Some dilemmas of complexity are illustrated, such as: setting goals *in spite of* the fact that basic underlying conditions are uncertain; *balancing* short-term return and long-term development; *keeping informed*; and criticizing *and* motivating subordinates. These are issues without analytical solutions.

Kotter found that the managers he studied were not analytically inclined, but were not 'generalists' either. Managers are socially talented and they have usually acquired an extensive knowledge of an industry in their career to be able to be accurate in intuitive judgement. In this sense they are 'specialists'.

Kotter found that managers took on their tasks in a similar manner. Early (six months to a year) after their appointment they devoted their attention to the establishment of an agenda and building the necessary network to carry it through. The establishment of an agenda (partly coinciding with the business plan of the organization) has content as well as process aspects. Whilst establishing himself or herself the new manager 'aggressively' seeks information, primarily from those he or she already has trustworthy relations with, by asking questions using his or her own experiences to guide the direction of the questions. The sequence of meetings and discussions with co-workers are often unplanned and disjointed. Choices are made on intuitive grounds to achieve specific programmes or projects that can be expected to contribute to several goals at the same time, and for which a mandate to implement is sought. This goes on continuously, bit by bit in a time-consuming manner during the first phase. The content of the agenda is characterized by loosely coupled goals and plans based on business ideas with mixed time horizons and covering a broad spectrum of issues. They were not put in writing and were related to, but separate from, the formal plans of the company. Managers seem to be oriented towards changing their organizations.

Building networks is time consuming; it means spending time with others, and managers devoted considerable time to building relations, assuming it beneficial to the implementation of the agenda. These relations often reach far beyond the immediate co-workers and cross formal organizational boundaries.

The manager is naturally interested in promoting teamwork and eliminating politics in his or her immediate neighbourhood, but obviously sees a need to build networks that can be used to 'short-circuit' the formal organization to promote implementation of the agenda.

Kotter attributes differences in the manner in which all this is done to background and career experience. The more comprehensive the experience of the industry, the less time was devoted to agenda and network building and more to implementation. Such differences in the allocation of time to networking have also been documented by Luthans *et al.* (1988). Here focus is on 'successful' (fast career) and 'effective' (good responsibility centre performance) managers. While successful managers spent 48% of their time networking, effective managers spent only 11% of their time on these kinds of activities.

Once the agenda and network were established they asserted a more direct influence on the daily work of the manager. The agenda directed attention to its issues and the network framed how they were approached. In this way the managerial agenda affects, significantly, the behavioural patterns of the company. On the issue of whether it is possible to detect differences between more or less effective managers, Kotter claims that even the small sample that he studied gives reason to conclude that several completely different behavioural patterns, seemingly based in contingency-specific solutions, seem effective.

These empirical studies of managerial work, and many others, have some commonalities that have not been properly noted. (1) Managerial work is mostly done in groups and in face-to-face communication. (2) Decisions are rare events. Asking questions and getting information is the most frequent activity. (3) Managers work with verbal fresh information in a fashion characterized by brevity, variety and fragmentation in a stream of events where agendas related to, but separate from, the formal plans of the company are at work. Managers want to shape and change the organization to something better. To achieve that they build networks of personal relations. They may be assumed to behave this way not because they are stupid and ignorant, but because it works.

What would it mean to approach management accounting from the 'management' side?

Given that the account of empirical studies of managerial work is a reasonable one, what conclusions should be drawn concerning management accounting? We would not want to diminish the usefulness of analytical applications of management accounting techniques in any way, but we would be interested in how management accounting information is used in managerial discourse. It seems safe to assume that the analytical use of management accounting information is mainly referred to staff units. Line managers, working in real time in management situations characterized by "brevity, variation and fragmentation" are likely to use information in different ways and they may be expected to use it in conversations with others in joint problem solving or implementation processes to achieve the establishment of rules of the game, commitment to tasks and policies, and for attention direction. Conversations are cooperative games rather than competitive ones and they do not only convey information but also serve to generate symbolic capital and trust.

Management as a cooperative game

Rule-following

According to Wittgenstein (1953) and Winch (1958), meaningful behaviour must meet two criteria:

1. the actor must be able to give a reason (account) for an action, and

2. the actor must be bound by the act now to do something consistent with that act in the future (seen as following a rule).

When these two criteria are met, the actor's behaviour may be said to have a sense.

The first criterion means that the actor must be capable of providing a justification or account for the act. The actor will usually not have to specify all the alternative acts that were at hand, but it is obviously necessary to show that there was a choice (at least not to act) and the reason for the actual choice. (If there was no choice there is no initiating actor and no responsibility.) The reason does not have to be true but must be recognizable as a reason, and not incompatible with other information about the situation.

The second criterion establishes the rule-following or commitment aspect of action. As the actor makes public the reason for the act he or she also announces an intention to behave accordingly in the future. A principle that has been applied is elevated to be a rule in the repertoire of rules that generates the behavioural pattern that in turn constitutes identity. Hereby accountability is established. The actor declares a willingness to be held accountable for this and consequent acts. This giving of reasons for acts constitutes explanation to the environment. As such it has to be geared to the conceptual framework (paradigmatic meaning) or constitute a self-contained story (narrative meaning). The environment will signal its acceptance of the explanation by holding the actor responsible for this and future acts. Competent rule-following will lead to increased trust and a granting of a status of self-management, i.e. to be allowed to handle sensitive matters and warranty relations on behalf of the group without interference from other members of the group. This is akin to being considered 'Mündig', which means having the right to sign contracts, and being bound by one's word.

When a person understands the reasons for the acts of others and expects them to be bound by their commitment to behave consistently in the future, he or she may act confidently and effectively because of the trust in the rules of the game. Garfinkel (1963) illustrates a conception of trust via a description of games. The basic rules of a game are:

- frame a set of 'moves' which the player has to choose from,
- which the player expects to be binding for him or her as well as other players; and
- the player expects other players to expect the same thing in return.

This gives rise to the *constitutive expectancies* of the game. Trust could be defined as constituting a situation where individuals in their interpersonal relations are governed by constitutive expectancies.

When trust is broken, for example when an actor makes moves that violate the rules of the game, Garfinkel (1963) found that individuals engage in vigorous efforts to 'normalize' the situation, that is to return it to the original constituent expectancies. He also found that people who tried to retain the original rules of the game were more frustrated in their normalizing efforts than people who were willing to redefine the game.

Wieder (1974) extracted 'maxims' from interviews with inmates in a half-way house for reformed drug addicts that seemed to guide behaviour. He could then demonstrate how these maxims were used to regulate conversation. Potter and Wetherell (1987) illustrate this kind of rule use/rule following in an example:

> One of the 'maxims', in fact the first one, was "above all do not snitch". When Wieder had a friendly conversation with an inmate it was sometimes abruptly stopped by the inmate saying "you know I won't snitch". Analysing what this utterance achieved Wieder found that: (1) it defined what Wieder had just said as a request to snitch which allowed the inmate not to answer. It would have been illegitimate for an insider to answer in this situation; (2) it also served to confirm that Wieder was an outsider and not a friend. If Wieder had continued his line of questioning he would have risked being seen as an incompetent, as someone who did not understand the code. These expectancies and codes of conduct set limits to individual member behaviour. Opportunism and other breaches of such social bonds result in loss of membership.

Roles

When an actor meets constituent expectancies and engages in meaningful behaviour every act, consistent with the expectations, serves as confirmation of a role in the game. Consistency in behaviour provides a stable base for other actors' rational calculation and efficient response. It binds the actor further to role consistency.

In sociology there has long since been a clash between two approaches to role theory, structuralist and interactionist. Structuralists see the role concept as a set of social norms constituting a part of the culture that influences actors in a given situation (Turner, 1985). Society in principle is a system of social norms and behaviour is an expression of how well the individual has internalized and adapted to these norms. Critics of this view ask how were these norms established in the first place and how did they achieve a status independent of the role?

The symbolic-interactive view sees the role concept in more of a communicative light. The role has a character of a relation and the individual assumes and forms the role in interaction with the environment. The communicative capacity of humans makes it possible for them to see a situation not only from their own perspective – not even only in 'alter's' perspective – but also from a third position and sees the interaction between 'ego' and 'alter' from the outside, objectively, as it were. This interactive ability is central in making sense of behaviour, that is the ability to foresee the reactions of others to one's own behaviour. Role expectations are mutual and situation-specific. The role is formed in interaction on specific problems.

The fundamental difference between these two views; the role given by the expectations of the environment (with role conflicts if the individual is unable to meet them), on the one side, and the role emerging and changing in communicative interaction in a situation, may not be as fundamental as it once seemed. Turner (1985) sees convergence between the views over the last decade. The differences seem to have been inspired by the different modes of data collection and analysis that the two schools have practised. In both cases it seems reasonable to assume that rule following is a generator of roles. When people assume roles they certainly put limitations on their repertoire of behaviour, but they also become more predictable and they may also reduce complexity (Wildavsky, 1975).

Teams

A set of mutually constituted cooperative roles is a team. The members of a team establish a division of labour and constituent expectancies in an inner dialogue (Jönsson, 1992) in which a unit is chiefly concerned with translating its experiences from narrative meanings to paradigmatic ones, i.e. from stories to principles. Bruner (1990) maintains that there are two modes of cognition, the paradigmatic and the narrative. The paradigmatic mode starts from definitions, models and deductive logic, and provides a rational analysis inside a problem frame. Data become meaningful by being processed through a model. A 'technology' is applied to the data.

The narrative mode builds on our capacity to make sense of our experience by narrating it, telling a story, putting it into 'script', as it were. The narrative gets its meaning from the internal configuration. The narrative is good and worth remembering if it is exciting, plausible and persuasive. Paradigmatic information is acceptable if it is logical, non-contradictory and consistent. The narrative is social and it is through narrative that we build and maintain culture and praxis. When the narrative is established well enough to be taken for granted it has been conceptualized into the paradigm or integrated into background context.

This translation work gives members of the unit opportunities to build trust and professional competence in experiential learning cycles

(Kolb, 1974) and builds on the giving of accounts. A competent person must be able to account for what happened. It is part of the definition of competence. You should always know what you are doing and why. If you are competent then you are responsible for the consequences of your actions. If you cannot account for your whereabouts at the time of the crime you will be suspected of being an outcast.

Everyday life is built around giving accounts (Garfinkel, 1967). The network of social life is constituted and maintained by storytelling, or 'accounts' (explanations) of things that seemed to have no meaning before. Once we are given the account that bridges between that which we had already taken for granted and that which seemed odd, we can extend the area of normality yet another inch. Inside the constituting network of the social we can then use the paradigmatic for effective communication in coded messages. Management accounting is such a paradigmatic code used by responsible, competent people who manage resources and personnel over which they are granted jurisdiction by others. The technical aspect has its own rules of communication. By applying them properly membership in the class of responsible team members can be maintained (Munro, 1994). When there is error, when there is a variation from budget or some other expected performance target, an explanation is in order. Typically we use a story of some kind. If we say "it was due to the fluctuating currency situation", that may be an acceptable explanation, but if we say "the deviation from budget is due to my wife being seriously ill (I cannot concentrate on my job)" it will probably not be accepted as a legitimate explanation. At best we might get away with "don't let it happen again!" (which means that we lose part of the trust that was put in us). The manager receiving our explanation may feel sympathy with our problem, but the role of principal does not allow exceptions from the rules of the game. Membership puts limits on what kind of narratives we may allow ourselves as explanations of error (Munro, 1994).

Membership work thus amounts to giving accounts for our activities and developing routines for doing so. In this way routines become the constituents of social order (Giddens, 1984). But routines are also there to keep things apart. Not to mix up company time with personal time, company money with private money and admissible accounts with inadmissible ones. A constant labour of division goes on and part of membership work is to keep a clear distinction between what is 'in' and what is 'out'. This requires attention to the rules of the game by members: "the activities whereby members produce and manage settings of organized everyday affairs are identical with members' procedures for making those settings 'account-able'" (Garfinkel, 1967, p. 1).

Between teams – discourse

Communication between teams is complicated. Interaction between teams is less frequent than in the inner dialogue of teams and it is more abstract in the sense that it rarely takes place in the work process. Communication typically takes place in a meeting between representatives (who take 'time out' to attend the meeting) of the involved teams. If teams develop special expertise ["communities of knowing" (Boland *et al.*, forthcoming)] – which might be the main purpose of a decentralization, but also a consequence of evermore differentiated technology – they may also become intolerant towards information, advice, orders and intervention from other groups. If teams have developed a role in a large unit it will be expected to behave consistently with that role and may need to negotiate 'contracts' to change that role. It is also likely that the same data will be interpreted differently by different communities of expertise owing to the different experiential basis for the interpretation. Then narratives will be used in reaching an understanding. But a precondition for reaching an understanding is that the conversation develops as a cooperative game.

From discourse to conversation

The basic factors to consider in the study of conversation and discourse are shown in Fig. 9.1.

Complexity arises from the fact that information emerges as the receiver interprets the message. The sender may have an intended meaning with the message, for example, to arouse a certain pattern of behaviour in the receiver, but the extent to which that intention is realized is largely dependent upon the meaning the receiver ascribes to the message (if the message is at all noticed in the noise of everyday urgencies). This 'emergent view' of information (Moore and Carling, 1982) is crucial for the analysis if narratives constitute a significant part of the conversation.

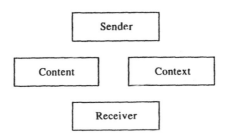

Figure 9.1 The factors of discourse.

If sender and receiver have developed mutually understood codes in earlier interaction they may have little difficulty in reaching similar or the same interpretation of the content of the message. In such a paradigmatic situation (Bruner, 1990) the content of the message is a matter of coding and decoding (plus channel capacity). Information may be said to be contained in the message. Moore and Carling (1982) call this "the container view". This case is, however, of less interest in a managerial perspective, where teams are assumed to have different experiential bases for their interpretive work. Then it is likely that the same message is attributed different contents by different participants. Variability in interpretation must be assumed to be the normal situation in communication between communities of expertise. In order to achieve coordinated action the two teams have to relay their interpretations. Consider the two hunters. The first says: "Hey, do you see the moose over there?" and the second responds: "Oh my God, don't shoot! It is our friend Peterson!". They interpret the same visual stimulus differently and can avoid a tragedy by interaction: "do you see what I see?".

The fact that sincere interpreters can arrive at different understandings of the same message brings out the issue of truth. How can it be determined that the story contained in the message is true? Most of the time we cannot be sure. We have to rely on trust. Even if it could be determined that the story was untrue, it could be persuasive. The story could have internal consistency and reveal a connection between variables that is interesting, or lay the basis for a useful concept. Such generation of relations, concepts or models of interpretation that seem useful in understanding other situations have a value. They contribute to the language of organizational interpretation. Stories are instrumental in generating language. The meaningfulness of them consists of their 'making sense'. The truth concept of pragmatism (James, 1974; Mead, 1934) comes to mind. If it works in your experience, if you are ready to act on this new insight after having been frustrated, the information has truth-value in a pragmatic sense.

If action fails, data will be reconsidered, but if it succeeds this experiential confirmation will constitute learning and the portfolio of practices or the interpretive repertoire (Gilbert and Mulkay, 1984) may expand. Repeated successful action will 'prime' interpretive patterns (Wilson, 1980) of actors and teams so that they are more likely to be evoked in similar situations in time forming custom and even culture.

There are two, possibly alternative, approaches to the tools people use to make sense of the world which are of interest here; Moscovici's theory of social representations (Moscovici, 1984) and the conception of interpretive repertoires (Potter and Wetherell, 1987).

Social representations are mental schemata with abstract as well as concrete elements (concepts and images). In most representations concrete images are the most important ones. The representation is built up around a 'figurative nucleus'. These social representations are assumed to "underpin attributions or the causal explanations people give for events" (Potter and Wetherell, 1987, p. 140). The representations are 'social' because they originate in the course of social interaction and because they provide an agreed code for communication. By providing a conventional code of communication the social representations will also provide a unifying and homogenizing force. Since the code of communication is used in the sense-making process, all who share a representation will agree in their sense-making. The members of a group will share representations and therefore representations can be used to identify a group. (This is a problematic statement that we will come back to.)

Social representations have a constructive effect. When a group makes sense of the world it is constructed in terms of social representations. Two mechanisms are proposed for how people cope with new experiences – anchoring and objectification. First anchoring is used to assign the new object to an element or category in an earlier representation, then the new object is transformed into a concrete, pictorial element of the representation to which it is anchored, and the new version of the representation is diffused in conversation (objectification).

The theory of social representation has been received enthusiastically by social psychologists because it offers an antidote to the "increasingly common cognitive reductionism" (Moscovici, 1984, p. 142), but there are some difficulties with it.

Potter and Wetherell (1987, p. 142) challenge this theory of social representation (referring to their own research and that of colleagues) and the thrust of the critique is directed (1) towards the assumption that the community of representations establishes group identity. This assumption is problematic because it creates a viscous circle of identifying groups through representations and representations through groups. (2) There are also empirical problems connected with the underlying assumption that there is consensus in representations for the people in a group. Such presuppositions will tend to smooth over internal diversity. Specifically there are distinctions to be made between actual use of a representation ("the riot was caused by poor housing") and mention of available representations ("the left-wing press have claimed that the riot was caused by poor housing") and between use in generalized formulations (about police behaviour in riots) and in specific situations (police behaviour in this riot). (3) Finally there is the issue of whether social representation should be operationalized as cognitive or linguistic. Moscovici seems to view them as cognitive phenomena. Researchers are then faced with the problem of constructing a neutral record of secondary phenomena on the basis of interviews, etc. How could one recognize an instance of anchoring in the interview transcript? Social representations, if they are seen as cognitive phenomena, will simply be difficult to observe.

To remedy some of these problems Potter and Wetherell offer the notion of interpretive repertoire which has been developed in collaboration with several colleagues in empirical discourse analysis. The point of their offer is that they focus on how members cope with accounts in interaction – discourse in context – rather than on cognitive aspects – what 'lies behind.' A study by Gilbert and Mulkay (1984) is used to illustrate this.

After identifying a group of biochemists in the U.K. and U.S.A. who worked in the same area, Gilbert and Mulkay collected publications of respondents and conducted interviews where accounts of biochemical research work were elicited. There were two competing theories in this prestigious area and adherents to both were represented in the network of 34 of the most productive biochemists. In this area of theoretical competition, two contexts, the 'formal' one of scientific writing, and the 'informal' one of interviews, seemed to generate different accounts of the same research activity. In the article account it was the *results* (of standard experimental work) that suggested the model, but in the interview it was *the model* (a dramatic revelation) that suggested the results. On the basis of numerous differences in accounts Gilbert and Mulkay arrived at the conclusion that two broad interpretive repertoires existed that explain the differences in accounts. These were labelled the 'empiricist' and 'contingent' repertoires, respectively.

"Interpretive repertoires are recurrently used systems of terms used for characterizing and evaluating actions, events and phenomena" (Potter and Wetherell, 1987, p. 149). The basic principle in the *empiricist repertoire* is that actions and beliefs are a neutral medium through which empirical phenomena make themselves felt. The scientist is forced by the observations and professional rules of scientific work to take certain actions. In the *contingent repertoire* the basic principle is that actions and beliefs are crucially influenced by factors other than the empirical phenomena (subjective factors like power and lack of skill). The scientists used both repertoires.

They used the empiricist repertoire to justify their beliefs by referring to how experimental evidence and correct application of rules prevented them from having any other beliefs.

However, given the obligations of the empiricist repertoire scientists can make no mistakes. When an error occurs scientists use the contingent repertoire to explain.

The contents of the contingent were more varied than the empiricist one. Subjective elements were included like prejudice, narrow disciplinary perspective, threat to status, lacking experimental skill, personal rivalry, etc. When all the accounts of these researchers were combined virtually everyone in the network had their work explained away by at least one other scientist. Gilbert and Mulkay found that researchers used asymmetrical patterns in explaining 'right' and 'wrong' beliefs. The empiricist repertoire – facts arise naturally from empirical findings – was used to explain 'right' beliefs (other scientists regularly seem to get them wrong), and the contingent repertoire – provided a package of non-scientific resources for explaining error (Potter and Wetherell, 1987, p. 152).

Scientists manage to live with this asymmetry in accounts of scientific work by using the 'truth-will-out' device. Even if the progress of science is sometimes hindered by personality problems and power struggles, the truth will win in the end through experimental evidence. This rhetorical device serves to reconcile potential contradictions between the two repertoires, but it also re-establishes the primacy of the empiricist repertoire, which may be its main contribution.

Social representation or interpretative repertoires?

The choice between the two approaches when studying communication between teams is fairly simple. Since the social representation approach is so closely linked with the identity of groups and their sharing of representations, it will be less suited for analysis of communication between teams. Repertoires, on the other hand, are not assumed to be intrinsically linked to specific groups and they are assumed to be used in different sorts of accounting tasks. This provides for greater flexibility in the analysis. The analyst does not feel obliged to squeeze observations into shared representations. Instead it is possible to deal with variation and contradiction as fairly common phenomena in discourse. Furthermore the repertoire notion is not presented as a theory, but as a component in the systematic study of discourse.

Between teams conversation

The most important medium of interaction in management, no doubt, is conversation. Conversations have some systemic and ritualistic constraints that have to be met if they are to function as a medium of interaction. Goffman (1981, p. 14) specifies the following systemic requirements:

1. A two-way capability for transceiving acoustically adequate and readily interpretable messages.

2. Back-channel feedback capabilities for informing on reception while it is occurring.
3. Contact signals: means of announcing the seeking of a channelled connection, means of ratifying that the sought-for channel is now open, means of closing off a hitherto open channel. Included here, identification–authentication signs.
4. Turnover signals: means to indicate ending of a message and the taking over of the sending role by next speaker. (In the case of conversation with more than two persons, next speaker selection signals, whether 'speaker selects' or 'self-select' types.)
5. Pre-emption signals: means of inducing a rerun, holding of channel requests, interrupting talker in progress.
6. Framing capabilities: cues for distinguishing special readings to apply across strips of bracketed communication, recasting otherwise conventional sense, as in making ironic asides, quoting another, joking and so forth; and hearer signals that the resulting transformation has been followed.
7. Norms of obliging respondents to reply honestly with whatever they know that is relevant, and no more.
8. Non-participant constraints regarding eavesdropping, competing noise, and blocking pathways for eye-to-eye signals.

Inside such a framework there are numerous ritual constraints at work to regulate how participants should act to preserve everyones' face, express disapproval, sympathy, greetings, etc., and also how potentially offensive acts can be remedied, and offended parties can induce remedy. There is also a specific ordering device, adjacent pairs, which caters for the flow of conversation by statement–response links. The variations within such a framework are overwhelming and the microanalysis of discourse through conversation analysis has to deal with them. Here is not the place to go deeper into these matters. It seems in order, however, to present one more aspect of conversation analysis before an illustrating case is introduced; Grice's cooperative principle (originally presented in 1975).

Conversations are typically cooperative efforts and could be thought of as quasi-contractual in the sense that there is a common immediate aim, contributions are mutually dependent, and the interaction should continue until all parties agree to terminate. The general formulation of the cooperative principle is: "make your conversational contribution such as is required at the stage which it occurs, by the accepted purpose or direction of the talk exchange in which you are engaged" (Grice, 1989, p. 26). Grice distinguishes four categories under which fall maxims to be followed to live up to the cooperative principle. These categories are:

Quantity: make your contribution as informative as is required and no
   more!

Quality: try to make your contribution one that is true!

Relation: be relevant!

Manner: be perspicuous!

Conversational *implicature* can be achieved by failing to fulfil the maxims
(violate a maxim, opt out, clash between maxims, flouting) under these
categories. A hearer will repair the failure by finding an implication that
will restore the cooperative principle. (He said that *p*; he is following the
maxims of the cooperative principle; he could not have said that unless
he thought that *q*; he knows that I will recognize that he thinks that *q* is
required; so he has implicated that *q*.)

   Example:

A: How is X getting on in his new job?
B: Oh, quite well, I think; he likes his colleagues and he has not been to prison
yet. (Grice, 1989, p. 24.)

Here B fails to fulfil the maxims of quantity and provides more information than requested. A will have to work out the implications.

   One of the points with Grice's cooperative principle is that it uncovers,
in an intuitively satisfying way, the work participants in conversations do
to bridge gaps and rectify failures in conversational cooperation. The
analyst requires background information as well as participants' help in
arriving at conclusions. Grice's approach as well as the discourse analysis
represented by Potter and Wetherell (1987) indicate that we should expect
variation in understanding between participants to be the normal condition. Misunderstandings may not be the sign of inefficiency we normally
ascribe to them. A case to illustrate the potentials of implication and the
use of interpretive repertoires follows.

Setting rules for internal rents

The conversation about to be analysed is a sequence about halfway through
the videotaped meeting on a day in May 1993 of the top management
group of one of the downtown municipal districts in one of the major cities
in Sweden. The background to the study was that the city had decided to
reform its organizational structure in 1989. The new organization meant
that the city, which was previously organized in large functional departments (social, school, culture, leisure were involved in the reform), was
now divided into 21 districts, each with its own political executive
committee. Some of the catchwords used to describe the objectives were,
democracy, effectiveness, local solutions, integration, service. Each district

has a district manager, but the middle management levels were organized differently. Some districts used a geographical subdistrict division, charging subdistrict managers with the task of finding local solutions to the integration of activities that were formerly managed by different functional departments, for example, between schools and kindergartens. Others maintained a functional structure on the district level and others again used target groups, like 'children and youth', to organize integration.

The problem with the reform was that a very severe economic crisis struck the Swedish economy at the time the reform was launched. The city quickly found itself in financial difficulties due to the fact that significant parts of the welfare system were managed by municipalities and unemployment reached levels that had been unheard of since the 1930s. The newly-formed districts came under orders to cut their budgets drastically before they had a chance to organize properly. By 1993 the best managed districts had emerged from a very turbulent period with their finances in order and an organizational structure that might have to be pruned further because new cuts were to be expected.

A contract with the university was included in the reform decision to evaluate reform over a five-year period. This gave rise to a very large, multidisciplinary research project from 1990 onwards. The research team which did the videotaping of the meeting focused their interest on the role of the district managers in the reform process. Annual interviews had been conducted with the 21 managers and measures of their conceptions of effectiveness, etc. were made. Large repeated survey studies of citizens, politicians, professional groups and personnel provided background. To be able to study the city manager at work the research team was given permission to videotape a meeting of the top management group in one of the best managed districts. In preparation for the interpretive work, all 11 members of the group had been subjected to interviews on two topics: the (four-year) history of the organization and the group; and the roles of members in the group. Further background knowledge was based on the extensive studies of the districts over the previous years and studies of the budgetary process of the city some 15 years earlier (Jönsson, 1992).

As there were 11 members of the top management group, we had 10 descriptions of each member. They were remarkably similar. For the purpose of this analysis we may note that the leader, A, was seen as dynamic and driving. There were also four female subdistrict managers described as 'talkative' and sometimes referred to as the 'four sisters'. It should be noted that the participants had considerable experience of management groups in the old, functional organization. One of the advantages with the current group, in comparison with the earlier functionally organized ones, was said to be that if you are a subdistrict manager and you bring up a problem there will be three other subdistrict managers who recognize the problem and can contribute. In the functionally organized groups of earlier experience everybody was a specialist in his or her area and the meetings were just for reporting and information (except budget meetings). It was only natural that the four subdistrict managers form an active subgroup. We called them the 'activists'. **G**, 'the opposition,' is a committed social worker in charge of the 'drugs and prostitution' department. He speaks his mind and is likely to be the one to interfere when the group gets talkative and flimsy. "A breath of fresh air!" as somebody described him. Another person in the group is the controller, **B**, a quiet and able person who always sits to the left of the leader, **A**. The other members, some of whom are generally less active and called 'the peripherals' by us, are not active in the sequence that follows. The group functioned well together and members were proud of its achievements. It met every fortnight to discuss and settle policy matters and rules of the game. It was implicitly understood that these meetings were not for matters concerning individual departments. The whole district employs a little more than 2000 people with social services and schools dominating.

The method of data collecting beside the preparatory interviews was to videotape a whole meeting. The resultant tape was transcribed and seven sequences of about one to two minutes each were edited to a separate tape. This tape of sequences was then replayed some time after the meeting, individually, to each group member. For each sequence the respondents were asked to explain "what goes on here?". These post-meeting interviews we have called self-confrontation interviews because part of the task for the respondent was to interpret her or his own performance. In all we thus have 11 self-confrontation interpretations of each of the sequences.

The following sequence is the first on the edited tape. The item on the agenda was 'rents to charge when letting premises'. The district has a lot of different rooms, from gyms to conference rooms, that are not used for municipal activities all the time. What rent should be charged when letting those premises? An officer had investigated and produced a memo that was presented to the group. The presenter had been interrupted by questions and discussion several times. "Who gets the revenue?" was a question that turned the conversation towards accounting and fairness. It was posed by one of the peripherals who did not participate in the following sequence. Somebody had introduced the example that a certain school rented the gym from another school and would have to pay that rent from their operating budget, while the receiving school did not include the costs for the gym in its budget. Budget responsibility at this time did not include rent. Cost for premises was a central responsibility. This meant that cashing in rent from the other school would be sheer profit and no costs for the receiving school! The sequence below starts with the leader, **A**, trying to sum up the principles that should apply for internal rents:

The text

Videotaped 06.05.93, sequence time 13.06.30–13.09.10.

(Summary after a lengthy presentation of a memo on the proposed changes of the ground rules for charging rents.)

Personage:
A = the leader
B = the controller
G = the opposition
C, D, I, = activists.
X = persons unidentified by the transcriber.

(...) indicates words that cannot be heard, usually because people are talking at the same time.
[ ] denotes overlapping speech.

A: We will, [1 we could]1 start from how we basically treat 'premises', sort of, and there the rule is that rents, base rents, are decoupled from budget responsibility ... ehhh ... and if we then take ... ehhh ... this case with the school then, we do in fact pay full ... ehhh ... base rent, sort of independently of how it ... ehhh ... adds up in the Burred school or the Guldheden school. It is then reasonable that we pay full base rent, that is the rent for the gym of the Gustavi school as well, huh. You can argue that one should, sort of, start from that which is the ... ehhh ... base premises for the activity. Then we could charge internal prices for the rest which are transactions. In that way ... that would be a way to
...
B: [1 yah]1
  (There is a silence for a long while.)
G: ehhh ... I am not sure that I understand, but ...
C: no, me neither
I: no [2 take it]2 once more
D: [2 yah]2
A: Well ... ehhh ... the basic rent for a premise is outside budget responsibility. That means that for the Guldheden school WE pay full rent for premises so to say also for the gymnastics activities. If we then come to the Gustavi school, one could say like this ... ehh ... they would pay for ... ehh ... the gym and that would come out of the operating budget.
D: m =
A: = and that [3 would be]3 inside budget responsibility
B: [3 m]3
I: = m =

A: and then we would use a different budget principle for the Gustavi school than we have for the rest of the school activities ... that ... and that is not reasonable

I: no

G: no, that's not why (...) I agree about that but I am of the opinion ...

A: Therefore I am of the opinion that [4 in this type of case]4 I believe that it is reasonable to argue [5 on this issue]5 that ... ehhh ... we do not use internal charges, while we should do it in the rest of the cases, where this does not apply.

I: [4 yes, it is]4

X: [5 (...)]5

X: yes

G: I [6 think that]6

A: [6 Shall we]6 [7 si]7

I: [7 (...)]7 [8 (...)]8

G: [8 (but what the hell)]8 I think that it can be a bit unfair (...) huh =

I: = yes there are many other examples like this then where you find yourself [9 puzzled]9. I have been thinking about many. I could think of ... in my office it would be the same effect. When we want to have a meeting at the office there is no room big enough to [10 take]10 us all. Will I then have to pay every time I want to be somewhere for a meeting ... or doesn't one have to [11 others]11 so to say huh. What I mean is that it will be [12 exactly]12 the same stuff and there will be an [13 awful]13 (...)

X: [9 (...)]

X: [10 (...)]10

X: [11 mhm]11

X: [12 mmm]12

X: [13 mm]13

A: "yes" [14 we will take]14

I: [14 or is it]14 maybe, too hard to drive it home, I don't know

A: D!

D: [15 ehhh]15

I: [15 yes]15 that is exactly what I think

D: I also think we should have a special rate for senior citizens.

What is going on here?

The first reason we cut out this 2.40 minutes from the meeting of four hours was the long pause in the beginning where the picture seemed to freeze. It was a comic effect. Then there was an outburst of demand for clarification with **G**, the opposition, breaking the silence. Then there is a much clearer summary that focuses the problem illustrated by the Gustavi school paying for the use of the Guldheden school gym which was not responsible for the cost of premises in the first place. The proposed principle was that for planned regular use of premises there should be no internal rent charges, but for the rest, occasional use, as it were, which are called transactions, there should be a charge. **G** has something on his mind and tries to break in, but never gets to the point of articulating his problem. Instead I, one of the activists, thinks of another example. When she has a meeting with her subdistrict management team there is no room big enough in the office and she usually holds the meetings in the neighbouring old-age home where they have a nice room. That would mean some kind of bureaucratic costs of charging rents. Then A, the leader, breaks out of the example-giving exercise by giving the word to D, who comments on the original memo on external rents and proposes that there should be a special rate for senior citizens.

In terms of interaction in the group A the leader is the dominating actor. He seeks to conclude a diversion on internal rents by analogy reasoning. He does not get it right and it is in accordance with G's role that he breaks the silence of confusion. A gives it another try by relating the summary to the example in focus. Then I, an activist, thinks about other examples and the paperwork it implies to have these internal charges. A marks irritation (that the matter is not closed due to I's bringing up of another 'case') by saying "yes" (in English) and moves the meeting back on track with the help of D. Actor behaviour fits nicely into the roles group members have assumed over time. (We are not told what it is G is annoyed about, only that he thinks there is unfairness hidden somewhere.)

We gain further insights into what was going on by examining the context of this exchange. There was a memo that had been circulated to partici-pants the day before. In the meeting there was a presentation (sometimes interrupted by questions) of the main points of that memo. Then there was the innocent question by H; "who gets the revenue?". This question alerts the participants to the added freedom of action (in a budget straight-jacket) that rent revenue would give. Then comes the fairness question of the school with the gym (Guldheden) getting revenue from the Gustavi school without having responsibility for the costs of the gym.

This point on the agenda, which was the first one, ends with a decision to go to the council with a formal memo to request a decision on a price list for external rents. This is a rule of the game – only the council can decide on fees and charges to outsiders. Revenues would go to the activity centres, but if revenues grow exceptionally there will be a review of the rules. There are also a number of points in the meeting minutes about further development of the internal rents issue. The task is given to B, to devise administrative routines and the appropriate changes of the account-ing system. The matter of rents is fragmented into 13 statements in the minutes. The original issue was external rents but the crux was definition of territory and 'revenue sharing'. The group discovers several new prob-lems by solving the original one. It is not without consequences for internal relations to behave in a more business-like manner towards outsiders!

What did (s)he mean? Self-confrontation interviews

The videotape containing this sequence (together with six other sequences from the meeting) was replayed to participants in individual interviews three (summer) months after the meeting. The structure of the interview was the following; each sequence was dealt with separately and the opening question concerning each sequence was "what goes on here?". The follow-up questions on the first statement of interpretation varied depending on the specific circumstances that developed in the interview. In the following, only those aspects of the interview that seem to add to the interpretation of the sequence are touched upon.

We chose to start with **B**, the controller (a peripheral), because he gives additional perspective to the sequence. He says that the reason for this becoming a bit complicated is that the district managed to take only half the step when they designed economic responsibilities in the beginning of the reform period. There are 'rates' for schools, child care, home service, etc. (making resource allocation automatic and based on volumes). When they did this there was no time to work out 'rates' for office space and premises. They had to keep 'premises' a central cost responsibility. Now there was an opportunity to take a further step towards more complete economic responsibility for the 'profit centres'/activity centres by including cost for premises. **B** did not see the sequence as complicated at first but, (**R** = researcher):

> **R:** But participants did not seem to understand. **A** had to repeat before getting any reaction.
> **B:** Well, I do not see that as indicating that people did not understand. We were in agreement on this issue.
> **R:** Why did he have to repeat then?
> **B:** Well I suppose he wanted some kind of response. The fact that **I** brings up (the example of paying for a meeting room) is for clarification.

B sees the incident as a natural continuation in the design of financial responsibilities.

In addition, the leader, **A**, is of the opinion that there were no difficulties in understanding. This was not a complicated issue. When asked why he had to repeat his points he says, "perhaps members had not done their homework properly". **A** was more prepared. It is difficult to 'jump aboard' if you are not prepared. The fact that **I** brought up the example with a meeting room is interpreted by **A** as a *questioning* of the solution. The researcher says, when you say "yes" that means that you recognize the consequences of the rule and you realize that there may be problems with it. **A** responds with "maybe".

In the self-confrontation interviews, these two actors convey the opinion that this rent incident is a natural continuation of the work on delegation of financial responsibility. A *recipe* that has worked well for the district.

I, who brought up the case with the meeting room, admits that she did not understand the opening summary and she adds that it felt like nobody really grasped what he was talking about. When **A** repeated it, it was much clearer. It sometimes happens to all of us that we do not understand.

She would prefer to have the money for rents in her budget and pay when she borrowed somebody else's rooms. This is a manager of a subdistrict. If she could get budget responsibility for premises in *her area* she obviously sees opportunities for good business for her district, but does she really want *the activity centres* to have the budget allocations for internal rents? Better to have the budget item 'premises' on the subdistrict level and avoid internal rents between activity centres?

One cannot avoid the impression from the self-confrontation interview that **I** has not really understood what the decision was. She understood the principles adequately and she wants to increase her responsibility area to include internal rents provided that there is money in the budget for it.

G, the opposition, interprets the sequence as:

G: As usual **A** gives a long harangue.
R: Don't you understand what he says?
G: No not always, sometimes he speaks in a way we don't understand.
R: And then everybody is quiet?
G: Yes I think so.
R: And then several people ask for clarification?
G: Yeah, there is something there that isn't right! Sometimes I think that it is some bloody tactic of his just to get a decision through.
R: He dominates a lot?
G: Yes he does, but we let him!

Among other participants that did not take part in the exchange of the sequence we note that the record keeper of the group (a peripheral) finds the matter easy to understand when the summary is repeated. The same goes for other participants. The example with the meeting room brought up by **I** was to confirm that she had understood and she got that confirmation. On the matter of not understanding what goes on, the record keeper complains that her greatest trouble is that there often is no clear signal that a decision has been taken. It might be like this "yes" – statement in the sequence – and then you have to go back and try to interpret what the decision was. She usually tests her interpretations with the others and if **A** is available she will check with him. Sometimes it is clear from the whole atmosphere of the meeting which way the group wants to go, but it is still difficult to formulate the decision. The group has discussed how to be clearer about decisions and there has been improvement. As record keeper and information officer, she cannot doze off like some of the others do at times. She likes being well informed and keeps alert through the meetings.

Text in context

The centre piece of this sequence is the role of the concrete case of the Gustavi school paying internal rents for using the gym at the Guldheden school, should the proposed principle for internal rents be implemented inside the current responsibility system. On the basis of this illustration a first general principle is (not very clearly it seems) formulated. A second version of the general formulation is clearer. This could be the end of the matter because the original issue was external rents, but now a second candidate for concrete illustration is introduced by I. This is the case of regular, but less frequent, use of premises belonging to an activity centre, and it is a higher organizational level (the subdistrict) using the premises of an activity centre. The matter of internal rents is much more complicated than asking the council to confirm rates for external rents! It has to be investigated further and it cannot be solved here at the table today as it involves budget allocations as well as principles for what is to be considered a transaction between responsibility centres. A cuts the discussion short and moves the meeting back to the agenda, already set on a decision to give somebody the task of preparing a memo on principles for internal rents. What is established in the sequence is a concrete case (the Gustavi school) to be used as a touchstone in formulating the rules for internal rents. The pronounced fairness criterion is that there should be a match between cost responsibility and budget allocation. The alternate candidate for 'test case', the meeting room, is cut short by "yes", meaning that the rule would be generally applicable, but this is not the time to come up with a lot of tricky cases.

This point on the agenda resulted in a list of 13 points in the minutes. Several of them contained principles and expressions of desirable orientations in the continued work on the issue. The 'decision' was to investigate further, and separate the external rents issue from the newly 'discovered' internal rents issue.

The external rents matter will go to council, after some adjustments which provided for more differentiation (base rate plus cost, and special rate for pensioners). The management group discovered the complexities of charging internal rents, and this matter was given to the controller to work out a memo (rules, changes in accounting system, administrative routines). We find that in the context of discovery the group used the concrete case of the Gustavi school to make sense of what it would mean to use a sketched set of rules. It is also clearly signalled by **A** to the controller that he should use the concrete case as a thought-out model in his drafting of his memo for a later meeting. We conclude that on this level of interpretation *the concrete case, as a narrative illustration to general principle*, is the context that gives meaning to a proposed change of rules.

The larger context: district finances

The economic situation of the district is excellent. The financial reporting model that the city imposes on districts generated the array of surplus shown in Table 9.1.

The focus of attention of the management group ever since the inception of the district organization has been to rationalize activities in order to save money. It has not been possible to avoid being exposed to the fact that the city has been in financial crisis. The city allocated a budget cut of 15% over a three-year period, evenly distributed over the years. The district decided to cut the costs quicker and get done with it. This policy was successfully implemented and the accumulated surplus (= equity) by 1993 was approaching 10% of the budget total.

The practical methods of cost cutting have varied from closure to dilution of personnel density in child care. To support action **A** has taken measures to enhance 'cost consciousness' and to articulate responsibility in cost control models on the lowest possible operational level.

The logic of resource allocation inside the district has been to allocate through standardized rates. A specified amount of money per school child, nursery kid, home service receiver, etc. This has given a certain transparency to the allocation system and a direct link between performance and resource allocation. Responsibility centre heads are able to calculate the consequences of their actions.

Table 9.1 Financial outcomes (surplus) 1990–1993

Year	Mcr
1990	5.2
1991	10.8
1992	28.8
1993	20.7
Total	65.5

This rate system could also have been used for the cost item 'premises', but there were complicating factors and the small team of accounting staff did not have the time or inclination to work out the necessary rules and prices during the first years. A complicating factor was, for instance, that a number of school gyms are not used by the schools in the evenings. They are contracted out to the city's leisure department, which in turn rents them out to sports clubs, folk-dance ensembles, etc. These evening activities incur costs and the rates the leisure department charges can be questioned. There are, for example, pensioners from the district that are not given space for their activities because some outside floor ball club is given priority by the leisure department. A confrontation with the leisure department is on the cards.

The district has many other kinds of premises in its possession, and more could be done here, but the rates are not easy to calculate and keep transparent. The controller said in the self-confrontation interviews reported above that top management did not have the energy to do the necessary ABC-analysis to include costs of premises in the rates at that time. Now it was natural to take this step and make the successful recipe for economizing complete. There are more savings or revenues to be won on premises, which is a significant cost in the district's budget (see Table 9.2).

Initially, the item on the agenda and the memorandum on external rents were not seen as very effective ways of relieving some of the budget pressure. But the businessmen among the participants were aroused by the innocent question from a member: "who will get the revenue?". The need for rule-making concerning internal rents is obvious to the members and the starting point is fairness, as illustrated by the Gustavi school example. The decision on this point of the agenda includes a policy statement about the desirability to rent out premises as much as possible, and it is up to the activity centre heads to judge. As a consequence they need rules and the Gustavi school exemplar is given to the controller as a touchstone in forging the new set of rules. For him it is a natural

Table 9.2   Cost items in the district 1993

Cost item	Mcr	%
Personnel	256.7	41
Premises	105.2	17
Transfers	218.2	34
Other	53.4	8
Total	633.5	100

continuation of the so-far successful recipe of specifying responsibility and delegating to activity centres to decide about action. This recipe has generated a transparency that has made business-like behaviour on the part of activity centre heads natural. The success of the management group in rule making, as well as in implementing cost cutting action, confirms the soundness of the approach.

We conclude that on this level of interpretation *the recipe gives meaning to the accounting rules*.

Transparency, confident action, success and increased belief in an established recipe gives members of the management team a nice feeling of being part of a well-managed organization. The recipe has the capacity to 'explain' a large number of concrete cost-cutting cases. It is also a useful source for arguments in a more teleological discourse with City Hall.

The further enlarged context: city financing

Control strategies have an interesting history in the city. When the city was modernized in the 1950s, the economy at large grew and a rapid inflow of people to the city made large housing commitments necessary, which caused financial difficulties. The budget system was reformed but basic-ally it was the booming economy that generated the good times of planning. An adapted version of programme budgeting was introduced and the only problem seemed to be to find land and infrastructure for all the housing projects, and to build schools where the children live, closing down the ones not needed in the city centre. Great challenges for planners!

The oil crises came and proved many plans illusory. The 'planning craze' was replaced by a new austerity management marked by a shift in political leadership. The rest of centralized planning control remained in the expan-sion of services financed by state subsidies, health care continued to expand and needed space. When the influx of new employees to expanding industries did not meet expectations, empty flats and deteriorating finances for municipal housing companies made corporate financial planning on the municipal level necessary. The continued expansion of the 'soft' municipal services (like child care) with their 'housing' needs continued to add to the municipal 'premises' assets. The difference was that now the state no longer had the financial power to back up its reforms. The financial situation for the city deteriorated in the squeeze between growing personnel costs, decreasing transfers from the state, decreasing tax revenue and increasing welfare costs due to the economic crisis.

In a symbolic sense the reform (geographical decentralization) itself signifies that the city is no longer accommodating the traditional welfare state structures. The old organization with its departmental structure matching the state structures of grants and subsidies was oriented towards the causal centre of the welfare state – parliamentary reforms implemented via state agencies through the municipal sector and supported with a flow of grants. Now the flow of state grants was, if not drying up, changed much to the disadvantage of big cities, financial markets were deregulated providing more room for manoeuvre for the finance department of the city. Since the political situation did not allow tax increases, borrowing was the main source of financing the deficit generated by the economic crisis. The credit rating of the city affected its cost of borrowing. Financial reporting and financial management have come increasingly into focus in City Hall during the last few years. A compelling reason is that the debt–equity ratio which was approximately 50/50 in the beginning of the 1980s had reached values of 90/10 by the beginning of the 1990s.

One way of dealing with the financial crisis – and the balance sheet – was a large sale–lease-back deal in 1991, including mainly schools, between the city and one of the larger pension funds. This provided spending money and looked better on the balance sheet than a loan. Deregulation had provided this new kind of space for financial management. A by-product of the deal was a 'market-based' price for leasing 'premises'.

During the past five years city leaders have been preoccupied with ordering cost cuts, pleading with the state for financial relief measures, and preventing a too rapid decline in balance sheet-related indicators. For them there has been no room for discussion of concrete cases or recipes. The thing that matters is whether financial indicators maintained the levels that left the credit rating intact, while the city weathered the storm and waited for better economic times to improve revenues. A conceptual financial model gives meaning to rules for internal rents. If the market-based rents can be transferred down the organization to activity centres and then be felt by responsible managers, so much the better.

On this level of interpretation we conclude that the context of *financial crisis gives meaning to managerial decisions*. The sale–lease-back deal on the schools was a financial operation motivated by *conceptual* reasoning on financial costs which transfers down to districts in terms of rents on premises.

Discussion

We have presented three distinct interpretations of the conception of costs of premises in possible accounting discourses on different levels of organization. Two of the 'readings' were based on recorded conversation and the related self-confrontation interviews, and one on our extensive background material on extended context (cf. Jönsson and Solli, 1994).

It seems reasonable to claim that these interpretations are well founded and will be considered facts in the sense of 'social accomplishments' (Atkinson, 1988). The epistemological status of these interpretations remains a problem. Clearly all three interpretations emerge when we relate the recorded conversation to context. We have used the transcripts and interviews to detect cues indicating interpretive repertoires (Potter and Wetherell, 1987, p. 138), but we have not documented the repertoires as such. Interpretive repertoires are described as "recurrently used systems of terms ... used in particular stylistic and grammatical constructions ... organized around specific metaphors and figures of speech" (Potter and Wetherell, 1987, p. 149). It might be ventured that this kind of definition is anchored too deeply in the text itself (and in form) to be optimally useful. Context is in a sense given in the case (Gilbert's and Mulkay's study, 1984) used to narrate the concept. If context was permitted to vary, as in our different levels of interpretation, some definitional dimensions could be added.

First, it should be noted that our three interpretive repertoires represent a progression of increasing conceptualization. This illustrates how a translation from narrative meaning to a paradigmatic one could occur in an organizational setting.

At the group level the meaning of accounts (rules for accounts as well as accounts for rules) seems to be *generated from the concrete case*. The battle for control over the rule-making process (to the extent that there was any) is interpreted to have been about what concrete case should be the touchstone for the rule formulation work to be done by the controller.

At the organizational level the meaning of accounts seems to be *generated from the successful recipe*. The interview statement of the controller (that the intended solution is a natural continuation of the approach used earlier) bears evidence, as well as the fact that the leader, A, saw this as an unproblematic issue.

At the corporate level (in the municipality itself this term is used) the meaning of accounts seems to be generated from the *conceptual models related to financial reporting and financial management in a crisis*. We do not have evidence of this in the conversation or interviews, but the contextual evidence, for example, the design of the models that specify the financial responsibilities of the district and the budget documents, support the conclusion.

We seem to have a distinct relation between context and interpretative repertoire here. We are inclined to assume that all three repertoires are present (potentially) to be used in giving accounts in all three contexts, but that one of them is dominating on each level. We do not have sufficient evidence for this claim at this time, but it seems intuitively appealing to assume that there is a relation between repertoire and context. This is after all, also present in the Gilbert and Mulkay (1984) data since the 'contingency repertoire' of that case was used to explain error and deviations from the 'right' beliefs, while the 'empiricist repertoire' was used in 'formal' occasions and as an overriding legitimizing device.

The arguments for the tendency of the three repertoires to dominate each one in its specific context would run as follows.

The *case* is concrete and offers associative links in analogue descriptions of cases. The discussion in the meeting started to generate alternative cases and parallels. The concrete case allows 'testing' of how a principle would 'work' (relate to the pragmatic truth concept). Thinking through the consequences presupposes that the thinker has a 'thick' description of the case. Controlling what case is used for this 'touchstone' purpose will make it possible to control the outcome of such contemplation. Narratives have great power in normative discourse (Bruner, 1990).

The *recipe* is experiential (Kolb, 1984) in the sense that it accounts for a behavioural pattern, and is condensed in the sense that it summarizes confirmed (successful) action. A recipe has a history and the specific associative link to consider here is the question of whether the definition of the current situation is similar enough to the experience condensed in the recipe. The recipe also has a 'teleological' end. The recipe informs us about what to do to achieve certain ends – what it is good for. Learning to apply the recipe includes experience of earlier applications as well as the ability to determine a diagnosis of what immediate objectives have priority now.

The code of the (financial) *conceptual model* is known by outsiders. The financial crisis is constituted by the lack of revenues to cover budgeted (and non-budgeted) costs. In such a situation negotiation with outsiders on conditions for granting additional resources are focal. It may be adding persuasive power to the argument if the recipes applied to achieve improvements are described, but the effects in terms of financial indicators are the crucial arguments. In a financial crisis political leaders are open to advice from experts who can show beneficial effects on financial indicators from, e.g. a sale–lease-back deal on 'premises'. The language will be financial and conceptual.

The three interpretive repertoires indicate three different discourses; a normative one concerning how the contemplated rules would work in the concrete case; an instrument one on how the recipe will contribute to the achievement of immediate objectives; a contracting one on the conditions for the disposition of resources.

If interpretive repertoires differ how can organizational levels communicate?

A nice thing about communication is that it gives opportunities to check up on your senses. If you do not quite believe your eyes you can say to your hunting colleague (to repeat the story): "Hey do you see the moose over there?" When your colleague says "Oh my God, don't shoot! It is our friend Peterson!", it offers an opportunity to adjust action accordingly. What happens here is that one party focuses attention on a phenomenon and the conversation serves to classify it and confirm that the participants are talking about 'the same thing'. This classifying of the intended phenomenon seems to be a crucial function in communication and in giving accounts. Once the situation is defined the repertoire of activities can be scanned and the adequate response chosen.

When Simon *et al.* (1954) talk about the *attention directing* function of accounting information, they mean that accounting information may serve as an indicator that 'something' is wrong. There is however one more step, the identification of relevant cause–effect relations, before a link between accounting and control can be established. Jönsson and Hedberg (1977a, b) advanced the idea that 'semi-confusing' information could serve the function of alerting managers to the need to investigate what cause–effect mechanisms were at play.

Here we are considering the role of communication in focusing attention. What are the chances that participants from different levels will 'talk about the same thing' if dominating interpretive repertoires differ? On the team level we have pointed to the concrete case or narrative as a meaning generator in normative discourse. This level is likely to be able to communicate without structural misunderstanding with the organizational level in the sense that 'recipe' is compatible with the 'concrete case'. A case can be compared to the recipe to determine whether the case is 'in line' with the recipe or not. It also seems that a recipe can be compared with a financial model to see what effect it might have on the indicators. If we, however, consider communication directly between the concrete case and the conceptual model, misunderstanding seems unavoidable.

The worrying aspect is that there seems to be an *asymmetry in the relation*. Different time scales and learning styles are applied to achieve communicative competence in the concrete case and conceptual modes. One repertoire will not be well served by a conceptual 'grammar' since it is the particular effects that are of interest. The other will find it too time-consuming to build the experiential repertoire to appreciate the generality of the concrete case. Furthermore a conceptual argument can be broken down to the appropriate level of application through deductive reasoning, while the concrete case is difficult to build up to a general level without a detailed experiential context even if metaphors offer an opening. Proponents of the general and the particular, respectively, may conceive the resulting communication problems differently. Suffice it to say that here is an interesting area of research that management accountants could benefit from exploring!

The recipe of the middle level can serve a communicative link in that the practice contained in the recipe is an enrichment of the historical concrete cases constituting experience. It is also rationally principled in that the recipe is a solution to intentional problems – if this recipe is applied it will lead to improvements in relevant outcome variables. The principles of a recipe provide conceptually-based justification and the practices of a recipe summarize historical concrete cases. Thus the recipe holds promise by being a two-way meaning generator in normative discourse. Perfect for middle management!

What do these interpretive repertoires mean for the work of managers in different organizational units?

We have stated earlier in this chapter that managerial work is verbal and characterized by brevity, variety and fragmentation. Communication is crucial and dependent on context. Control of the 'world' will require taking control of the language used to describe it. But taking control of a language cannot be done other than in communicative interaction.

The recorded interaction discussed earlier was between insiders of a team and we can note some differences in the understanding of the norms that were under discussion. It is easy to see the need for further interaction, especially interaction on implemented practices, before the narrative of the concrete case has been boiled down to a taken-for-granted managerial practice. The advantages of teamwork in this connection seem to lie in a speeding-up effect from conversation in accomplishment of Kolb's (1984, p. 42) experiential learning ("concrete experience – reflective observation – abstract conceptualization – active experimentation"). Teams, with their internal network of trust relations, will be able to assimilate and conceptualize experience differently, and probably more robustly, than the individual. The conception of managerial work which was extracted from previous research is situated in this discourse on experience (do you see what I see?).

If different teams understand the intended process differently a negotiated contract, if implemented, will provide opportunities to develop a discourse on joint experience. The same kind of problem-solving process as we have observed inside a team may occur in time. A precondition is that communication is kept open. Transparency of activity improves chances of constructive communication.

In the meantime managers on different levels of organization will be immersed in different contexts and they will communicate differently with their co-workers. Different information will emerge from the same kind of accounting reports. 'Training' is not the solution. Discourse is.

And what does this mean for management accounting research?

The main consequence of orienting management accounting research towards the information that emerges when managers manage would be a focus on communication. Instead of assuming that management accounting information goes directly into decision-making models of some kind, we would assume that information comes to use in varying communicative contexts. Decision-making would be one of them. The traditional (Simon *et al.*, 1954) categories of 'score keeping, attention directing and problem solving' constitute a good starting point and studies could be designed to elaborate these and other contexts. 'Improving understanding' could be added, since we have ample evidence that the most significant part of managerial work is asking questions.

The assumptions of rationality and opportunism, implicit in most decision-making models, are sometimes criticized as not descriptive of real humans. This may no longer be an issue. If focus is on managers at work the question of rationality will be an empirical one. It will not come to any researcher's mind to postulate that a manager should behave in accordance with some abstract conceptual model of decision making. The situation of managerial work will be in focus rather than some 'natural law' of rational decision making. The observational data may be explained by a rational model, or some other model may make better sense of the observations. In both cases it is possible to conduct a constructive debate on the merits of theoretical statements against the background of empirical observation.

Epistemological aspects

So much for ontology (what it is we are studying when we study managerial work). Now the question is what can be said about the epistemological status of the kind of studies the approach sketched in this chapter would have. What kind of criteria for what can be accepted as knowledge are applicable in this kind of study? How can we know that we have learnt something?

First, if empirical observations are focused on managers at work, that is individuals in communication, much can be gained by taking advantage of the rapidly developing area of ethnomethodology.

Ethnomethodology aims to understand 'folk' (ethno) methods (methodology) for organizing their world (Garfinkel, 1967). Those methods are laid down in the skills ('artful practices') through which people develop, jointly, an understanding of each other and their social institutions. Bruner (1990) uses the same 'folk' approach in defining the narrative mode of cognition.

Even if ethnomethodology is not well defined there are a number of misunderstandings about its methods. In particular, it is said that it is tarnished by voluntarism and subjectivity. This is a misunderstanding attributed to Bourdieu among others (Watson and Seiler, 1992, p. xiv). On the contrary:

1. Ethnomethodologists agree on anchoring their analysis in 'texts' of behaviour (that is not to engage in sophistry where arguments are borne solely on the wings of language). This has given rise to the labelling of ethnomethodology as 'new empiricism'.
2. They also agree that 'social facts' are not out there to be encountered, but are continuously constructed through interaction. The subjectivity is virtually eliminated by the fact that the registered 'text' is a conversation between competent persons (Atkinson, 1988) in their area of competence in a situation where their purpose is to reach a solution that works. The statement participants make are public and stand to be corrected by other competent participants. The statements are empirical facts. What went on in their minds while they were making them cannot be registered. Researchers can come back to the empirical facts, the text, when discussing interpretations.

Conversation and discourse thus allow and require interpretive feedback (note, in the earlier case, how A was obliged to repeat the proposed principle of accounting for internal rents) and so provide for a negotiability of meanings which includes corrections and retrospective reinterpretations (Blimes *et al.*, 1992, p. 97). Participants reflect on what they are doing while doing it.

Ethnomethodologists are not interested in individuals or reading people's minds, but in describing the methods people use when they generate accounts of 'the way things really are'. This means that ethnomethodology focuses only on social phenomena – 'how participants use the tools, rules and machinery of conversation to accomplish their purposes, and to expose and test their mutual understanding' (Moerman, 1992, p. 33).

It should be noted that 'understanding' is not an unproblematic concept. An early interpretation of Weber's 'verstehen' was that it means to relive the experience of the actor to understand decisions and actions – getting inside the actor's head, as it were. Later it was understood to mean gaining access to 'subjective meaning', but lately the view, inherited from Wittgenstein (?), is that subjective meanings are unavailable to research and that only public meanings, (developed in conversation or discourse), are available.

Meaning is negotiated interactively in conversation and the parties participating in the conversation are not alone. There are others present in the form of expectations that constitute role and competence, and there are sources of norms like the city council demanding action on cost cutting. The more demanding the interpretation of what goes on in conversation, the denser the presence of such situational structures. The researcher needs contextual information for interpretation.

These requirements are rather exacting and may explain why ethno-methodological studies in sociology have tended to focus on everyday conversation in short sequences, and order, in terms of the sequencing (turn taking, etc.), of the conversation itself rather than content. But there are also studies of scientific work (Gilbert and Mulkay, 1984) and we propose that more daring applications to accounting work are desirable and possible. The epistemological problem is related to the problem of accounting for 'context' in the research report and the demonstration of how context implies a certain interpretation. In the case presented in this chapter I have tried to use my familiarity with the focal organization of the case to show that multilevel interpretations can give new insights into communication in organizations. But it has not been possible to demonstrate that familiarity. There remains the need to seek support for the proposed conclusions in the narrative meaning that the account conveys. In this sense the criterion of success will be if it 'works' in the mind of the reader – whether the reader feels that the conceptualizations help understanding and are useful in discourse on the matters at hand.

This kind of narrative meaning cannot meet criteria of generalizable knowledge. Such knowledge is of interest only under ontological assumptions of organizations following laws of nature. Surely such assumptions are no longer tenable in the social sciences (Harré and Gillet, 1994).

10

Conclusion

One could say that all the cases presented in this book are about management, and then ask what is this 'management' anyway? A little reflection
tells you that management is interfering in other people's lives and it should
not be taken lightly. Work is important for most people, not only because
it provides for the family, but also because you *are* your work. Work gives
people identity – something to relate to. It makes quite a difference
whether it is something tedious that a machine could do better or something that you can talk about with friends. Heroic problem solving, unusual
situations, work well done, are all events that are worthy subjects of
conversation and useful building material for a work role identity.

This author is a professor. A privileged position by most standards
(except pay!), but also an identity. I am the professor who has, with the
help of colleagues, carried out this series of action research studies of
information support for operational management. This book, reporting
on them, will hopefully add to the respect colleagues and practitioners feel
towards this kind of research. There will be invitations to talk about the
results, and people will refer to these studies in their argument for this or
that solution. I will be identified with this work. I will be my work. Even
if everybody thinks that it is all unscientific quackery it will be part of my
identity. So there is a risk. The image I exhibit of myself may not be very
flattering, at least not according to the feedback signals I may get from

others. That is the only feedback available for a person. I read my own identity in the mirror image of me that my immediately surrounding environment provides. There is some choice as to what signals to include in the pattern, but I need the feedback to know who I am; and in order to elicit reactions I have to act. My actions demonstrate my intentions and my skilfulness in carrying out my intentions. (In some departmental budget matters I might find it feasible to disguise my intentions but I cannot overdo that without loss of trustworthiness.) I must mind my identity. It is a most valuable asset!

In doing my job I take the risk of losing face. I am tempted to try to control the reactions of others in order to get a favourable reading of my identity. There really is not much choice, I will simply not get a reaction of others unless I act. If I am successful in controlling the reactions of others I will get a distorted reflection of myself. This kind of reasoning is likely to have gone on in the minds of every person engaged in the projects which have been described in the preceding chapters, and it goes on in my mind as I write. How can I make the reader see the point of all these tales from the field? How can the theoretical importance of it all be conveyed? It is best to summarize the empirical findings first, then draw conclusions concerning the use of economic information in operational activities in organizations and how further studies can be conducted.

Summary of the cases

First, it should be noted that the field studies reported here have all been done over considerable periods of time. It has therefore been possible to observe changes in the organizations while observations were being made. Any researcher exposed to this fact is affected by it. Seeing organizations change is an effective antidote against static views, but it also generates a certain humbleness in drawing conclusions. Since organizations changed while we observed them it is likely that they continued to change after we left. All the cases thus are testimony to the fact that organizations are dynamic entities. The changes are mostly for the better in terms of generally accepted values. There are some examples of when improvement has not been achieved, but the bulk of the material shows how organizations improve by acts of management. We will return to the question of what management is.

The first three chapters set the stage.

Chapter 1 was intended to give an overview of the problem area we are dealing with. What actually is improvement is difficult to define if one wants to reach consensus. The orchestra was thought to be a good metaphor since the 'blueprint' is given in the sheet of music, but concerted action must be reached by keeping an eye on the man up front waving his arms, and, primarily, by listening to one's colleagues and acting accordingly. Acting is signalling, and the meaning of the act emerges as the receiver does the interpretation in context. (When moose hunting it is wise to ask your friend if he also sees the moose over there – it might be your friend Peterson.) Repeated action primes associations and learning from experience occurs. Learning and improvement presuppose trust, when trust is breached crisis occurs. Breaking out of crisis starts with explaining why the crisis emerged in the first place.

Chapter 2 outlined the theoretical basis in Bourdieu and Habermas for the work with the empirical material.

Finally, Chapter 3 tried to sketch the Swedish managerial culture in which the observations have been made, and the narrower context of management control (given a desire to encourage participation). Swedish management has been characterized as 'ambiguous and obscure', meaning that there is a tendency towards consensus and delegation of decision-making authority. This requires that matters are not settled from the start, that there is some room for discussion. Otherwise there would be nothing to delegate and reach agreement on. The general work values among Swedes have been measured by Hofstede. The most distinguishing factor is the extremely high value attributed to relationships and teamwork. Institutionally Swedish industry, located in a small country, had to go international early-on to grow, since the home market could not support economies of scale. A well-developed (and expansive) welfare state provides for a view towards long-term employment and a reciprocal loyalty to the company. The state cooperated with organized labour and industry federations to promote modernization, and when the oil crises and un-realistic ambitions forced the state finances out of control a new period of learning to compete started.

A short section of this chapter was intended to show that our knowledge of budget control in terms of the effects of participation on motivation and performance is limited.

The empirical part starts with a case from the car industry where two studies done at about the same time illustrate: (1) a breakdown in budget communication between the plant level and European headquarters; and (2) a case of improvement work that turned into organizational problems. A very steep improvement in productivity was interrupted and succeeded by a steep decline. There is no proof that the 'kink' in the productivity development was caused by a break in morale owing to lack of communi-cation with other organizational levels, but it is quite likely that this was the case. The moral is a simple one; improvement work will be much more difficult without the support of higher organizational levels. It is not a question of whether the budget allocations are cut or not but whether there is a feeling that the upper levels listen and care.

Chapter 5 presented the basic model of how improvement work is done. It is the Floby team which alerted the author to the mechanisms of joint problem solving in teams. Leadership is crucial since it serves to focus attention on problems, but the core mechanism is attention focus, collecting data on the problem, presenting data to the group, discussing causes and remedies, deciding what to do and allocating responsibility, confirming improvement and the new routine. The Floby team also focused on one problem at a time and did not choose to start with the most difficult problem. The team was in firm control of its problem-solving process. Once it had established itself as a competent team an increasing proportion of the problem solving involved contacts with other departments. We recognize that there was an inner dialogue at first and later an increasing amount of outer dialogue (with surrounding departments). This inner dialogue does not always involve a lot of talk. If you know your machines and have been present during production runs you know what is going on and what symptoms are present. A suggested solution may be accepted with a nod and the group can go almost directly to action sometimes. It seems likely that the data that were collected in the problem-solving process served mainly as reminders. One of the operators said his main experience of the project was that he learned that he had a 'short memory'. The data helped to see patterns.

As far as the outer dialogue goes the fact that responsibility centre boundaries were crossed meant that initially a confrontational atmosphere was evoked. By providing facts and professional arguments a communication channel could be established. Soon the foremen on the opposite side realized that the new customer relationship could be used to make needs for improvements in their own department visible. The fact that Börje was hired by the division head to develop a one-day course in 'local economy' and that this label in time became a household word in Volvo Components testifies to the power of communication in improvement work.

Chapter 6 concerned a project that was designed to study the effects of individually designed accounting reports. The participants were trained in the accounting concept of their organization and were then allowed to design their own reports. The plan was to monitor how these new reports were used by regular interviews every month. These interviews started with the question "How are you doing?". It was found that participants valued these interviews higher than the other interventions. The dialogue with the visiting outsider allowed participants to:

- first ask questions about what was included and what was not included in the report (responsibility territory and time);
- then increasingly discuss impediments to activities to lower costs;
- finally to test half-baked ideas about improvements ("what if?" issues).

The latter kind of issues came up towards the end of the period when trust had developed, not least by the outsider (controller or researcher) helping with elimination of impediments to improvements. By acting to help eliminate rules that prevented rational solutions to problems the outsider could demonstrate that headquarters was serious in its delegation of responsibility and efforts to improve efficiency. The outer dialogue was seen to serve a committing purpose in this case. By being provided with the opportunity to reason through arguments, be it only by having a sympathetic, passive listener in the room, the participants mustered a will to act which initiated the learning process.

Chapter 7 was about planning your own work and being able to cope with complexity. The Road Authority has a history of planning since it is a manifestation of the modernity project. It is the state's agency for transportation infrastructure. In time it developed a top-heavy structure with central experts for every conceivable aspect of road transport. A decentralization project was initiated and the idea was to support decentralization by a grand information system which contained all relevant information in many different data bases. The unintended (?) result of this integrated planning structure was that work for the people tending the road was fragmented. A reason for this was that the new trend of behaving in a business-like manner was superimposed on the planning structure. The case of the Road Authority illustrates how a couple of districts conquered their work and could start dealing with whole jobs again. The model-building activities of young engineers in foreman positions constituted the instruments of taking back command over the work situation at the same time as it provided information bases which served well in communication with customers as well as with budget people on the regional level. The project had difficulties catching the attention of headquarters, possibly due to the fact that headquarters was focused on governmental agencies and parliament. It is at that political level where decisions to go ahead with large projects and to release funds are taken. Given this kind of structure the Road Authority was under dual pressure. It was required to appear business-like at the top and at the bottom. The middle part suffered and had to develop communicative skills which were not as obviously required under the old regime where plans and authority came from the top. It is doubtful whether the project described in the case led to any improvement in collective communication skills across organizational levels in the Road Authority, but it certainly improved the capacity of the operational level to communicate its views and provide data to back them up.

Chapter 8 was about work that is never done and where consequences are only visible indirectly. Managing maintenance is like chasing ghosts. The trick is to eliminate potential monsters, but since they are potential you will not know if they are eliminated. Perhaps they were not there in the first place.

The problem with the monsters is that the repairman feels really wanted when they appear. All attention is focused on the stopped line and the repairman is the hero who will fix it. A perfect opportunity to demonstrate competence!

Preventive maintenance, on the other hand, is routine and has a high level of drudgery. It is undramatic and seemingly without any effects. Since the theory is that 50% of the breakdowns are caused by uncleanliness, you clean a lot, but cleaning is not production is it? It is what apprentices do!

So in maintenance, focus is on the efficiency of machines. It is possible to calculate the value of an improvement of 1% unit in machine use, and most of the time it is worth the effort and cost. But then again the more one manages to bring down unplanned stoppages the more the Maintenance department loses opportunities to maintain their repair competence, and the process of preventive maintenance implies giving competence away to the production departments. Attention in a project, like the one carried out in the Volvo Floby plant, will focus on competence. Part of the project was to develop a bonus mechanism tied to an indicator which would measure efficiency as well as costs and value of production gained. A quality bonus was also included.

This project, dealing as it was with ghosts, involved abstractions to a degree that the other cases did not. The point was that there are effects beyond the routine maintenance work which are important. You see them in the efficiency statistics and in the new orders that come in. These new orders and the upgrading of technology changes the learning environment continuously. In preventive maintenance it is easy to see the effects of leadership in improvement work. A good leader is able to make ghosts visible.

Then, finally, in Chapter 9 we encountered the top management group of a beleaguered part of the public sector, a downtown district of a city. When the new decentralized structure was launched some four years ago the city council had set up the abstract objectives 'democracy, efficiency, local solutions and integration' for the reform. Activities should be directed from positions closer to the concerned citizens and solutions adapted to local circumstances. Services should be more efficient and integrated. This was a radical reform for a society built on equal treatment of every citizen and used to social reforms being initiated in parliament and implemented through structures which channelled finances and rules in tandem. Now integration across professional and bureaucratic borders was elevated to the status of a goal. On top of these goal dimensions, which were difficult to manage in themselves, a financial crisis was added. The complicated managerial problems of efficiency, integration and local solutions had to be solved with decreasing resources and every district had its own traits. The downtown district of this case has, besides the extra social work related to drugs and prostitution, an unusually large population of very old people. Also schools and child care can be problematic since renovation of housing tends to come in blocks and suddenly an area may be housing young families with small children.

Our management group developed a reputation as able managers of a large district who had gone through difficult cost-cutting programmes over the last few years, at the same time as a more integrated administrative structure had been built. The group met every second Thursday to discuss policy issues and lay down rules of the game. "Management is 3% analysis and 97% implementation" said one of Sweden's most prominent business leaders, but still it is a thoroughly verbal activity.

The case in Chapter 9 was about managerial talk and the point of it is to show the importance of context in communication. With this case the book takes a 'linguistic turn' and focuses on what managers do when they manage. Learning is rendering new ways of action meaningful. Attributing meaning to an occurrence includes finding an intention that 'explains' it. With an intentional actor responsibility is readily allocated and trust relations may develop.

In this case it was possible, by gradually expanding the conception of context, to demonstrate how the same situation of rule setting can be understood differently depending on the context in which rules are made. Furthermore it is likely that communication problems will arise in discourse where several levels of organization are involved. In particular, direct communication between a conceptual top level and a concrete operational level is likely to evoke misunderstandings. It is indicated that the recipe-based understanding on the middle management level provides a channel of communication that might have been overlooked in these days of 'flat organizations'.

It is a remarkable fact that all these projects were started with the focus on action and problem solving, but in time the communicative aspects of improvement work were discovered.

It is also worth pointing out that almost any kind of improvement generates complexity since change, if it is at all significant, will have effects on others and thus will generate demands on the environment. Therefore improvement work requires leadership and support from management.

It seems significant that in all the cases there is a movement from the inside out in the projects. The process starts with the group developing an intimacy around problem solving and demonstrates its competence to the environment. Then all sorts of interaction with units in the environment may follow. Being competent is to be recognized as somebody to do business with (this was what Thatcher said about Gorbachov, wasn't it?). Like individuals, who get to know who they are by mirroring themselves in the responses of others to their own action, an organizational group builds identity by its business dealings. Being true to its role in the organization is essential to the group. Changing the role in concerted action with other units is difficult and time consuming.

Theorizing improvement work

Action in context is specific and loses its point when reduced to generalized statements. The point of all this empirical evidence, anecdotal as it may be, is that the common problem in improvement work is to overcome the inability to deal with situations in context. Every organizational unit has its own specific context and it is in that context that action must be taken. Action is necessary to achieve improvement, because improvement means changes in the world for the better. Talk and proclamations, manuals and goal statements cannot deliver the goods, it is what people do that counts.

Action has an initiator with an intent (otherwise it would be an 'event'), somebody who is responsible. Making sense of action means allocating responsibility. It is in context we lose face. If we don't do anything but just carry on as before, follow praxis, we cannot lose face. The risk of initiating improvement is socially constructed as are the rewards. Improvement has taken place when it is recognized as such by those concerned, that is in context. This means that an organization oriented towards improvement should pay primary attention to establishing an improvement-inducing context. Such a context will be demanding and rewarding concerning initiatives and it will discuss real-life phenomena, seeing accounting figures as indicators (only) of what really goes on. Since it is oriented towards real actions it must provide ample opportunities to discuss these actions – 'Do you see what I see?' – in order to achieve joint, coordinated action across organizational territories. This is the first general conclusion: improvement requires space for people to talk about what they are doing. The relevant context of improvement is its embeddedness in discourse.

Context is not enough. There is a need for leadership and configuration of skills. There is also a need for a will to improve. This latter aspect is an interesting and age-old problem discussed by Aristotle as well as Plato under the label 'akrasia'. "Weakness of the will" is a heading used by Harré and Gillett (1994) in discussing our difficulties of getting around to do what we wish to do – our incontinence of action. What is it that drives us to do what we wish to do and what is it that sometimes keeps us from doing it? Harré and Gillett, arguing for a second cognitive revolution, maintain that those theorists who assume the mind to be a "rational preference-serving mechanism that causally produces behaviour" (Harré and Gillett, 1994, p. 118) are considerably embarrassed by the fact that people sometimes act as they would prefer not to. All theories which regard the reasons for our action (be it motives, attitudes, desires or preferences) as 'causal', with the mind choosing what we do, have difficulty in explaining why we do things we really do not want to do. We all know that this phenomenon is common. We justify such action by referring to loyalty, friendship, love, etc., but this does not mean that those feelings 'caused' the action. A theory that resorts to this kind of 'revealed preferences' mode in explaining action becomes a rhetorical device rather than a proper theory. We need to view the ability of making up one's mind as a learned skill. 'Overcoming akrasia involves a discursively learned skill of regulating one's behaviour so that it conforms to the rule-governed significations one endorses in a given context' (Harré and Gillett, 1994, p. 119). This would mean that the study of improvement work would include the study of discursive learning, i.e. how we learn to regulate our behaviour so that it conforms to what is right and proper in a certain context.

The discursive mind (Harré and Gillett, 1994; Potter and Edwards, 1992) is perceived as a mind in context rather than a set of cognitive states. The discursive constructions, which we can observe, are examined in their context of occurrence, rather than as expressions of some mental states, which we cannot observe. They are constructs in context which make sense to the participants in terms of the social action they accomplish. In this way the individual builds identity and commits himself or herself to rules and story lines. The norms and rules that emerge in historical and cultural circumstances structure what people do, and what people do has effects on narrative conventions. It is high time that we throw our Cartesian dead weight overboard and with it the biologically unsound (Edelman, 1992) idea that there is a homunculus sitting inside our head directing our information processing. There is now plenty of evidence that the work of our mind is social, that attention is a social act (Luria, 1973), and that even perception is influenced by discourse.

With a discursive view of the mind we might even be able to account for how our feelings come into play in our developments of norms and rules of proper behaviour. Displays of emotions are, as we easily realize, "expressions of judgements, and, in many cases, though not in all, they are also ways of accomplishing certain social acts" (Harré and Gillett, 1994, p. 146). When we identify a feeling or display of emotion there are four different features to attend to.

1. First there is a bodily disturbance related to feelings. Sometimes it is easily identified (blushing), at other times more diffuse (what do we refer to when we say 'elated'?)
2. Then there are conventional display rules. There are several ways of displaying 'elation'. Conventions may be specific to each group of speakers.
3. Then there is the choice of what judgement the emotional display expresses. Elation may express that something good has happened to me and that my actions have some part in bringing it about.
4. Finally there is the "illocutionary force" (Austin, 1962) or the effect of what is said or done, of the social act.

It seems quite obvious from our fieldwork that emotional display is very often used in regulation of behaviour in improvement work. We have not had the foresight to register such incidents to the extent that we are able to analyse them, nor do we have the tools yet, but there is certainly potential in closer study of the discursive use of emotional display in improvement work. Harré and Gillett illustrate how such work on 'emotionology' could be conducted by showing how Lutz (1988) analysed the emotional practices of the Infaluk people.

She started by studying the diversity of emotion terms and the rules of their use. Then she analysed the situations and episodes that people described when using these words (context). Finally she could see how these emotional displays were integrated into the episodes of everyday life of the Infaluk. The problem was that the emotional vocabulary of the Infaluk could not be simply translated into English equivalents. Whole clusters of words had to be used to indicate. *Metagu* is an illustrative example. The closest English words would be *fear, anxiety* and *embarrass-ment.* The issue here is to show how the display of this emotion functions socially. To do that Lutz has to use two other emotions, as shown in the following:

> A is seen to do *ker,* which is an expression of excitement. (He caught a large fish.) But such expression of excitement is inappropriate for a person of A's social status in the presence of a very important person B. B displays *sort,* which is an expression of justified indignation at A's presumption of doing *ker* in his presence. When A is confronted with B's display of *sort* he will display *metagu,* and when B sees this the episode is over. The emotion of metagu is given meaning in context (*ker:* I am a great fisherman; *sort:* you are a brash fellow; *metagu:* I behaved

improperly, sorry) and the cycle serves to restore the social fabric in the presence of a member's success.

Emotionology may provide keys to an analysis of how social practices are preserved and change in groups and between groups.

Conclusions for the practice of improvement

The main practical conclusion from these empirical studies of improvement work is probably the insight that improvement is accomplished in specific situations with specific groups of people doing their specific things. Any general recipe for improvement work should be looked upon with suspicion.

1. First it has to be stated, even if it is a cliché nowadays, that improvement work (by this we mean, changes in organizational practices that survive over a reasonable period) requires leadership and support from superior levels of organization. 'Weakness of the will' or akrasia lurks in the shadows of every improvement project. Therefore leadership has to be applied in the closest possible vicinity of the relevant operations themselves.

2. Improvement work focuses attention on real activities (even if the discussion may at times be abstract to the outsider). It probably does not damage improvement work to elaborate statements of objectives and general principles, but the heart of the matter is to assume the pragmatic attitude of learning from experience and find out what works.

3. Improvement work is interactive in the sense that the group establishes what the problem is, what the causes might be and what data will inform decisions about action. Participation does not have to be measured in terms of influence, but should be assured in terms of group members being well acquainted with the particular improvement discourse under way.

4. The learned skill of taking action to improve should be trained in cycles of problem identification, data collection, problem solving, action, satisfaction. One problem at a time. The easier the better in the beginning. Success in problem solving generates the ability to overcome akrasia (the weakness of the will). Problems must be solved and declared solved within a reasonable period otherwise the improvement project will lose impetus.

5. Improvement work entails increasingly a focus on competence. Competence in the sense of authority to make decisions and make binding commitments on behalf of the organization, as well as competence in the sense of capability to apply a portfolio of skills to problems.

To leave room to develop these competencies as well as apply them is a necessary part of the improvement project and in line with the management of intensification of knowledge. When the group has demonstrated competence it can enter into 'outer dialogue'.

6. People grow with success. All cannot become leaders, but working in a group means that there is room for specialization. As the individual competencies of members change the composition of the group may have to be adapted to the emerging situation. If, for example, Börje in our first case is found to be an excellent pedagogue he should be encouraged to develop a one-day course in improvement work and to run it in other plants. The management of the production department will have to adapt accordingly.

7. Improvement work is verbal in the sense that it requires time out from machine tending chores for discussion of diagnoses and therapies. Such time outs are usually easier to accomplish the more automated the production is. Reflection on concrete experience allows conceptualization which in turn is the basis for further experiment. Completion of the cycle is facilitated by time outs.

Afterword on accounting

The title for this book was decided long before the content was produced and that took much longer than anticipated. This was due to the complexities of the cases we have presented but also to the gradual realization that accounting in the bookkeeping, number-crunching sense plays a different and more modest role than originally visualized. This might be conceived as a difficult lesson for an accounting professor, but it has, in fact, been very exciting and it has illustrated quite distinctly the other side, perhaps the front side, of accountability. A person may be accountable for the activities carried out (and their consequences) in his or her area of responsibility. But then it is vitally important that he or she is able to account for what goes on in order to demonstrate competence. In order to be able to account for activities it is necessary to make the activities account-able, that is, think through every detailed activity and infuse it with intent. Only then will it be possible to account for it in a manner that gives it meaning for outsiders, only then is it related to context and available for reasoned discourse.

'Account for' in terms of providing with meaning is more central to improvement work than 'account for' in terms of allocating costs to activities. We do need accounts for the role of accounting in improvement work. Please do not misunderstand me, I don't mean that accounting is not important, not at all! But it isn't everything!

References

Agar, M. H., *Speaking of Ethnography*. Beverly Hills, CA: Sage, 1986.

Arendt, H., *The Life of the Mind*. San Diego, CA: Harcourt Brace Jovanovich, 1978.

Argyris, C., *The Impact of Budgets on People*. Ithaca, NY: Controllership Foundation, Cornell University, 1952.

Argyris, C., *Reasoning, Learning, and Action – Individual and Organizational*. San Francisco, CA: Jossey-Bass, 1982.

Argyris, C., Putnam, R. and McLaine Smith, D., *Action Science – Concepts, Methods and Skills for Research and Intervention*. San Francisco, CA: Jossey-Bass, 1985.

Argyris, C. and Schön, D., *Organizational Learning: A Theory of Action Perspective*. Reading, MA: Addison-Wesley, 1978.

Ask, U., Ax, C. and Jönsson, S., Cost management in Sweden: from modern to post-modern. In *Modern Cost Management: European Perspectives*, ed. A. Bhimani. Oxford: Oxford University Press, in press.

Atkinson, P., Ethnomethodology: a critical review. *Annual Review of Sociology* **14**, 441–465, 1988.

Austin, J., *How To Do Things with Words*. London: Oxford University Press, 1962.

Barnard, C. I., *The Functions of the Executive*. Cambridge, MA: Harvard University Press, 1966. (Original 1938.)

Barnes, B., On the conventional character of knowledge and cognition. In *Science Observed*, eds I. D. Knorr-Cetina and M. Mulkay. London: Sage, 1983.

Becker, S. and Green, D., Budgeting and employee behavior. *Journal of Business*, 392–402, 1963.

Blimes, J., Mishearings. In *Text in Context*, eds G. Watson and R. M. Seiler. London: Sage, 1992.

Boland, R. J., Tenaski, R. V. and Te'eni, D., Designing information technology to support distributed cognition. *Organization Science*, forthcoming.

Bourdieu, P., *Outline of a Theory of Practice.* Cambridge: Cambridge University Press, 1977.

Brownall, P., The role of accounting data in performance evaluation, budgetary participation and organizational effectiveness. *Journal of Accounting Research* (Spring), 12–27, 1982.

Brownall, P. and Dunk, A. S., Task uncertainty and its interaction with budgetary participation and budget emphasis: some methodological issues and impirical investigation. *Accounting, Organization and Society* **16**, 693–703, 1991.

Brownall, P. and Hirst, M., Reliance on accounting information, budgetary participation, and task uncertainty: tests of three-way interaction. *Journal of Accounting Research* (Autumn), 241–249, 1986.

Bruner, J., *Actual Minds, Possible Worlds.* Cambridge, MA: Harvard University Press, 1986.

Bruner, J. S., *Acts of Meaning.* Cambridge, MA: Harvard University Press, 1990.

Brunsson, N., *The Irrational Organization.* Chichester: John Wiley, 1985.

Brunsson, N., *The Organization of Hypocrisy.* Chichester: John Wiley, 1989.

Brunsson, N. and Jönsson, S., *Beslut och Handling.* [*Decision and Action.*] Stockholm: Liber, 1979.

Burns, T. and Stalker, G. M., *The Management of Innovation.* London: Tavistock, 1961.

Carlsson, S., *Executive Behavior: A Study of the Work Load and the Working Methods of Managing Directors.* Stockholm: Strömbergs, 1951.

Carmona, S. and Perez-Casanov, G., Organizational forgetting and information systems. *Scandinavian Journal of Management* **9**, 29–44, 1993.

Cyert, R. M. and March, J. G., *Behavioral Theory of the Firm.* New York: Prentice-Hall, 1963.

DI, News item: Renault-order på 50 Mkr till Volvos fabrik i Floby. [50 MSEK order from Renault to Volvo's Floby plant.] *Dagens Industri,* 19 August 1992.

de Geer, H., *Arbetsgivarna – SAF i tio decennier.* [*The Employers – Swedish Employers' Federation over ten decades.*] Stockholm: SAF, 1992.

Edelman, G., *Bright Air, Brilliant Fire – On the Matter of the Mind.* London: Penguin, 1992.

Fernandez Perez, L., Budgeting Construction. Working paper, WP 3/1993. Department of Business Administration, University of Almeria, 1993.

Ericsson, A., *Stagnation, kris och utveckling.* [*Stagnation, Crisis and Development.*] Gothenburg: BAS, 1978.

Garfinkel, H., A conception of and experiment with trust as a condition of stable concerted action. In *Motivation and Social Interaction*, ed. O. J. Harvey. New York: Ronald Press, 1963, pp. 187–238.

Garfinkel, H., *Studies in Ethnometodology.* Englewood Cliffs, NJ: Prentice-Hall, 1967/1984.

Garfinkel, H. and Sacks, H., On formal structures of practical actions. In *Theoretical Sociology: Perspectives and Developments*, eds J. C. McKinney and E. A. Tiryakian. New York: Appleton–Century–Crofts, 1970, pp. 338–366.

Garner, S. P., *Evolution of Cost Accounting to 1925.* Alabama: University of Alabama Press, 1954.

Giddens, A., *The Construction of Society.* Cambridge: Polity Press, 1984.

Gilbert, G. N. and Mulkay, M., *Opening Pandora's Box. A Sociological Analysis of Scientists' Discourse.* Cambridge: Cambridge University Press, 1984.

Goffman, E., *Forms of Talk.* Philadelphia, PA: University of Pennsylvania Press, 1981.

Grice, P., *Studies in the Ways of Words.* Cambridge, MA: Harvard University Press, 1989.

Grönlund, A. and Jönsson S., Managing for cost improvement in automated production. In *Measures for Manufacturing Excellence,* ed. R. S. Kaplan. Boston, MA: Harvard Business School Press, 1990.

Habermas, J., *The theory of Communicative Action. Volume 1: Reason and the Rationalization of Society.* London: Heinemann, 1984.

Halldin, B. and Schiller, S., Förslag till ett forskningsprogram inom området "Underhåll med inriktning mot ekonomisk styrning". [A proposed research program for "Management Control in Maintenance".] Working paper, GRI-rapport 1992: 4, University of Gothenburg, 1992.

Harper, R. R., An ethnographic examination of accountancy. Unpublished Ph.D. thesis, Sociology Department, University of Manchester, 1989.

Harré, R. and Gillett, P., *The Discursive Mind.* Newbury Park, CA: Sage, 1994.

Hedberg, B., How organizations learn and unlearn. In *Handbook of Organizational Design,* Volume 1, eds P. C. Nystrom and W. H. Starbuck. Oxford: Oxford University Press, 1981, pp. 3–27.

Hedberg, B. and Jönsson, S., Designing semi-confusing information systems for organizations in changing environments. *Accounting, Organizations and Society* 3, 47–64, 1977a.

Hedberg, B. and Jönsson, S., Strategy formulation as a discontinuous process. *International Studies of Management & Organization* (Summer), 88–109, 1977b.

Hedberg, B. and Jönsson, S., Between myth and action. *Scandinavian Journal of Management* 5, 177–185, 1989.

Hedlund, G. and Rolander, D., Action in heterarchies – new approaches to managing the MNC. In *Managing the Global Firm,* eds C. A. Bartlett, Y. L. Doz and G. Hedlund. London: Routledge, 1990.

Hirst, M. K., Reliance on accounting performance measures, task, uncertainty, and dysfunctional behaviour: some extensions. *Journal of Accounting Research* (Autumn), 596–605, 1983.

Hirst, P. and Zeitlin, J., Flexible specialization versus post-Fordism: theory, evidence and policy implications. *Economy and Society* 20, 1–56, 1991.

Hofstede, G. H., *The Game of Budget Control.* Assen: Koninklijke Van Gorcum, 1967.

Hofstede, G., *Culture's Consequences: International Differences in Work-related Values.* Beverly Hills, CA: Sage, 1980.

Hopwood, A. G., An empirical study of the role of accounting data in performance evaluation. *Journal of Accounting Research* (Suppl.), 156–182, 1972.

Humphrey, C. G., Reflecting on attempts to develop a financial management information system for the probation service in England and Wales: some observations on the relationship on the claims of accounting and its practice. *Accounting, Organizations and Society,* 147–181, 1994.

Ims, K. J., *Leder i dialog. [Manager in Dialogue].* Oslo: Universitetsforlaget, 1987.

James, W., *Pragmatism – and Four Essays from The Meaning of Truth.* New York: New American Library, 1974. (Original 1907.)

Johnson, H. T. and Kaplan, R. S. *Relevance Lost. The Rise and Fall of Management Accounting.* Boston, MA: Harvard Business School Press, 1987.

Jönsson, S., Budgetary behaviour in local government – a case study over 3 years. *Accounting, Organizations and Society*, 287–304, 1982.

Jönsson, S., Stadsdelschefernas förväntningar – resultat av intervjuer med Göteborgs 21 stadsdelschefer inför genomförandet av stadsdelsnämnds-reformen. [The expectations of the district managers – results of the interviews with Gothenburg's 21 district managers facing the implementation of the district reform.] KFi report No. 6, University of Gothenburg, 1990a.

Jönsson, S., Action Research. Paper presented at ISRA-90 IFIP TC 8 WG 8.2 Working Conference on "The Information Systems Research Arena of the '90s", Copenhagen, 14–16 December 1990b.

Jönsson, S. Role-making for accounting while the state is watching. *Accounting, Organization and Society* 16, 521–546, 1991.

Jönsson, S., Accounting for improvement: action research on local management support. *Accounting, Management and Information Technologies*, 2, 99–115, 1992.

Jönsson, S., *Goda Utsikter – Svenskt management i perspektiv.* [*Good Prospects – Swedish Management in Perspective.*] Stockholm: Nerenius & Santerus, 1995.

Jönsson, S. and Grönlund, A., Life with a sub-contractor: new technology and management accounting. *Accounting, Organization and Society* 13, 513–534, 1988.

Jönsson, S. and Lundin, R., Myths and wishful thinking as management tools. *TIMS Studies in Management Sciences 5.* Amsterdam: North Holland, 1977, pp. 157–170.

Jönsson, S. and Solli, R., Stadsdelscheferna i Göteborg och reformen – Erfarenheter 1990–91. Delrapport i SDU-projektet. [The district managers and the reform – Experiences 1990–91.] Progress report, Department of Business Administration, University of Gothenburg, 1992.

Jönsson, S. and Solli, R., 'Accounting talk' in a caring setting. *Management Accounting Research*, 301–320, 1993a.

Jönsson, S. and Solli, R., Organisering för mobilisering – strategisk förändring i ett komplext politiskt fält. [Organizing for mobilization – strategic change in a complex political field.] Paper presented at the Conference "Organizing and Management Control in Public Sector Organizations", School of Economics, Stockholm, 27–28, May 1993b.

Jönsson, S. and Solli, R., Stadsdelscheferna och reformen. Sammanfattning efter 4 år. [The district managers and the reform. Summary after 4 years.] SDU-report 94:1, University of Gothenburg, 1994.

Kaplan, R. S. (ed.), *Measures for Manufacturing Excellence.* Boston, MA: Harvard Business School Press, 1990.

Katz, D. and Kahn, R. L., *The Social Psychology of Organizations.* New York: John Wiley, 1966.

Katzenbach, J. R. and Smith, D. K., *The Wisdom of Teams. Creating the High-performance Organization.* Boston, MA: Harvard Business School Press, 1993.

Kolb, D. A., *Experiential Learning. Experience as The Source of Learning and Development.* Englewood Cliffs, NJ: Prentice-Hall, 1984.

Kotter, J. P., *The General Managers.* New York: Free Press, 1982.

Lawrence, P. R. and Lorsch, J. W., *Organization and Environment: Managing Differentiation and Integration*. Boston, MA: Harvard University Press, 1967.

Levitt, B. and March, J. G. Organizational Learning. *Annual Review of Sociology*, 319–340, 1988.

Lundberg, E., The rise and fall of the Swedish model. *Journal of Economic Literature* **XXIII**, 1–36, 1985.

Luria, A. R., *The Working of the Brain*. Harmondsworth: Penguin, 1973.

Luthans, F., Hodgetts, R. M. and Rosenkrantz, S. A., *Real Managers*. Cambridge, MA: Ballinger, 1988.

Lutz, C., *Unnatural Emotions*. Chicago, IL: Chicago University Press, 1988.

Macintosh, N., *The Social Software of Accounting and Information Systems*. Chichester: John Wiley, 1985.

Mannheim, K., *Structures of Thinking*, eds D. Kettler, V. Meja and N. Stehr. London: Routledge & Kegan Paul, 1982, pp. 31–139.

McCarthy, T., *The Critical Theory of Jürgen Habermas*. Cambridge: Polity Press, 1984.

Mead, G. H., *Mind, Self & Society. From the Standpoint of a Social Behaviorist*. Chicago, IL: University of Chicago Press, 1934.

Milani, K., The relationship of participation in budget-setting to industrial supervisor performance and attitudes: a field study. *Accounting Review,* 274– 284, 1975.

Mintzberg, H., *The Nature of Managerial Work*. New York: Harper & Row, 1973.

Moerman, M., Life after C. A. An ethnographer's autobiography. In *Text in Context. Contributions to Ethnomethodology*, eds G. Watson and R. M. Seiler. Newbury Park, CA: Sage, 1992.

Moore, T. and Carling, C., *Understanding Language: Towards a Post-Chomskyan Linguistics*. London: Macmillan, 1982.

Moscovici, S., The phenomenon of social representation. In *Social Representations*, eds R. Farr and S. Moscovici. Cambridge: Cambridge University Press, 1984.

Munro, R., Calling for 'accounts': monsters, membership work and management accounting. Paper presented at the 4th Interdisciplinary Perspectives on Accounting Conference, University of Manchester, 11–13 July 1994.

NASA, Guidelines for application of learning/cost improvement curves. Technical Memorandum X-64968 (by L. M. Delionback). Marshall Space Flight Center, Alabama, 1975.

Otley, D. T., Budget use and Managerial Performance. *Journal of Accounting Research* (Spring), 122–149, 1978.

Pascale, R., *Managing on the Edge. How Successful Companies use Conflict to Stay Ahead*. London: Penguin Books, 1990.

Porter, M. E., *The Competitive Advantage of Nations*. London: Macmillan, 1990.

Potter, J. and Edwards, D., *Discursive Psychology*. London: Sage, 1992.

Potter, J. and Wetherell, M., *Discourse and Social Psychology*. London: Sage, 1987.

Samuelson, L. A., The development of Accounting Information Systems in Sweden. *Scandinavian Journal of Management*, 293–310, 1989.

Samuelson, L. A., *Models of Accounting Information Systems: The Swedish Case*. London and Lund: Chartwell-Bratt/Studentlitteratur, 1990.

Schiller, S. and Jönsson, S., Managing maintenance in automated production. Paper presented at the First Internationa Federation of Scholarly Associations of Management (IFSAM) Conference, Tokyo, September 1992.

Schroder, H., Driver, M. and Streufert, S., *Human Information Processing*. New York: Holt, Rinehart, and Winston, 1967.

Scott, W. R., *Institutions and Organizations*. Thousand Oaks: Sage, 1995.

Searle, J. R., *Intentionality. An Essay in the Philosophy of Mind*. Cambridge: Cambridge University Press, 1983.

Silverman, D., *Interpreting Qualitative Data. Methods for Analysing Talk, Text and Interaction*. London: Sage, 1993.

Simons, R., Planning, control, and uncertainty: A process view. In *Accounting & Management: Field Study Perspectives*, eds W. J. Burns and R. S. Kaplan. Boston, MA: Harvard Business School Press, 1987.

Simons, R., Strategic orientation and top management attention to control systems. *Strategic Management Journal* **12**, 49–62, 1990.

Simon, H., Guetzkow, H., Kozonetsky, G. and Tyndall, G., *Centralization Vs Decentralization in Organizing the Controller's Department*. New York: The Controllership Foundation, 1954.

Solli, R., *Ekonomi för dem som gör något – En studie av användning och utformning av ekonomiinformation för lokala enheter. [Economics for People that do Something – A Study of the Use and Design of Financial Information to Local Units.]* Lund: Studentlitteratur, 1991.

Starbuck, W. H., Organizations as action generators. *American Sociological Review* **48**, 91–102, 1983.

Stedry, G. H., *Budget Control and Cost Behavior*. Englewood Cliffs, NJ: Prentice-Hall, 1960.

Turner, R. H., Unanswered questions in the convergence between structuralist and interactionist role theories. In *Micro-sociological Theory*, eds H. J. Helle and S. N. Eisenstadt. Beverly Hills, CA: Sage, 1985.

Van de Ven, A. H. and Polley, D., Learning while innovating. *Organization Science*, in press.

van Gunsteren, H., *The Quest for Control*. Chichester: John Wiley, 1976.

Walker, C. R., Guest, R. H. and Turner, A. N., *The Foremen on the Assembly Line*. Cambridge, MA: Harvard University Press, 1956.

Watson, G., The understanding of language use in everyday life. In *Text in Context. Contributions to Ethnomethodology*, eds G. Watson and R. M. Seiler. Newbury Park, CA: Sage, 1992.

Watson, G. and Seiler, R. M. (eds), *Text in Context. Contributions to Ethnomethodology*. Newbury Park, CA: Sage, 1992.

Westin, O., *Informationsstöd för lokal ekonomi. [Information Support for Local Control.]* Göteborg: BAS, 1993.

Wieder, L., *Language and Social Reality*. The Hague: Mouton, 1974.

Wildavsky, A., *Budgeting – A Comparative Theory of Budgetary Processes*. Boston, MA: Little, Brown, 1975.

Wilson, K., *From Associations to Structure. The course of Cognition*. Amsterdam: North Holland, 1980.

Winch, P., *The Idea of Social Science and Its Relation to Philosophy*. London: Routledge & Kegan Paul, 1958.

Wittgenstein, L., *Philosophical Investigations*. Oxford: Basil Blackwell, 1953.

Zuboff, S., *In the Age of the Social Machine. The Future of Work and Power*. Oxford: Heinemann, 1988.

Author index

Subject index

Printed in the United Kingdom
by Lightning Source UK Ltd.
135116UK00001B/296/P